RADIO KNOBS
— AND —
SCOPE DOPES

BEHIND THE SCENES IN THE AIR NAVIGATION SYSTEM

To Roberta

Enjoy the stories

All the best

Bruce

BRUCE LeCREN

Tellwell Talent
www.tellwell.ca

ISBN
978-0-2288-7105-7 (Hardcover)
978-0-2288-7104-0 (Paperback)
978-0-2288-7106-4 (eBook)

For my friends and colleagues who never
got the chance to read these stories.
You are remembered.

FOREWORD

Radio Knobs and Scope Dopes is Bruce LeCren's first-person account of his 30 plus years as a Transport Canada electronic technologist, project manager, and instructor. During LeCren's time, ground-based navigation was critical for all-weather marine and air transportation as well as defence in Canada.

His memoir is highlighted with many photos and amusing anecdotes featuring the people in LeCren's career. The result is an easy-to-read insight into living and working in different and often remote parts of Canada on a variety of projects with a cross-section of characters.

Radio Knobs and Scope Dopes should stand as an entertaining perspective on an interesting era in Canada's navigation history.

Garth Wallace, author and pilot

Table of Contents

I WAS A RADIO KNOB

For more than 33 years throughout my working life I was fortunate to have had a job that took me to every part of Canada and exposed me to a variety of people and cultures. I had two employers during that time, but only one career with four distinctly different paths.

I was an electronic technologist within Canada's Air Navigation System (ANS), familiarly known to the public as Air Traffic Control. From the 1970s into the new millennium my colleagues and I lived through the development of aviation electronics from steam-powered analog equipment using vacuum tubes to the latest digital satellite-based systems, and at every step along the way I can attest that while we worked behind the scenes and out of the public eye, the controllers would be deaf, dumb, and blind without the equipment we installed for their use and maintained at the highest state of readiness.

Over the course of my career the ANS became more automated and checklists replaced the individual initiative required from technologists in the 1970s. Many who I worked with, including myself, miss those days. I worked within a large bureaucracy that had its origins in Canada's military, so our everyday language was replete with acronyms. It was also very technical work, but this is not a technical book. I have tried to keep the use of acronyms and technology to a minimum. Each acronym is spelled out the first time it appears, and usually once or twice more later on as a reminder. I have also tried to explain the technology in layman's terms.

I defined both acronyms and terms in the Glossary, which can be found on the following pages for easy reference. For those readers whose curiosity demands a deeper dive, there is Wikipedia!

This is our story told through my experiences as my colleagues and I travelled the country. All the stories in this book are true, although not necessarily in chronological order and some are composites of more than one anecdote. The cast of characters are real people but I have disguised some names and details to spare the feelings of some participants.

They called us Radio Knobs, we called them Scope Dopes....

Most of the time in fun.

GLOSSARY

AASR	Airport and Airways Surveillance Radar. A long-range radar for the surveillance of aircraft.
Ab-initio	Latin for "starting from the beginning." Air traffic control ab-initio training assumed zero prior knowledge of the air navigation system.
Ace McCool	Chief pilot of the fictional Down East International airline, created by Jack Desmarais. The adventures of Ace and his crew were featured in *Canadian Aviation* magazine for over 14 years.
ADS-B	Automatic Dependent Surveillance - Broadcast. A high-tech system for the surveillance of aircraft. In its basic form ADS-B transmits the position received by the aircraft's GPS to air traffic control via telecom or satellite link. Computers at the operations centre then plot the aircraft's position on the controller's monitor without the need for a radar signal, thus enabling worldwide aircraft surveillance.
AMC	American Motors Corporation. United States automotive manufacturer that operated from 1954 until 1988.

Amauti	Plural: Amautiit. The traditional parka worn by Inuit women incorporating a built-in baby pouch just below the hood.
Anik	A series of Canadian geostationary communications satellites first launched in 1972 and still in use today.
ANS	Air Navigation System. The entire apparatus dealing with air transportation safety, including air traffic controllers, flight service specialists, technologists, and their equipment and support services. Formerly part of Transport Canada, Canada's ANS is now owned by Nav Canada but still regulated by Transport Canada.
APM	Airport Manager.
ATB	Air Terminal Building.
ATC	Air Traffic Control. That part of the Air Navigation System dealing with positive control services to aircraft.

Also Air Traffic Controller, a trained specialist who provides guidance instructions and safety separation services to aircraft. |
ATV	All-Terrain Vehicle.
Beacon	See NDB.
Bear	A Russian Bear is a type Tu-95 strategic bomber first flown by the Soviet Union in 1952 and still in service with the Russian air force today. Built by the Tupolev Design Bureau and code named 'Bear' by NATO, Bears also come in maritime patrol and airliner versions.

BIC	Basic Installation Competency. A component of the engineering competency program initiated by Nav Canada that focusses on equipment fabrication and installation techniques.
CAF	Canadian Armed Forces, most commonly used today in reference to Canadian army units and the unified joint services.
CARS	Community Aerodrome Radio Station. Manned stations located at airports north of 60 degrees latitude. They are staffed by community residents who have received training in weather observation and radio procedures, and provide an advisory service to pilots.
CBC	Canadian Broadcasting Corporation, a Crown Corporation and national radio and television network. Until the advent of satellites the CBC was often the only service available in rural or remote areas of Canada.
Crown Corporation	Entities that are owned and regulated by the Canadian Government or a Province, but structured and operated as a commercial business. Examples include the CBC, VIA Rail, and Canada Post.
DEW	Distant Early Warning. The DEW line is a chain of Arctic radar stations operated by the military and designed to alert NORAD of an aerial invasion over the North Pole.

DME   Distance Measuring Equipment. The aircraft DME transmits pulses to the ground-based DME system, which returns them back to the aircraft. The timing of the pulses gives pilots their distance in miles to the DME site. Usually paired with a VOR or glide path (see ILS).

DUE   Dial-Up Equipment. DUE is used at some low-traffic remote communication sites to enable communication between pilots and flight service stations over regular telephone lines instead of dedicated telecom circuits.

FSS   Flight Service Station. An air traffic facility providing flight information and planning, weather, and advisory services to pilots. In Canada most FSSs have been consolidated into large regional centres made possible by the use of remote communications (see RCO and DUE).

             Also Flight Service Specialist, the operations people manning an FSS.

GIC   General Installation Competency. A component of the engineering competency program initiated by Nav Canada that focusses on project management.

Glide Path   See ILS.

GMD   Ground Meteorological Device. An electronic system built around a movable dish that automatically tracks the weather sensor packages (radiosondes) carried aloft by high-altitude weather balloons.

GNWT

Government of the Northwest Territories. The Northwest Territories included Nunavut prior to that territory's creation in 1999. Now they are the "Northwest Territory," singular.

GPS

Global Positioning System. A GPS receiver in an aircraft uses a precisely timed satellite signal to display aircraft position to a pilot in latitude and longitude. At least three satellites must be visible to the GPS receiver for an accurate position to be resolved. Modern GPS uses computer processing to visually represent the aircraft's flight track and position on an electronic map.

Ham

This book refers to Ham as an amateur radio operator. First used to denigrate a Morse code operator with poor skills, Ham operators now wear the label with pride in their skills and achievements, including significant contributions to science, engineering, industry, and social services.

Heathkits

The Heath Company produced high-quality electronic kits and other products from 1947 until 1992. Today they offer newly designed products and some vintage kits through their website.

Herman Nelson

An eponymous line of gasoline or diesel indirect-fired portable heaters designed for brutal winter conditions.

HR

Human Resources, formerly Personnel. The part of an organization responsible for hiring, firing, and the working condition policies of employees.

HVAC	Heating, Venting, Air Conditioning. The term describing the mechanical heating and cooling systems in a building.
IBEW	International Brotherhood of Electrical Workers. This book refers to IBEW local 2228, the union representing the electronic technologists in Transport Canada and Nav Canada.
IFR	Instrument Flight Rules. Aircraft flight within controlled airspace under the positive guidance of air traffic control and without visual reference to the ground.
ILS	Instrument Landing System. A system of electronic beams that guide aircraft along an approach path to a runway's touchdown point. The localizer beam keeps aircraft aligned with the runway centreline. The glide path beam guides aircraft down a slope, usually three degrees, to the touchdown. Marker beacons were formerly used to tell pilots how far they had to go to the touchdown point. Now, a DME system located at the glide path site provides that information.
INCO	International Nickel Company.
Localizer	See ILS.
MiGs	Soviet, now Russian, aircraft. Primarily fighter planes manufactured by the Mikoyan-Gurevich Design Bureau.
MLO	Maintenance Liaison Officer. A technologist who used to act as the interface between controllers and electronic maintenance. Replaced by Technical Systems Coordinators.
Mulies	Mule deer.

NCTI	The Nav Canada Training Institute, formerly TCTI, located in Cornwall, Ontario. It is now operated primarily as a conference centre.
NDB	Non-Directional Beacon. A non-precision navigational aid, essentially the same as an AM radio broadcast station, whose signal gives the pilot directional bearing to the NDB site relative to the nose of the aircraft.
NORAD	North American Aerospace Defense Command, formerly North American Air Defense Command. A joint U.S. and Canadian military organization that provides early warning, air sovereignty, and protection for North America.
NRC	National Research Council. The science and technology research and development arm of the Canadian government.
Omni-Range	See VOR.

Radar	Radio Detection and Ranging. Primary radar systems send out pulses that reflect off solid surfaces and back to the radar. The timing of the reflection combined with the bearing of the radar antenna relative to North allows the target to be plotted on an electronic display. Formerly an acronym, radar is now part of the common lexicon. The Airport and Airways Surveillance Radar (AASR) mentioned in this book is an example of a primary radar.

Secondary radar systems are sometimes co-located with primary radars. Their pulses are processed by a transponder in the target aircraft before being reflected back. The transponder allows positive identification of the target aircraft to air traffic controllers and can also give them the aircraft altitude and other information. |
| RCAF | Royal Canadian Air Force. |
| RCMP | Royal Canadian Mounted Police. Canada's federal police force. |
| RCO | Remote Communications Outlet. RCOs consist of transmitters, receivers, and a control system that allows remote communication between pilots and a flight service station or other manned centre.

Also refers to the name of the site into which the equipment is installed. |
| Siegfried Line | A defensive chain of concrete fortifications erected by the Germans just prior to WWII along their border with France. |

Tacan	Tactical Air Navigation. A military electronic system giving pilots of Tacan-equipped aircraft their precise distance and bearing from the Tacan site. Civilian aircraft can use the distance portion of the Tacan signal in lieu of a DME.
TCTI	Transport Canada Training Institute, now known as NCTI. Once the site of all ANS operational and technical training, it now operates primarily as a conference centre by Nav Canada.
TIRL	Technical Institute Recruiting Level. A probationary hiring classification for technologists coming out of college. It was dropped shortly after the author joined Transport Canada.
TSM	Telecom Station Manager. The senior technologist in charge of a team of maintenance technologists and sometimes FSS specialists at the manned station level.

Vacuum
Tube

An electronic component built into a sealed glass vial typically the size and shape of a human thumb, but these can differ depending on function. Also known as 'electron tube', 'valve', or simply 'tube', it was invented by J. A. Fleming in 1904 and consisted of an anode and cathode. Later, a third element called a grid, or screen, was added by Lee de Forest. A vacuum tube's basic parts include a filament, cathode, grid, and anode. The cathode is heated by the red-hot filament causing it to emit electrons, which are drawn in a stream to the high voltage present on the anode, also known as the plate. The grid is a wire mesh located between the plate and cathode. A low-voltage signal on the grid will modulate the high-voltage electron stream, resulting in amplification. Often multiple grids are installed allowing the tube to perform other functions. Vacuum tubes were key electronic circuit components for the first half of the 20th century, essential to the development of radio, television, radar, telephone networks, and early computers.

Picture tubes, also known as cathode-ray tubes, are a special development of the vacuum tube having a very high voltage anode and a focused electron beam that is scanned across the anode's screen. Modulating the beam illuminates phosphorescent pixels on the screen to form a visible picture.

Vig	Vigorish, also called the juice, the take, and other terms related to gambling or loan-sharking. In this book it refers to the cut taken in merchandise in lieu of paying freight charges.
Voodoo	CF-101 jet fighter interceptor built by McDonnell Douglas and used by the RCAF from 1961 until 1984.
VOR	Very High Frequency Omni-Range. An electronic system whose signal gives pilots their bearing to the VOR site relative to North. When co-located with DME or Tacan equipment the combined signals give pilots their precise position relative to the site.
VorTac	A combined VOR and Tacan site.

EARLY DAYS

As with so many things that happen in life, it was chance that brought me into electronics and then the Air Navigation System. I grew up in a military family; my father served as an air gunner in the Royal Canadian Air Force during WWII and afterwards stayed in the service as a photographer. His career caused us to move every few years; we were living in Germany from 1959 until 1963, at the height of the Cold War when the Berlin Wall went up, the Soviets shot down Gary Powers' U-2 spy plane, the Cuban Missile Crisis almost brought about WWIII, and President Kennedy was assassinated by Lee Harvey Oswald. At that time the RCAF with their Canadair Sabre fighters were the elite air force in Western Europe. Our pilots flew their Sabres to routinely intercept Soviet MiGs probing NATO's defences, won all the gunnery competitions, and generally demonstrated that there were none better. Heady stuff for a 10-year-old!

The Siegfried Line bunker seen from our apartment window.
It was blown up by the French after the war.

Zweibrücken, home of Number 3 Fighter Wing, was a great place for a boy to grow up in! We lived on the former Siegfried Line beside an old German bunker across the street from our apartment building, and unexploded ordnance from WWII could still be found in the woods and fields. We did not have television or telephone. We knocked on other kids' doors to get together and play, or met in the local park and walked to wherever we wanted to go. We read books and magazines or picked up English-language broadcasts on short-wave radio. We listened to vinyl records, built model airplanes, played unsupervised outdoor games of our own invention, and we never felt deprived or disadvantaged by not having the electronic devices essential to today's youth. We made our own fun and went home when the street lamps came on. My friends and I joined the Scouts and learned outdoor camping skills, woodcraft, and tracking. We aspired to be Mercury astronauts like John Glenn and Gus Grissom; our fictional heroes were the Hardy Boys, Tarzan, Superman, Dick Tracy, and Sergeant Rock.

On Armed Forces Days we got to tour the restricted parts of the base and see the aircraft up close, sitting in fighter cockpits on the laps of steely-eyed Ace McCools, awed by all the instrumentation.

"Kid, stop pulling on the yellow handle."

The highlight was climbing into an armed Sabre at the gun butts, and being allowed to pull the trigger! The gun cover panels were off, and the tracer bullets, noise, and smoke from the six machine guns were breathtaking! After we climbed out, we could pick up some .50-calibre souvenirs!

Canadair Sabre test firing at night. DND photo,
Canada archives PL-55764.

We also experienced the sober side of the Cold War when it
nearly went hot during the Cuban Missile Crisis. Each family
had to keep six weeks' worth of food in our basement locker
and we practised retreating there during air-raid drills. We
were confidently and optimistically told that 'duck and cover'
would save our asses if the Commies dropped a nuke on the
base. We had our first lessons in geopolitical history in Grade
4 told, of course, from the winning side.

After Germany we relocated to Winnipeg. The United States
was about to enter the Vietnam War, and I was entering junior
high school. I hung around with a few other boys from RCAF
families, and we largely kept to ourselves. Bob Crosby and
I shared many interests and we still keep in touch today. In
those days you could buy bulk chemicals off the shelves in
the drug stores, so we purchased saltpetre and sulphur by
the pound, ground up the carbon rods from dead batteries,
and experimented with our own fireworks, dynamite, and
rocket fuel. When we weren't trying to blow off our fingers we
were stargazing, collecting stamps and coins, going weekend
camping with our Venturer Scout Company, and dabbling in
electronics.

I got interested in electronics because Bob was. We took
apart radio and television sets, studying their parts and

schematics and discovering how they worked. We read *Popular Electronics* magazine and saved our money for parts to build our own amplifiers, radio receivers, and other arcane devices; some even worked! For Christmas I received Heathkits and built my own transistor radio and electronic test equipment. Bob got his amateur radio licence and went on the air as a Ham operator using an army surplus radio from a tank. I got a CB licence and set, and as soon as I acquired my first car I mounted the radio under the dash and went mobile. I divided my time between the Venturers and REACT (Radio Emergency Associated Communication Teams), a volunteer group whose primary role in those days was to monitor the emergency CB channel 9 and assist motorists, most of whom were lost or needed a tow. Our Venturer Company also owned a CB set and joined REACT, and we collaborated several times to provide safety communications and first aid at community events like outdoor festivals or marathons.

Bob Crosby, ca. 1973.

My interest in electronics continued to grow. In Grade 11 I made a digital adding machine for the school to demonstrate binary math, and in Grade 12 I made a pair of electronic dice using first-generation integrated circuits and, combined with a display on probability, won a gold ribbon in our school science fair. High school was certainly my nerdy phase!

After high school I went straight into Electronic Technology at Winnipeg's Red River Community College. I selected radar, radio communications, and control systems as my course options because they fitted into my interests at the time, not because of any tie-in with air traffic control. My first exposure to ATC came during a student visit to Winnipeg's airport control tower. The controllers explained how they kept aircraft separated visually and with radio and radar, but the thrust of our tour was the electronic equipment that enabled the controlling to occur. The actual radio and radar equipment was located remotely from the tower so there was a heavy emphasis on control systems, which in 1973 relied on electric relays and analog telephone system technology. Vacuum tubes predominated and digital technology had yet to make an appearance.

Towards the end of our two-year course, we survivors began scouring newspapers for job opportunities, and several recruiters came to the college to interview those of us who showed an interest in their companies. Most of us were looking for long-term career prospects. Company loyalty was an important concept then. Hopping from one employer to the next every few years seems to be commonly accepted practice now but in 1973 it raised questions about one's ability and personal suitability. Competition was fierce and I was fortunate to receive multiple offers despite finishing with an average GPA.

I declined the offer I received from Saunders Aviation, which was an aircraft manufacturer located in Gimli, Manitoba. The job would be installing wiring and avionics into their new ST-28 commuter airliners that were currently at the prototype stage. As interesting as being in on the ground floor of a new aircraft manufacturer was, the job I was being offered was assembly-line repetitive 'monkey work' with few opportunities for advancement. Not long after I passed on Saunders their ST-28 program ran into financial and regulatory difficulties and the company filed for bankruptcy.

Transport Canada was hiring technologists to perform electronic maintenance duties for the ANS. Initial training would be at Winnipeg airport followed by a mandatory one-year tour of duty at an isolated post in Canada's Arctic. Assuming I received an offer and passed the probationary period there would be job security with a good pension, and a diverse and interesting career path. This was a job requiring a variety of skills and competencies because of the wide range of duties that directly affected aviation safety. I could save most of my salary during my Arctic duty to launch myself and start a family once I returned.

In 1973 the organization was called the Department of Transport. Later the name changed to Department of Transportation, then Ministry of Transport, and the bureaucrats eventually settled on Transport Canada. With each new name came another reorganization which meant a new set of managers and several new sets of office acronyms. I am using the modern name throughout so as not to confuse you, the reader; unlike we who were constantly confused by what seemed like unending bureaucratic change.

I was very excited when I was offered the job as an electronic maintenance technologist. It came with the probationary classification of Technical Institute Recruiting Level, or TIRL, and the princely salary of $6,000 per year. I accepted with thanks and a couple of days later the neighbours reported to Ma that two Men-in-Black had been asking about me. Apparently the RCMP took Transport Canada's security clearances seriously, and I considered myself lucky that I had done my partying and tomcatting well away from home!

APPRENTICING

Transport Canada hired me in early June pending graduation later that month, which took a lot of pressure off my back and allowed me to concentrate on my upcoming final exams. When I got the call from Personnel (Humans were not Resources then), I was asked when I could start. I was thinking a couple of weeks' break after two years of hard study was not out of line; I had recently become engaged so my fiancée Val and I wanted time together before years' end when I would be leaving for the North, and I would have no vacation time for at least the next 18 months.

"How about the middle of July?"

"Well, your classmate Rod Coey just accepted our job offer and he said he could report for duty the day after your final exam!"

John Skitcko, Telecom Area Manager, Winnipeg. Winnipeg Free Press photo.

Thanks Rod.... Neither he nor I were quite sure what to expect on that first day. On June 25, the Monday after our final exam on the previous Friday, we stood in front of our new boss John Skitcko in his Winnipeg airport office. We each wore the only white shirt and tie we possessed (my tie was from my Venturer Scout uniform and Rod's was a snappy orange paisley number). John was about five feet four and built like a fire hydrant. His hair looked like Dagwood Bumstead's and he spoke with a heavy Ukrainian accent as he welcomed us to his team of about 40 professional electronic technologists.

If Rod and I harboured any thoughts about being turned loose to imperil the flying public on our first day we were sadly mistaken. First, we got an orientation lecture from Personnel that featured a large chart. At the top sat the Minister of Transport, described by our lecturer as one who talks to God, walks on water, and kicks airplanes out of hangars. I swear he actually bowed his head whenever he mentioned the Minister. One hour and many downward layers later, at the bottom of the chart among the weeds and assorted human detritus, dwelt us newbie TIRLs. We were left in no doubt that our place in Transport Canada's universe was somewhere below the Minister's shoe scrapings.

Following this humbling we were given a batch of forms to fill out in triplicate, several of which asked ominously about next of kin. We had our mug shots taken and ID cards made, were fingerprinted by the RCMP, and signed both Canada's Official Secrets Act and our International Brotherhood of Electrical Workers union cards. After a lunch in the airport cafeteria we were sent off to visit a Transport Canada-approved Aviation Medical Examiner, who for some reason had his office in the downtown railway station. Rod and I both concluded that this learned gentleman could not make a living in general practice so had to rely on government medicals to put food on his table. First up was the eye test. We were asked to read a paragraph in 10-point font that was highlighted in a *Reader's Digest* magazine while covering each eye in turn.

Next was the hearing test.

"Can you hear me now?" says the medico, sotto voce.

"Yes."

Then came the colour blindness test....

"What colour is that fire extinguisher?"

It was yellow, not red, and I am not kidding, he actually asked that! Rubber gloves played a prominent role in the rest of the exam as we underwent the standard test for hernia in males. Rod and I walked bow-legged out of our medical exams and into our careers. We parted ways at that point, each of us being assigned to work with different groups of technologists back at the airport.

Over the next few months until I received my northern duty assignment I observed and learned as much as I could by osmosis. The Transport Canada equipment I would be in charge of in the Arctic was basic enough that formal training was not considered necessary, however I would still need to know how to troubleshoot and repair it. The day after my orientation I reported to Winnipeg airport's radar group where I spent three weeks before rotating through the other maintenance specialties. This rotation gave new techs a chance to become familiar with the whole gamut of airport electronic systems and it gave the organization a chance to see where each of us might best fit in before making a permanent assignment. This policy was well intentioned but didn't make much sense because there was no guarantee we would be reassigned to Winnipeg after our Arctic duty, and there was no radar to look after in the Arctic.

Old Hat at the Radar Site

Don Strath, the radar group supervisor, announced that he and the new TIRL (me) would be joining the technologists assigned to perform radar antenna maintenance that day. Don was ex-military, like most senior ANS employees in the 1970s. He fancied himself a bit of a cowboy, so his walk was a cross between a march and a swagger. He was always kitted out in cowboy boots and an oversized Stetson that rested on his ears and eyebrows. When upset he would hitch his hands in his belt and thunder forth in a deep gravel voice, chewing nails and spitting rust. His formidable chin jutted forward and his head would tilt back to keep the object of his displeasure centred in his steely glare. I can say from personal experience that it was an effective technique. I can also add that I enjoyed my brief time working for him.

The radar site we were going to be working at was on the far side of the airport. I trailed Don and the two other technologists out to our government-issued Chevy and climbed into the back seat. Government cars were purchased from the lowest bidder and were low-end basic models; dark blue, no hubcaps or chrome, vinyl bench seats and no power accessories, radio or air conditioning. There was an orange gumball machine on the roof and a two-way radio that our techs had installed to communicate with the control tower.

The car did have a V-8 engine and our driver did a reasonable impression of A.J. Foyt as he peeled away from the admin building heading for the aircraft parking ramp, the gumball machine making grinding noises as it flashed brightly above us. We had to cross the ramp then use taxiways and runways in order to reach the site. A.J. hit the ramp doing 80 kph with Don's chin jutted out and the Stetson lowered. There was no conversation in the vehicle until Don picked up the microphone and spoke one long word to the tower:

"Telecom53mainramptotheAASR."

The controller in the tower was used to us and came right back with our directions to proceed to the radar:

"Telecom 53 tower, cleared to the AASR via Mike and Poppa to the Bay of 13."

As soon as our driver heard "cleared to" he cracked on more speed so we entered the taxiway called 'Mike' doing 100 and accelerating. You can't drive on airports like that these days. Now they have white lines painted to look like roads on the aircraft ramps and vehicles must be driven between them like your granny on her way to church. It was much more interesting then. We screamed off the end of runway 13 at the far side of the airport onto a dirt road leading to the radar site. Our driver skidded to a stop in a cloud of dust a couple of metres from the site door, and we all piled out.

Don dispensed some sage advice to me: "Don't ever let me catch you driving like that. You never want to find out the amount of paperwork you need to fill out if you bend a car, much less an airplane, which would be a career-ending move."

I was still trying to un-pucker my sphincter from the wild ride. "Yes sir."

"And don't call me sir, damn it."

"Yes sir, damn it, Don."

The AASR (Airport & Airways Surveillance Radar) site was a cinder block building typical of many Transport Canada electronic sites. It was painted in a white and orange checkerboard pattern so airplanes could see it before they hit it, with no windows and a single metal door. The steel mesh radar antenna rotated above us atop a 12-metre-tall platform tower similarly painted in alternating red and white bands. There was no enclosing dome; the antenna sail and its motor sat exposed to the elements and had rotated unfailingly since 1958. To ensure this unfailing rotation continued we had to shut it off once a year, climb up, and grease the bearings.

Today was that day. I got to carry the tool box, grease gun, and a wad of rags. There were stairs for the first nine metres and then a ladder leading up to a hatch in the floor of the platform. Don opened the hatch and I followed his cowboy boots up to the now still antenna. The view was great. We were right at the edge of the airport property and you could see for miles in all directions across the prairies and the city. Hay fields surrounded the site and the crops were coming in nicely. My old college was in view and I took a moment to wonder what my fellow grads were up to. I'll bet they weren't 12 metres up a radar tower.

The late June day was warm, low clouds scudded along by a moderate breeze promised rain later. The breeze combined with our height atop the tower kept the mosquitoes away. Life was good. Don explained and pointed. I listened, greased, and wiped. Half an hour went by and I noticed the

Don Strath wearing his stetson, photo taken in Resolute Bay by Paul Meyer. Courtesy Blomquist, James Edward, and James Dale Phillips. Canada Points North: The Untold Stories. Beaumont, Alta., 2016.

wind was picking up and the clouds were getting darker. A summer storm was imminent.

"Okay. Before we go down, we have to make sure all the mounting bolts are tight. Look them over and then give them a good shake, like this." Don proceeded to put all his weight into rocking the antenna back and forth. "See, no play in the gearbox and no movement in the mounts."

Now he climbed up the frame on the back of the sail to the secondary radar antenna mounted above. This he grabbed with both hands and attempted to rip from its moorings while balancing on the steel frame in his cowboy boots. He shouted down:

"You have to make sure this antenna is solid too!"

Air traffic control radar type ASR-8, similar to the one from which Don lost his hat. Accessed 2021, photo courtesy Radartutorial.eu.

At that moment a sudden gust of wind blew across the structure, causing Don to hang on tight to his exposed perch and lifting the Stetson off his head. It twirled away behind him as he made a futile grab for it with one hand. His silver-grey military brush cut stood up straight as the jaw jutted out and began dispensing a torrent of profanity while stomping down off the antenna.

I had to hang onto the railing because I was laughing so hard. The building door was open below us and the two techs came outside to investigate the commotion in time to see the wayward Stetson, spinning like a Frisbee, sail magnificently over the airport perimeter fence.

It then cleared the city road on the far side before vanishing inside a field of new green hay.

In the seconds it took him to get down to ground level Don showed himself to be a true virtuoso of colourful phraseology. Pausing only to draw breath, I don't believe he repeated himself once all the way to the ground. I stumbled down behind clutching tools, rags, grease gun, and my sides, while the two on the ground added their own witty repartee to the mix, which made Don curse all the louder.

As soon as he hit the deck Don demanded we all saddle up and go look for his hat. He laid a trail of dust out of the site while we were still getting the car doors shut. The radar stood silent and still behind us with the site door flapping in the wind as the first raindrops began hitting the windshield.

We sped along the airport perimeter road about half a kilometre to the nearest gate. Now the summer storm had really opened up overhead. The rain was bucketing down in true Prairie fashion, fed by a gale-force wind. This kept the dust down but now we were leaving two rooster tails of mud behind. We slid to a stop at the gate and the tech in the front seat tossed a huge ring of keys into my lap.

"TIRLs open gates."

"And hurry up!" added Don, "My hat is getting soaked!"

"Your hat is probably halfway to North Dakota by now!"

My two buddies were having a great time. There hadn't been this much entertainment in the radar section for months and it was only my first day on the job! I knew enough to suck it up and get wet.

"Which key is it?" There were about 20 unmarked keys on the ring, all opening different doors, gates, and sites in and around the airport.

"One of the small ones!" That narrowed things down by about half.

"Are you still here?" from Don.

That was my cue to exit into the pelting rain. The rain was warm, but pushed by the wind it came slanting down in sheets and I was soaked through before I made the 3 metres or so to the gate. As I began fumbling with the keys, I realized there were three padlocks linked together on the chain that held the gate closed, and I didn't know which one was ours (the others, I found out later, were for the airport firefighters and the airport manager's people). It took the fourth key in the second lock to open the gate and by then I knew how a drowned rat felt. The car slid past me and stopped just long enough for me to splash down into the back seat after refastening the lock. There was no sympathy from my professional colleagues.

"Geez, you're getting us all wet!"

"Watch where you're shaking yourself!"

"You smell like wet dog!"

"You piss yourself? You're leaving a puddle on the seat!"

"TIRLs are sure great gate openers; every one of us should have one!"

In the time it took to drive back along the city road to the hay field the rain had ended as quickly as it began, and we could see the storm cell making its way towards the homes of St. James. Don barked out more orders as he stopped the car beside the field opposite the radar site.

"Okay, I saw where my hat came down. LeCren, you come with me since you're already wet. You other two wait here."

On the drive around to the field, Don must have changed his mind about ordering the more experienced techs out of the car to help search. They seemed a bit disappointed that he didn't make the effort; no doubt they had suitable rebuttals at the ready that would feature words like 'job description' and 'grievance.'

Don and I squelched our way through the steaming mud. It was not so bad if we mashed the hay down under our feet as we went. We spread out when Don figured we were getting close. I wasn't holding out much hope that the hat was still where he said he saw it land, but it was Don's turn to catch one on the fat part of the bat. The brown hat showed up clearly against the new green hay. I think the weight of rain water it had absorbed had something to do with its staying more or less in place.

He ran up to the hat, arms akimbo and cowboy boots making little mud fountains with each step, like he was recovering a lost child. Perhaps he was. He picked the hat up and held it aloft in triumph as he turned around to face us; then, with a grin splitting his face he jammed it home with both hands. The hat made a 'splotch' sound as it settled over the brush cut onto his ears and jets of water squirted out from underneath. Don didn't care that the water was running down his face and head as he swaggered as best he could through the mud back to the car. He was whole again. On the drive back he turned to me and said:

"You did good for your first day. Next week we get summer students. They'll open the gates."

We maintained four radar systems on the airport including one used by the military for precision runway approaches and a weather radar owned by Environment Canada. Signals from our two long-range surveillance radars were converted into television displays that the Scope Dopes sat in front of to watch airplanes. By the middle of July I had a basic knowledge of how all these systems worked and it was time to rotate from radar into the navigation aids (navaids) group.

Life in the Navaids Group

The navaids, communications, and radar group's desks were all next to each other in a bullpen so I had already met most

Cliff Somers. Winnipeg
Free Press photo.

of the techs I would be working with, including the navaids supervisor Cliff Somers. Cliff was the antithesis of Don, mild mannered, taller, rounder, and a consummate gentleman. He wore dark suits and reminded me somewhat of the family uncle who became an undertaker. I don't think he ever threw out a piece of paper and you didn't dare rearrange anything on his desk because he had his own order amidst the chaos. A few years later Transport Canada recognized him for overseeing a special team of technologists who designed and built a new public address system for the Winnipeg airport terminal from scratch; featuring digital queuing for users and audiophile-quality sound, it was definitely state-of-the-art!

The navigation aids we maintained consisted of three Instrument Landing Systems (ILS) that gave pilots precise guidance to runway touchdown points in bad weather. We also looked after a military Tacan system as well as an Omni-Range and several beacons. Each of these used different electronic signals to guide pilots along various airways and air routes between airports. The first GPS satellite would not be launched until 1978 so even with these electronic aids pilots still relied heavily on paper maps and pencils in the cockpit.

Our ILS and Omni-Range systems radiated precise electronic beams that were periodically checked for accuracy by a specially equipped aircraft. These flight checks required techs on the ground to track the aircraft using an optical telescope called a theodolite. Comparing the aircraft and theodolite tracking data told us whether or not the navaid was performing as it should. On the day in question, I had helped set

A maintenance technologist using an optical theodolite to track a flight-check aircraft.

up the theodolite to flight check that part of the ILS called the glide path. Aircraft followed the glide path's beam down a precise electronic slope to touch down just past the runway threshold. I was looking through the theodolite back up the glide path from the touchdown point waiting for the aircraft to appear in my lens. Every time it passed through my crosshairs, I would send an electronic 'blip' that would be recorded on the equipment in the flight-check aircraft.

Aha! Here was the aircraft now, about 16 kilometres back. Through the theodolite's eyepiece the Beechcraft King Air looked like a thin pencil line with a dot in the middle. The aircraft went up and down across my lens, and I blipped away at it. It seemed to my neophyte eyes that the pilot was having difficulty staying on the glide slope's beam, but I put that down to turbulence aloft. About the time when the run should have been half over the pilot said he was having a very hard time tracking my blips while staying on the glide slope and he speculated that either the theodolite was not calibrated or the glide path equipment must be way out of spec. As he said that the 'airplane' I was tracking started flapping its wings, then the seagull stopped soaring on the air currents and flew out of my view....

"Sorry about that; obviously we are going to need another run...."

"... Radio Knobs...."

Randy Peterson had a long and varied career with Transport and later with Nav Canada. Randy Peterson photo.

When the flight check was over and we were packing up, the pilots called the tower and said they could not get their landing gear down. We hung around to follow what was happening on our radio. The pilots flew away from the airport to put the plane through some violent manoeuvres to try and shake their gear down. After trying that to no avail and with fuel running low, they declared an emergency and announced they would belly land. They were talking to one of their mechanics on the ground who said that one way to release the jammed gear might be to remove the floorboards and operate the mechanism manually. Our flight-check technologist on board, Randy Peterson, had a Swiss army knife in his pocket. Following instructions from the ground he was able to lift the floor panels and MacGyver down the gear. The wheels thumped down reassuringly but the landing was still tense until it was clear the wheels were going to stay where they belonged. Randy was the hero of the day and did not have to buy any beers for some time after that!

Many of our navaid sites were off the airport which meant some travelling, which I always enjoyed. The latest low bidder to supply our vehicles was AMC, and their Matadors were delivered from the dealer with AM/FM radios as standard equipment. The bureaucrats decreed techs did not require the luxury of listening to the radio while driving so Transport Canada paid hundreds of extra dollars to the car dealer to rip out the standard radios. We navaid techs filed grievances with our union stating our safety was being put at risk because we could not receive road condition and weather reports when driving off the airport. Eventually we won those grievances because we did have to drive hours away to reach the furthest of our sites. Management then paid hundreds more dollars for the dealer to refit an AM only radio into one vehicle and it would be only that vehicle that could be driven off the airport. They didn't even try to save cash by buying a cheap 20 dollar set from Radio Shack for us to install ourselves, but the navaid group got a car radio. In case readers think we spent the time on our journeys enjoying the latest hits, our AM radio usually picked up only the CBC's farm reports once we were outside Winnipeg.

I would be maintaining navaids and weather equipment in the Arctic so I learned as much as I could from my colleagues about common faults and troubleshooting, subjects that were not taught in college. After my time in navaids I had become fairly conversant with the beacons and their monitoring systems that I would soon have to look after on my own. Navaids was my favourite assignment because of the variety of equipment and the many different sites; also some of the equipment actually used modern solid-state transistors instead of vacuum tubes!

Some of the navaid group's off-airport travel was to Environment Canada weather stations. Environment did not have their own maintenance technologists at that time; instead they had an agreement with Transport Canada to look after their equipment. I found this interesting work because the weather stations were two of the first generation of unmanned automatic reporting stations. One was near the U.S. border at Gretna, and the other in Hecla Island Provincial Park, about half way up Lake Winnipeg. We always packed golf clubs or fishing rods when travelling to Hecla, knowing that if a fault delayed our return the supervisors would authorize an overnight stay at the park's hotel rather than pay us overtime to drive home. It was necessary to cross the driving range of the Hecla Island Golf Club in our car to reach the weather station site. With the orange light on top, we were a moving target for the duffers and occasionally came home with some 'hail damage.'

Vince Warszycki on the stand of a visibility sensor like the one at Gretna. W. Warszycki photo.

One morning when reporting to work I was told that the visibility sensor at Gretna was unserviceable, and Frank Gaudet and I were to leave right away and take care of it. On the drive out of Winnipeg we stopped at a hardware store to buy a packet of duct seal. I figured it was for

Frank's personal use and said nothing. When we got to Gretna, we had to approach the site by driving over a set of train tracks, and there was the site on the right. The sensor was a spot light, like a kind of high beam, which shone onto a photocell 200 metres away. Rain, snow, or fog reduced the amount of light reaching the photocell thus indicating a measurement of reduced visibility.

As we parked the car Frank asked me if I noticed anything.

"The light is out?"

"Right ... bring the duct seal and tool box, I'll get a spare bulb from the building."

Okay ... why would we need duct seal? The answer was clear when we climbed up onto the light platform. The bulb was shattered and there was a nifty .308-size hole in the rear case. There were three other similar holes of various calibres already plugged with duct seal. Frank explained:

"Farmers drive up to the railway crossing at night and see the light. They stop for what might be a train, and when they realize it isn't they get their rifle off the window rack and kill the light. This happens once or twice a year, but we can't get approval to move our sensor. With four bullet holes we should probably order a new case."

Fresh Sea-Bugs!

Frank and his wife were originally from Nova Scotia and still had family and friends there. One day he passed the hat to collect 10 dollars per person from anyone who was interested in buying fresh-cooked Nova Scotia lobster. These days 10 dollars doesn't buy a lot of lobster but in 1973 'sea-bugs' were going for a dollar a pound. A couple of days after placing the order Frank headed over to Air Canada's cargo facility at the end of his day shift. He returned with his pickup truck full of garbage bags each containing some ice and nine one-pound lobsters. One lobster from each bag of 10 had gone to pay the 'vig' to Air Canada's cargo folks in lieu of us being charged for the freight!

Frank's buddies back home had caught and cooked the lobsters that very morning so they couldn't be any fresher! We met up with Frank in the parking lot of the local bar to receive our lobsters. I sat on Frank's tailgate with a frosty bevvie in one hand and a cold cooked lobster tail in the other. I knew then I had made the right career choice!

Communications Group

Shortly after enjoying the lobsters it was my time to rotate again, this time into the communications group. Comm not only looked after all the radio transmitters and receivers used by ATC, but also the tape recorders that logged all voice communications, the vehicle radios and walkie-talkies used by everyone on the airport, and the airport security and public address systems. The comm group technologists also maintained the control systems used by the air traffic controllers and FSS (Flight Service Specialists) to communicate with everyone in their world via the radios, teletypes, and telephone hotlines that tied the whole Air Navigation System together across the country.

Despite this variety of equipment, I found the comm group to be a bit boring. I was already familiar with receivers and transmitters because we had studied them at college. Ours were manufactured in the electronic equivalent of tank factories so they were built like brick outhouses, rarely failed, and required little in the way of routine maintenance. The control systems we looked after were built up from standard modules connected together using a structured wiring system. This part was new to me and I needed to learn about it for my now imminent northern assignment. John Vereyken took me under his wing and explained the mysteries of sectionalizing, normalizing, wire charts, and distribution frames. He was not assigned to do this and without him taking an interest in my ongoing education I would have faced a steep learning curve on my own. John, I thank you to this day for giving me your time, and I'll have you know that none of it was wasted! On August 23, not long after my comm group assignment began, John Skitcko came to me with two telegrams. They read:

"LeCren, DB, confirmed GMD-2 course Sept. 4–28 Scarborough."

"Initiate relocation LeCren, DB, YWG - YZS October 8."

These telegrams meant that I had one week until the month-long GMD equipment training course began in Scarborough, Ontario, then only another week after that before I had to get myself and my worldly possessions to Coral Harbour, known throughout the aviation world as YZS, and located some 1,800 kilometres north on Southampton Island at the top of Hudson Bay.

Ground Meteorological Device Mk. 2 (GMD-2), colloquially known as the Grand Mother Duck, was an Environment Canada system that used a moving dish to automatically track weather

A transportable radio direction finder type AN/GMD-1. Photo courtesy radartutorial.eu.

balloons. Externally, it looked identical to the earlier Mk. 1 version shown in the previous photo. Weather balloons were launched twice every day at the same time from upper air observation sites around the world. They carried a weather sensor package and soared to around 30 kilometres high before the balloon burst and the package fell back to earth. In the pre-satellite days these packages, called radiosondes, were the only way of sampling conditions within the atmospheric layers to forecast the weather. Modern radiosondes are still launched today from 31 Canadian sites.

Coral Harbour had a GMD and I would spend a lot of my time there babysitting it. It was designed to military specifications and built by another electronic tank factory. Originally a military device, the GMD was designed to be taken apart in a hurry for transportation by truck. It came with its own speed wrench for this, so three of us, on the final morning of the course before we headed home from Scarborough, snuck into the room where it sat and quietly reduced it to its component parts in about ten minutes, scattering the pieces around the room and hiding the wrench in the janitor closet. We never heard anything about the prank and it may not have been the only time it was pulled, but when I returned to Scarborough two years later for training on another system, I looked in and noticed that the speed nuts were now self-locking types and the wrench had been taken away.

After the GMD course I shipped my personal freight to Coral and went through the necessary paperwork to get myself clear of the Winnipeg organization. There was surprisingly little else to do to relocate since I was leaving my parent's home to live in a furnished barracks. My stuff was packed into Dad's two RCAF footlockers, which were taken to Transair to be freighted north.

During my last week in Winnipeg, I managed some extra time at home and with my fiancée Val. She lived with her parents in the village of Anola east of Winnipeg. I left my car with her because she needed the transportation, even if it was only a 1959 Hillman Minx!

GOING NORTH

On the day I left my parent's home Dad came to the airport to see me off. Mom did not want to take the long two-transfer bus ride home by herself and Dad needed a different route to continue on to his work. That was fine with me because we were not an outwardly emotional family; few hugs and kisses, certainly none involving my father although we knew we loved each other. Neither of us wanted an emotional scene at the airport; we had done that earlier in the kitchen. I had called a taxi since my parents did not drive. At the airport I was pretty sure Dad was thinking about his own departure from his parental home some 30 years prior. He left by train to go to a shooting war in 1943, but the family scene was similar nonetheless.

"So, don't forget to write."

"Every week."

"And send us lots of pictures so we can see how you're living."

"Of course. I'll get extra copies made for you and Val."

We were both shuffling our feet and not making eye contact ...

"Be safe."

"I will."

"Do you have everything?"

"I think so, yes. Anything I've missed I'll ask you to send up."

Besides my freight that was already shipped I had Dad's large Gladstone bag containing clothes and other necessities. Mom had helped to pack.

"Do you have enough underwear?"

"All I own, Ma."

"I went to Sears and bought you some more socks …"

"Thanks, Ma."

"… and a nice pair of woollen long johns."

"Ma!"

"But I don't want you catching cold!"

Well, she was right about that. It would be cold where I was going. Dad and I were trying to think of things to say. There was so much but we were both a bit choked up and neither of us trusted ourselves to break the ice. I just wanted to be on the plane and on my way.

"Things go okay with Val?"

"I guess so, as well as they could I suppose."

Val and I had said a tearful goodbye the previous night. The plan was I would save my money while she completed her college training as a medical laboratory technician, and then we would start our life together when I returned. We were both young and naive and this separation would prove a blessing as well as a test of our commitment to each other. Dad rested his hand on my shoulder:

"I'm very proud of you, son. Your mom and I love you very much. You've taken on a lot in a short time, and I know you'll do your best and do well."

He was not speaking only of my engagement. Just three months out of college and after minimal training, I was now responsible for all the aviation and marine electronic systems at Coral Harbour. It was time to go....

"Are you all checked in?"

"Yes, got my boarding pass."

"Well, I should be getting to work ..."

"Thanks for seeing me off ... You and Ma take care. Tell her I love her and I'll write when I get there ..."

We gave each other a final hug and back slaps.

"You too. Love you, son."

"Love you too, Dad...."

"Here, take this in case you need something on the way."

He pressed a bill into my palm as we shook hands and gave each other one last hug in front of the ticket counter. Then he was walking to the terminal exit, I saw him wipe his eyes as he walked out to the bus, and I was on my own.

Airport security then was minimal and I walked through the metal detector in my government-issued parka and fleece-lined boots without setting off the alarm or receiving any attention beyond "Have a nice day" from the operator. We who were going north drew stares from the rest of the travelling public. They must have thought we were American tourists; after all it was a warm day in early October and the leaves were just changing colour, but here we were wandering around the terminal in Skidoo suits or parkas while everyone else sported tees and sunglasses.

Many travelling on the same plane as I wore military-style parkas and 'jingle boots' like mine, so called because the metal buckles were rarely done up and they jingled like sleigh bells when walking. These passengers would be army personnel from Fort Churchill or employees of other government departments returning to Churchill, which was Transair's one stop en route to Coral. The civilian travellers displayed patches from the Churchill Rocket Range, Port Authority, Pan American Airways, and Transair. There was a group of Inuit women wearing traditional Amautiit and one lady carried a baby in the pouch on her back.... between the military presence, rocket range, seaport, and tourists, Churchill was a going concern in the 1970s.

In our winter garb we looked like a gaggle of multi-coloured ticks about to pop as we filed through the gate, waddled across the ramp, then up the air stairs into the rear of the aircraft. There was no seat selection so I grabbed the first window I could near the rear, close to the lavatory and exit.

Transair operated YS-11 aircraft on their northern service that were configured to carry both freight and passengers. They were built by a Japanese consortium for their domestic market, powered by two Rolls Royce turboprop engines, and were referred to by us as 'rice burners.' They were not intended to carry North American-sized adults for hours over

the Precambrian bush and tundra in comfort, certainly not adults dressed to expect a blizzard. There was minimal stowage for carry-on baggage and none for parkas, so everyone scrunched into their too-small seat as best they could. We introduced ourselves to our neighbours with our elbows while trying to get our arms out of our parka sleeves. We who had the windows put our shoulders into the slightly wider window wells while those along the aisle slumped outwards. Our heavy coats forced us to sit upright even with the seats reclined, which they were despite instructions to the contrary from the flight attendant. Passengers could only lower the seatback trays halfway; if they had been able to come fully down our feet would not fit under the seat in front. We were cozy.

Transair's YS-11 'Norway House' arriving at Coral Harbour, weather permitting!

Soon the atmosphere became intense as the fresh air system failed to keep up with dozens of closely packed bodies and sweaty feet, many of whom had partied the night before and failed to shower. It was a two-and-a-half-hour flight to Churchill. The flight attendant could not get her cart down the aisle for the bodies and boots spilling out from the seats, so along about the time my butt went numb styrofoam cups of coffee and cardboard boxes started getting passed forward from the rear. These were our in-flight breakfasts. The regulars on board were used to inspecting the contents of the boxes and choosing extra juices or sausages before passing them on, and I suspect those in the front rows of the plane didn't get much except an empty box and the napkins. The smells of sausage patties and powdered scrambled eggs added to our olfactory experience. The large dude beside me tried to free his right arm trapped between us, which spilled my coffee into my lap. This was soon followed by my orange juice as he hoisted himself into the aisle to try and make his way to the single lavatory at the rear. As I contemplated another hour in the air with sticky balls, I noticed a trickle of fluid heading aft along the rubber floor mat. The atmospheric fug confirmed that at least one of my fellow flyers could not navigate the crowded aisle and did not possess a strong bladder.

There was a mad scrum for the exit upon landing at Churchill as everyone fought to be the first to the terminal bathrooms. Bad weather had delayed the onward flight to Coral Harbour by three hours which was not a hardship, except the airport restaurant closed on time leaving us nowhere to sit while we waited. By the time it was Dark O'Clock the weather in Coral had improved enough for us to make the two-hour flight. On this leg there were only a few Inuit returning home and me, so by folding down the seat ahead I was able to get my feet up and nap in reasonable comfort.

I awoke to a blast of frigid air and snow coming in the rear door … we had arrived! My misery was replaced by excitement as I thought about making new friends and experiencing new adventures. I bundled up and rolled down the air stairs to be met by another government-issued parka and set of jingle boots that were connected together with a pair of green canvas wind pants. The parka extended a gloved hand and the hood introduced itself as Marv Thordarson, airport manager.

"Welcome to Coral Harbour Airport!"

I looked around and saw nothing but blackness, blowing snow, and the dark shapes of other parkas outlined in the lights from a few idling Skidoos. There was no air terminal building. Seeing my parka swivel, my new best friend, who I still hadn't seen inside the fur-trimmed hood, hooked a finger over his shoulder and said:

"The station is over there. Let's get your stuff into my truck."

Coral Harbour Meeters and Greeters.
There was no air terminal in 1973.

I now noticed the checked baggage had been tossed onto a snowbank beside the apron, and a truck had backed up to the forward cargo door to receive the onboard freight and mail. I rummaged through the snow with the other new arrivals and found my Gladstone bag. It turned out my two trunks had caught the same flight I had, and had been tossed into another snowbank along with the rest of the airport's freight.

Welcome to Coral Harbour!

This hamlet with the beatific name was strung out along a cove on the south shore of Southampton Island like a Newfoundland outport, except here the little matchbox houses were frozen into the tundra and were not painted gay colours. Located just 160 kilometres south of the Arctic Circle, the island is covered with ice and snow for nine months of the year and muskeg, rocks, and tundra the other three. In 1973

Coral Harbour's airport boasted an upper air weather station, a flight service station (FSS) providing services to pilots, and a marine radio station that was only active during the brief summer shipping season.

The Inuit name for both Southampton Island and Coral Harbour is Salliq ('large flat island'). When I arrived, the hamlet was located about 14 kilometres via winding dirt road from the airport and had a population of about 400. It was named for the fossilized coral found in the shallow waters along the shores near the community. People had travelled through the area for thousands of years. In 1924 the Hudson's Bay Company sailed into the cove and established a fur trading post, followed closely by missionaries. The community coalesced in the 1950s when the government built an elementary school. Coral Harbour remains a traditional community preserving the Inuit language and culture. The land and sea are rich in natural resources and the people still live off the land pretty much as earlier generations have done, except Skidoos and rifles have largely replaced dog teams and spears.

Coral Harbour today. In the 1970s the community was half this size, occupying only the top half of the photo. Coral Harbour, Nunavut, Canada, accessed 2021. Photo courtesy Wikipedia.org.

The airport was built during WWII as a refuelling stop for aircraft being ferried along the Crimson Route to Europe.

Later, when it was understood that salt water and cool climates helped burn patients heal, the government built a convalescent hospital nearby. The community sank back into somnolence at war's end and the hospital closed. Coral Harbour was invaded a second time by the military and their civilian contractors when the DEW line was constructed. While not a DEW line site, Coral Harbour was a supply and staging base for construction further north. Things quieted down a second time when that work was finished, however the upper air and flight service stations remained due to their strategic location under the polar air routes to Europe.

About a dozen people lived on the airport. Eight were observers or specialists who carried out the upper air program and handled the flight service duties. Coral had a Telecom Station Manager (TSM) who was my on-site boss and who also managed the specialists through their FSS (Flight Service Specialist) supervisor. The TSM was an experienced technologist who volunteered, like the airport manager, for a six-month tour of duty. This was usually for one of three reasons: earn extra money, gain supervisory experience in hope of future promotion, or get away from their wives. The airport manager and two cooks rounded out our resident staff. Six Inuit were employed by the airport manager as airport maintainers, heavy equipment operators, kitchen helpers, and janitors.

Even though they are nearby the community and airport were isolated from each other and actually kept different times when I arrived. Southampton Island is in Canada's Eastern time zone, but the airport kept Central time because that was the zone our bosses in Churchill were in. Near the end of my tour the airport residents saw sense and we changed to Eastern time so our clocks would be the same as the hamlet's. There was socializing back and forth, particularly with the school teachers and nurses. We had scheduled air service once a week that brought fresh food, mail, and sometimes new people. By comparison, the High Arctic Weather Stations north of Resolute Bay had only eight people, no nearby hamlet, and a cargo plane only once a month, weather permitting.

In my opinion people coming from the south either loved or hated the Arctic, nothing in between those extremes. I heard the environment summed up as "magnificent desolation" by more than one person who appreciated the beauty of the land and the Inuit, and some of them never left. Others suffered through their time while counting down the days until the end of their sentence. I knew of one new employee who arrived at Resolute Bay from the south, looked around for the 20 minutes that the airplane was on the ground, then announced "I quit!" and re-boarded for the return flight to Edmonton.

Coral Harbour was and still is, like almost all Nunavut communities, dry. This was another benefit to living 14 kilometres away because we had an airport recreation association that maintained a well-stocked bar. The association membership was restricted to airport residents including the Inuit employees, and our invited guests. This did much to promote positive social interaction with the nurses and teachers.

What we did not have were long-distance telephones or television. We could listen to short-wave radio but there were no computers, gaming, or other digital technology. Music came on vinyl records or cassette tapes. Movies were 16-mm films that the rec association brought in every couple of weeks. If you wanted to talk to the folks back home you wrote a letter and waited about three weeks for a reply, unless you paid the high cost of a telegram that could be sent from the FSS. Social interaction consisted largely of pool and shuffleboard in the bar area, or leaving your barrack room door open as an invitation to passers-by to stop in and visit. I was fine with this, as it hearkened back to my childhood years in Germany.

When I arrived the Arctic winter had settled in, which pretty much confined us to the airport for the next nine months. There was no autumn.... One early September day the temperature was above zero and the land was green, the next day was a whiteout as the first blizzard of the season descended on the community. Temperatures would not see zero again until late May, and winter wouldn't release its grip on the land until June.

The most important people on the airport were the cooks! Our chief cook was Norm Frost, who learned his meat-and-

potatoes style of cooking in the British Columbia lumber camps. His food was satisfying and filling, even if a bit plain and predictable. He chewed snuff and kept a spittoon on the floor next to his food prep table. I don't ever recall any odd tastes or textures, so his aim must have been good.

Norm Frost, Chief Cook.

Our second cook was Bob Harron, who turned out some pretty decent pastries, sides, and desserts. Between the two of them we were kept well fed and happy, and struggled to keep our weights down!

During my time in Coral, I served with four different TSMs. All but one was a pleasure to work with and taught me a lot while pretty much leaving me alone to maintain the electronic equipment. Although we were always available if needed, we were not 'on call' and worked a scheduled 54-hour week. Having the TSM on-site meant that he and I each had one scheduled day off. Mine was Saturday, his was Sunday.

There was a diverse collection of equipment to look after besides the Grand Mother Duck. We had a radio communications suite for talking to aircraft and ships, short-wave radios for contact between communities, two navaid beacons used by both aircraft and ships, low-frequency radio teletypes for long-distance communication with the rest of the world, a dozen vehicle radios and miscellaneous odds and sods from the airport public address and fire alarm systems to a Ham amateur radio station and the movie projector. My only formal training was on the GMD and my Winnipeg osmosis experience suddenly seemed very inadequate. Repairs and maintenance came down to "read the manuals and figure things out on the learning curve."

I was also asked on occasion to repair personal stereo systems or the radio sets in the hamlet that belonged to the game warden, the Hudson's Bay store manager, or the two missions. I usually parlayed these favours into dinner invitations on my days off. Will Work for Food!

Marv, the airport manager, helped me square away my things that first night and told me that my boss, the TSM, had broken his ankle in a fight with a villager in our rec club bar and was in hospital in Churchill. The tech I was relieving had left the previous month so I would not get the customary handover briefing, but would be working alone for at least a week.

I met most of the staff the next morning at breakfast. Fred Lang, the supervisor of the flight service station, showed me

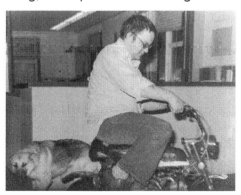

around his operation and introduced me to his specialists. He gave me a long deficiency list of unserviceable equipment that had been piling up for weeks and we sorted out which were his priorities.

Fred Lang, the FSS supervisor. He would drive his mini-bike to work in the summer, often accompanied by his dog.

Brian, the upper air supervisor, also informed me his GMD had not been looked at in a long time and was having issues so my first priority was to check it over before the next scheduled balloon release in about seven hours. His crew were sleeping after their 0700 morning balloon release and I would meet them later in the day.

It took a few hours to give the GMD a complete overhaul then over the next few days I worked through Fred's deficiency list. Fortunately, most of the problems were minor and dealing with them improved my confidence in my ability to maintain the equipment on my own. This older equipment dated from the mid-1960s but performed with a minimum of trouble provided it was kept clean and you stayed on top of the vacuum tubes, which wore out over time. Most of the tubes we used were no longer being manufactured except in Eastern European countries, which was ironic given the Cold War was still going strong, but their quality and life expectancy had certainly gone down from earlier years.

During this time alone I used my free time to go exploring. The single-storey facilities were built around the upper air station and FSS. The barracks block was 'H' shaped and in between it and the FSS was the mess hall and rec club. This middle building also had a few 'VIP accommodations,' which meant rooms with private baths. The airport manager, TSM, and chief cook all lived there. We in the barracks had single bedrooms with sitting areas and common washroom and laundry facilities. On 'plane days' we closed the bar so the rec club could function as a shelter for people meeting the flight, since there was no air terminal building. These three buildings were connected with a long wooden passage. This convenience was added in 1966 and allowed most of us to walk to work and meals without having to bundle up and go outside. Before we had the passage, safety ropes were strung between the buildings because people could become disoriented, lost, and freeze to death in a howling blizzard, even over short distances.

A short distance away towards the airport apron was the upper air station. The GMD lived in a dome above the station office and plotting room, and about 50 metres away was the

Coral Harbour airport main camp, FSS on the right, barracks on the left. Dining, rec club, and VIP accommodations centre.

hydrogen shed with its oversized door, where the radiosondes and balloons were prepared for launch. An electrolyser generated hydrogen gas from water for filling the balloons, and was about the only piece of electrical equipment I had no responsibility for besides the power house generators. The hydrogen shed was separated from the other buildings because a clear area was needed for launching the balloons, and because at least one shed had blown itself up when the electrolyser failed!

Coral Harbour upper air station.

A maintenance garage for our heavy equipment sat at the end of the aircraft apron, and a power house completed our airport camp apart from a few storage buildings.

There were three remote sites I had to maintain. Most of the radio transmitters and receivers were kept apart in their own buildings several kilometres from anywhere else because they operated best in an environment without interfering energy,

Coral Harbour airport, looking southwest from the dump along the receiver site road. The maintenance garage for the heavy equipment is in the foreground on the right, and the power house is in the centre. Keen eyes will make out the remote transmitter site antenna towers on the horizon, just right of centre.

and because the large number of antenna towers would be a hazard to aircraft.

Coral Harbour Remote Receiver Site, 3 kilometres east of the airport.

About four kilometres south of the airport on the shoreline of Hudson Bay was the third site, a low-powered beacon used by pilots for guidance to the runway. Also south of the airport was an old abandoned warehouse building, all that remained of the WWII camp and hospital. Besides the road to the hamlet there was nowhere else to go, and few personal vehicles to get you there anyway. I was fortunate to have a four-wheel drive pickup truck and a Bombardier snow bus, called a bomb, for my use. They were officially to access the remote sites but they also gave me the opportunity to roam around a bit in my free time. A corollary benefit was that I was the taxi service to the hamlet to fetch the weekly mail or whenever an errand needed to be run.

Both my truck and bomb, and indeed all our airport vehicles and mechanical equipment, were well maintained by our Inuit heavy equipment operators and gave me almost no trouble during my months at Coral. A previous tech had rolled the pickup out by the garbage dump, but our mechanics were very skilled and straightened out the cab so you wouldn't know it had been crunched.

CORAL HARBOUR MEMORIES, MAINLY PLEASANT

Home Renovation, Coral Style

Bob Harron, second cook.

Bob Harron, our second cook, was married to an Inuit lady named Harriet and so lived in the hamlet with his family. A month or two after my arrival I drove the off-duty airport staff into the hamlet for a social evening being held in the school gym by the teachers. The bomb needed to be plugged in to keep the engine from freezing so we arranged to use a cord that was hanging out the side of Bob's house. Come the wee hours we all piled into the bomb, which started just fine, and drove back to the airport. The next morning a very irate second cook told me I had forgotten to untie the cords, his end had been wrapped around the bathroom sink drain pipe, and his whole family thought their end had come when I drove off and pulled their sink out of the counter and nearly through the wall of the house! Fortunately, the hamlet authorities were able to install a new sink and vanity in his bathroom the next day, and there was no charge since this upgrade was considered part of routine home maintenance in Coral Harbour!

Hamming it Up

The amateur radio (Ham) station was installed in an empty barracks room officially as emergency communications in case all else failed, and only the flight service specialists

View of the barracks and centre block, looking south. The Ham antenna tower stands in the middle of the barracks block.

were supposed to use it. I, however, went on the air regularly in the guise of conducting preventive maintenance and usually had no trouble making contact with other operators down south. Many Hams were alert for rare call signs such as ours which began with VE8, signifying an operator in the Northwest Territories. Hams like to collect different call signs and a VE8 entry was a prize in many logbooks! On occasion I was able to work a Ham in Winnipeg who could patch our radio conversation into a local telephone line, allowing me a brief but public chance to call home! As my time at Coral increased and the days grew dark while the winter never seemed to end, these impromptu chats were confirmation that loved ones still inhabited a real world that continued to exist beyond our limited horizon, and did a lot to keep my morale high.

ND Returns

It was two weeks after my arrival in Coral before my TSM returned from Churchill, and by then I had figured out most of the station equipment and had it running smoothly. When I met ND at the plane and showed him that everything was working fine, I thought he would be pleased. Instead, I was treated to a barrage of nitpicking details, mostly administrative that were his responsibility and about which I knew nothing, but which he thought I should have taken care of and wanted put right before dinner. Okay, he was the boss and I was the lowly TIRL, but I felt his attitude was unwarranted since he was the one who had gotten into the bar brawl, leaving me on my own from day one with a long deficiency list that had all been remedied. It didn't take long to figure out that he was a very insecure micromanager who liked to find fault, as long as it wasn't his.

One Sunday morning I was driving back to the FSS when Marv flagged me down. His staff were not on duty on weekends and he needed help hitching his Caterpillar tractor to the big rollers used to keep the runway surface smooth. This job took about 20 minutes, and unbeknownst to me ND was watching out a window the entire time. When I arrived back indoors, he told me in no uncertain terms that I worked for him and not Marv; I must ask his permission before doing work for Marv; and he would now have to fill out a form and get Jake, his boss in Churchill, to recover the cost of my 20 minutes from the airport manager's budget! This was the kind of petty bureaucratic bullshit he dished out at every turn. Even I could see he was out of his depth and unsuited to supervision, especially in isolated conditions where everyone needed to pitch in together.

His attitudes probably had something to do with the bar fight, but to be fair he did step up when the chips were down. One night in the dead of winter a fire started in the hamlet's powerhouse. It was soon brought under control by their volunteer fire department, but three of their four diesel generators were out of action and most of the wiring was toast. Coral Harbour was now in the dark and without heat. Marv, who was an electrician by trade, and ND went immediately to the hamlet and worked tirelessly with their Inuit electrician for the next 48 hours. They managed to get a second generator on line. They bypassed the damaged switch gear and restored enough power to the community to run home oil furnaces and lights but not enough for appliances, street lighting, and other services. The residents used traditional methods of cooking over camp stoves or seal-oil fires for the next two days until Transair's Argosy freighter arrived and disgorged a new diesel generator set. Once that was trucked to the community and

Transair's Argosy delivers the hamlet's new diesel generator set.

installed into their powerhouse the crisis was over. The next summer the Northern Canada Power Commission took over the operation of our airport powerhouse and installed a power line between the airport and hamlet. Our airport generators were oversized and had enough capacity to power the entire island. You could also follow the pole line in bad weather so the chances of getting lost in a storm between hamlet and airport were greatly reduced!

Each of our remote sites were supposed to have a set of basic tools, but many had gone missing over the years. This was not a problem for me since I carried my own tools, but ND worried constantly that he would be held personally and financially accountable for anything still missing when the time came to hand over to the next TSM. He made me responsible for hunting them all down, which, of course, I was unable to do so his nagging got worse as his remaining time got less. We continued to tiptoe around each other for the remaining weeks until his time was up and I breathed a sigh of relief when he finally got on the flight home.

Elmer Klatt

Elmer arrived from Swift Current, Saskatchewan, to take over from ND early in 1974, and he was a joy to have on the station. I worked with him, not for him. The first thing he did as TSM was write off all the missing tools as either broken or worn out and uneconomical to repair.

Elmer was in his 40s and of average height, balding, and rotund. He always wore a bright smile to complement the fluorescent orange hunting hat that was part of our Arctic clothing issue. Elmer was the only person I knew who ever bothered wearing that hat, and he never took it off while at work including at meals. I think he slept with it on too. It made him resemble his Looney Tunes namesake, which was unfortunate because he was a very pleasant individual and always tried to please. Elmer was farm-smart and conscientious to a fault, that fault being he let insignificant things niggle away at him, like a worm in the back of his brain until he felt he had to act. Then insignificant things turned into big things.

That Left a Mark!

Elmer liked to keep his hand in, this time literally! We had an outdoor air sampler next to the FSS which was just a simple vacuum filter. The specialist changed the filter each week and mailed it to the National Research Council in Ottawa. There they looked for radioactive isotopes from atomic testing and other pollutants. We were never told the results but we didn't glow in the dark either so I guess the air was fit to breathe. The sampler was downwind from the cook's burn barrel so

I often wondered what the NRC boffins thought about our northern air quality!

A rather large electric motor and a pair of exposed belts on pulleys drove the sampler's vacuum pump. It bothered Elmer that we were not required to perform maintenance on this device. His farm smarts and the worm in his brain both told him that this was against all the laws of mechanical systems. The motor and pump were permanently lubricated but that did not stop Elmer from setting out one day to satisfy his worm by adjusting the tension on the belts. He decided not to turn the motor off while doing this so, of course, his finger jammed in the moving belts, which tore up the end of his middle digit. The first we knew of this was when he came into the FSS with his hand wrapped in an oily and bloody rag, looking for a Band-Aid. Despite his protestations that he was fine and it was just a scratch I drove him to the hamlet's nursing station where, after some antiseptic, a tetanus shot, and 16 stitches, he was good to go minus a fingernail and some pride.

"Elmer, why did you not turn off the motor? There's a switch right there!"

"Well, I did not want the filter to miss anything significant...."

"It runs 24/7 every single day, and it would have been off for only a minute. What significance would it miss—some ash from Cookie's burnt pork chops?"

Do Not Touch the Crank Ever Again!

Our FSS had one military-owned transmitter that guarded the Air Force's emergency frequency of 243.0 megahertz (MHz). It had eight tuning knobs on the front and a master crank that moved all the knobs at once. The idea behind the crank was to pre-tune everything together into the ballpark of the frequency you wanted, then each of the eight smaller knobs could fine-tune dead on to the frequency. The crank had an indicator dial, and ours pointed to 243.1 MHz, about 1 mm away from 243.0. This anomaly drove Elmer bat-shit nuts and it didn't matter that the crank would never be moved. The dial was only a suggestion to start the tuning process, and no one but us techs ever saw it anyway because the transmitter was located at the remote site. Every few days Elmer would visit the transmitter site on routine business. While there he looked at the dial reading 243.1 and his worm ate a little more of his brain. One Saturday, when it was my day off, he went to the remote transmitter site intending to correct the transmitter's dial position to read 243.0.

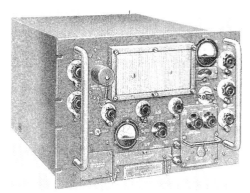

Radio transmitting set AN/GRT-3, June 1957, and the type Elmer disassembled. The master crank and indicator are to the right of the filter. Photo courtesy RadioNerds.com

The easy and correct procedure would be to turn the master crank the 1 millimetre to 243.0 then re-tune the other eight knobs on the transmitter. No one had ever gone to that trouble because the transmitter was operating spot on frequency and so the dial reading didn't matter. Elmer had not worked on this military equipment before and was unsure how to tune it. What his worm told him to do was loosen the master crank and tweak it the 1 mm onto 243.0 without moving the other knobs, and all would be made right with his world. He started by removing the transmitter from its equipment rack, which was no small feat for one person because it weighed about 30 kilograms. Then he manhandled it onto the site's workbench, undid the 30+ screws that held the lid on (remember electronic tank factories?) and peered inside.

What he saw was a gap between the electronic chassis and the front panel about five centimetres wide, inside of which was a bicycle chain wrapping around all the tuning knobs and the master crank like a modern car's serpentine belt. Each of the knobs and the crank had a gear for the chain, a shaft that the front panel tuning knob was attached to, a second shaft disappearing inside the electronics, and little universal joints that connected each assembly together. Rube Goldberg would be proud of the designers of this mechanical nightmare! The object of Elmer's effort was the crank's position indicator, which he could clearly see but the gap behind the panel was too narrow for him to get his fingers and tools in to make his adjustment.

Elmer decided to remove the front panel to get at the indicator. First, he removed the crank and all the knobs, then he undid another couple of dozen screws that held the front panel in place, took hold of each side of the panel, and drew a deep breath.

Like an oncoming train wreck that everyone could see but no one could stop, Elmer pulled on the front panel and all the shafts, gears, universal joints, and the bicycle chain clattered down into the bottom of the gap! Elmer spent the rest of that day and most of the evening trying to get it back together again without me finding out so he wouldn't be embarrassed. He had no hope of success. Finally admitting to himself that he needed help, he hauled all 30 kilograms of what was now a boat anchor back to our FSS workshop and quietly sought me out. I was dumbstruck. Words failed me. All the king's horses and men were never going to get Humpty back together again; Lord knows we tried!

The only spare transmitter in the country was at the Air Force stores depot in Trenton, Ontario. After an exchange of "What the hell did you do that for?" telegrams to us from Jake in Churchill and the Air Force in Trenton, and crow-eating replies in the reverse direction, they sent us the National Spare with the strict admonition DO NOT TOUCH THE CRANK EVER AGAIN!! When the transmitter finally arrived weeks later and we got it installed, Elmer noticed the infamous dial that started all this was reading 242.8. Fortunately, his tour of duty was up before the worm took over once again, but it was a near thing!

Does the Magic Tape Fit?

Our FSS was very much a paper operation and as a consequence used a lot of scotch tape. Fred asked Elmer to order Scotch® Magic™ tape because the regular tape we were sent quickly dried out and had to be constantly picked off the roll. Fred showed Elmer a magazine ad illustrating exactly what he wanted. Elmer sent the ad off to Jake in Churchill along with a rather long memorandum explaining exactly why this particular tape was needed and nothing else would do. Jake read this missive, scratched his head, and sent one of his minions shopping. In due course a padded envelope arrived back at Coral Harbour and Elmer ran into the FSS waving it while announcing in a stentorian voice:

"The magic tape is here! The magic tape is here!"

Everyone gathered round for the great unveiling. Elmer opened the bag, reached inside ... and pulled out a three pack of Nude Seam Control-Top Panty Hose! Jake had kindly returned Elmer's ad with a note saying "We aren't quite sure what panty hose has to do with FSS operations, especially since everyone on your station is male, but we know the nights are long and since you insisted, here they are. Enjoy them and yourselves with our compliments and we hope they fit!" Of course, turning the tape ad over revealed the panty hose ad on the other side! Elmer's reaction?

"After everything I explained in my memo and even giving them the picture, they still got it wrong!"

The Coral Harbour Curling Club

Winter had a solid grip on us even though the daylight hours had begun to increase. We were bored, everyone had cabin fever, and most of us, myself included, were drinking too much. Routine maintenance filled my mornings but unless a fault arose there was nothing much to do for the rest of the day except shoot pool or shuffleboard in the rec club. One of us had the scathingly brilliant idea to make a curling rink in the old WWII camp warehouse, so we drove down in my truck to check it out. Apparently there had been curling there at one time, because the framed outline of an ice sheet was still present, as was an old Perkins diesel generator that hadn't been run in years but which could probably be coaxed into generating some power for lights. What else could we possibly need? Marv generously allowed us to flood the old ice frame from the airport water truck. In February our curling sheet certainly didn't take long to freeze solid! Elmer and I removed the fuel pump and injectors from the old diesel, cleaned them out, and borrowed a 24-volt starter battery and five gallons of fuel from the maintenance garage. It cranked quite a bit but after some priming and verbal encouragement it finally fired up! After we got the lights on some wag remarked:

"What'll we do for rings?"

"Crap...."

"What'll we use for rocks?"

"Shit...."

"I'm not sliding frozen shit down the ice...."

We got one can each of white and orange from our never-ending supply of building paint and managed to daub some more or less circular rings onto each end of our ice sheet. Marv wouldn't let us use the water truck again so we had to make do with the paint being on the ice surface. One of our Inuit had shot a brace of ptarmigan which he had left in the back of Marv's truck, intending to take them home for his dinner. We absconded with eight to use as rocks. We figured if we used their heads for handles they would work just fine; after all, southern curling clubs have turkey bonspiels every Christmas! We got some corn brooms from the janitor supplies and were all set. Not bad for a couple of days' effort, and Red Green would be proud!

We slid the frozen ptarmigan back and forth on our curling sheet for an hour or so. Coral Harbour curling had some interesting variations on the southern game besides using only half the number of required rocks. For example, it was considered good form to bat your ptarmigan back onto the ice if it showed signs of sliding off the side. Scoring was problematic since all ptarmigan look the same so there were heated discussions over who owned how many birds closest to the button. We went for dinner full of high spirits and feeling quite pleased with ourselves. We couldn't wait to return after we had eaten but when we got back to our rink we found that foxes had made off with the rocks and the old diesel's lube oil had leaked out through a bad seal. That caused the unit to seize up so we had to tell the teachers and nurses that the planned Coral Harbour Bonspiel was cancelled forthwith!

I was sad when it came time for Elmer to leave Coral Harbour; he had been a good boss who was leaving the station a better place for his presence. As he was getting on the airplane, still wearing his orange hunting hat, he insisted on giving me his military-style flashlight. This was the kind with a waterproof rubber case and right-angled facing bulb that clipped to the front of your parka. He thought I needed it more than he did. That gesture summed up the kind of man he was.

A Date in Paris

The nearest radar to Coral Harbour was the military's DEW line station guarding Canada's northern frontiers at Hall Beach. Their Scope Dopes provided no civilian air traffic control services unless you were off course and unidentified. Then NORAD (the North American Air Defence Command) would scramble the Voodoos from Bagotville who, if you were a Russian Bear, turned you around and escorted you from Canadian airspace.

In the absence of radar coverage aircraft reported their positions to the nearest FSS by radio at regular intervals. The FSS then sent those position reports to Winnipeg's Air Traffic Control operations centre via radio teletype. The controllers in Winnipeg plotted the aircraft positions by hand on a map using a grease pencil. The process was reversed if ATC needed to contact the pilot. This was certainly primitive by today's standards but it worked to keep aircraft flying the transatlantic routes safely separated in the slower-paced environment of half a century ago. It was possible to chat with aircrews for extended periods as they passed overhead, if they were so inclined, so pilots and FSS often swapped news and gossip over the airwaves. One such conversation involved an Air France flight and one of our specialists who was nearing the end of his one-year sentence. After exchanging the usual pleasantries, the pilot asked our man on the ground if he would like to help one of their flight attendants practice her English. He would, so he and Thérèse passed a very pleasant 15 minutes or so chatting away, mostly en français. When the aircraft was about to go out of radio range our specialist informed her that he would be leaving Coral in a few short weeks, and asked if she would like to continue their conversation over drinks in Paris? She would, and they arranged a rendezvous at a club on the Boul. St. Michel.

That date was our specialist's sole topic of conversation as he counted down the remaining days to his departure. He became insufferable as he regaled everyone with images of how his evening would unfold with this paragon of Air France feminine pulchritude, who in his eyes was nothing less than Miss Universe material. We tried our best to burst his bubble, pointing out that it was almost certainly a hirsute male he had been talking to, but nothing would dissuade him from his dream date. Even the weather cooperated and we all wished him well as we poured him onto his departing flight. I know he kept the date but he left the public service so I have no idea if she did, or if she turned out to be all he imagined. I hope so.

Our Vancouver Symphony Concert

In the early summer of '74 we received unexpected visitors when the Vancouver Symphony Orchestra dropped in. This score of merry musicians was bringing culture to the North with their tuneful tour of major Arctic communities, of which

Coral Harbour was not. We were not on their itinerary. They had only stopped for fuel on their way to Iqaluit. When we told them that authentic Inuit culture lay just 14 kilometres away and the trip involved a chance of seeing a polar bear or walrus in the wild there was nothing for it but to call the hamlet and arrange an audience for an impromptu concert.

The snow had almost completely melted and the rising rivers had washed out the bridges on the road to town. We would travel around the coast on the sea ice to reach the hamlet, which only added to the spirit of adventure! We had three Bombardier snow buses on the airport, and by cramming seven or eight musicians with their instruments into each bomb we should be able to take everybody in one trip. We loaded up and off we went! I was following the airport manager's bomb, staying in their tracks because I was unsure about navigating over rotting sea ice whereas the Inuk driving ahead of me could read it like the back of his hand.

My passengers were very excited at their new adventure, taking turns rubbernecking out the escape hatch on the top of the vehicle while cameras snapped away at ice floes. They all wanted to know when they would see the polar bears and walrus! When we arrived at Coral's community hall it did not take the orchestra long to get set up and the hall was soon packed with almost everyone in the hamlet. There was great interest in many of the instruments because the Inuit had not seen such things as bassoons and trombones before. The musicians obliged with solo demonstrations as part of their repertoire. Our hamlet was probably the most appreciative audience they had played to up to that point. The polar bears and walrus declined to put in an appearance but the VSO returned to the airport laden with caribou roasts, Arctic char steaks, Inuit carvings, and the thanks of the community.

Ian Muir

Ian Muir during his time as TSM Coral Harbour.

Elmer left for Saskatoon, Saskatchewan, in the summer of '74 and Ian Muir arrived from that same city to take his place. Ian was probably the best TSM I had at Coral. His personality was full of humanity and humility; he was a real 'people person' who certainly knew his job and was very professional in carrying it out. I was enjoying my stay at Coral maybe a bit too much and had applied to extend my tour for a second year. In his memo on the subject to Jake in Churchill, Ian said my extension should not extend beyond six months as I needed to experience a wider variety of equipment if I was to progress in my career. Ian had realized as soon as we met that I was beginning to go 'bushy.' This common mental condition is like a severe case of cabin fever resulting from isolation and minimal human contact. Even though I didn't understand why he made that recommendation at the time, putting my reduced extension in the guise of career development was a benefit to me and demonstrated Ian's acumen as a leader of men.

Summer Idyll

Summer, although short, was an idyllic time in the Arctic. The spring breakup occurred in late May and took only a few days to transform the tundra from a barren white landscape into a wild riot of colourful flora as soon as the top layer of the permafrost had melted. Willow trees and flowering shrubs reappeared, only inches tall but decades old. There were roaring sounds throughout this time as the snow pack suddenly melted and the river ice let go. Water ran everywhere

Arctic wildflowers at Coral Harbour.

Purple saxifrage at Coral Harbour.

as creeks were created, rivers filled, and roads and bridges washed out. The water rushed with a vengeance either into low-lying ponds or onto the sea ice that still covered Hudson Bay. Millions of birds returned to Southampton Island and the sound of their calls filled the air as waterfowl, seabirds, songbirds, and raptors all competed for nesting sites and mates. Inuit left the hamlet for camping grounds along the south shores of the island where they spent the summer hunting and fishing in their traditional ways with their families.

Kirchoffer Falls near Coral Harbour, Southampton Island.

Tundra picnic near Kirchoffer Falls, with Bombardier snow bus.

We spent as much time as possible outdoors enjoying the 24-hour daylight. We travelled cross-country for picnics at nearby Kirchoffer waterfall and fished for Arctic char in the rivers.

FSS specialists Earl and Rene caught our goose dinner!

Polar bear swimming in Hudson Bay near Coates Island.

We hunted geese later in the season, played baseball against a hamlet team, and went with the game warden in his boat to nearby Coates Island to help count walrus.

Herd of walrus on Coates Island, Nunavut, Canada.
Photo courtesy Nunavut Tourism, Wikipedia.

We also explored for coral and fossils by the seashore while target shooting at empty beer cans. Ian was well aware of the morale-building advantages of these activities in the brief time we could enjoy them, and encouraged us by making the government vehicles available as much as possible.

Ian Muir and airport manager Bill Duffield getting unstuck.
Ian drove it in, so I watched and kibitzed!

The summer season allowed all of us on the airport to unwind and reset from the nine long months of winter. Habits had become deeply ingrained to the point where you always sat in the same chair at the same time for meals and never deviated from the daily details of your normal routine. The drinking slowed somewhat during the summer and just being able to get outside to enjoy the land with the fresh air and colours relieved a lot of the 'bushiness.' Three extra specialists arrived to operate the marine radio position in the FSS during the shipping season. Some of the airport staff and about half the teachers departed for new southern assignments at the end of their time in the Arctic. Of course others arrived to take their places so there were new faces and fresh conversations, which also did much to restore everyone's normal personality and good humour.

Land of the Midnight Sun

Noon, Dec. 23, 1974. The sun is due south, just above the southern horizon.

Coral Harbour lies just below the Arctic Circle so the sun never fully disappeared in winter. Not too far north of us began the winter period of full darkness. We had about four hours of twilight during the winter solstice with the sun poking up for about an hour. Not liking what it saw, Sol then ducked back down like the groundhog and announced a further five months of winter!

Things were reversed during the summer when the sun went around in a circle, only dipping below the northern horizon for about an hour. It never got completely dark for

Midnight, June 22, 1974. The sun is north, and ready to dip below the northern horizon.

about a six-week period. I found it hard to keep track of time during the 24-hour daylight period because I was always unsure if it was 4 p.m. and time for dinner, or 4 a.m. and time for bed! It was also interesting, and confusing if I was out on the tundra without any landmarks, to watch the sun set in the north in summer. I didn't have the same problem with keeping time during the dark period. Perhaps that was because I couldn't get out as much in the winter so it was easier to maintain a routine, or maybe because there was some sunlight even on the shortest and darkest day.

Morse Code Anyone?

Our marine radio equipment had been shut off since last fall so with the arrival of spring Ian and I kept ourselves amused for a week servicing those transmitters and receivers and making everything operational for the 1974 shipping season. Soon the chirping of Morse code mingled with voice communications in our speakers and headphones. In July a steady stream of ships began sailing past us in and out of Hudson Bay, mostly shipping grain from the port of Churchill.

Bob Crosby and I had practised Morse code with each other back when he was getting his Ham radio licence and I could follow along as long as it was slow, about five to eight words per minute (wpm). Our marine radio operators would usually make initial contact at 12 wpm but then work up to about 20 or 25 wpm, whatever speed the ship's operators were comfortable with. Fred was a dab hand with the Morse key and I once observed him tapping out 35 words in a speed contest with a Russian radioman. That was as fast as our teletype equipment!

Swarn Bains

Swarn was one of our seasonal marine radio operators who hailed from Thunder Bay at the western terminus of the Great

Lakes. He lived in the barracks room next to mine and I soon discovered he took a keen interest in personal fitness. Early

Swarn Bains as he is today, still running marathons! Swarn Bains photo.

every morning before breakfast Swarn liked to jog the four kilometres down the road to our low-powered beacon and back. He was cautioned about polar bears but kept jogging anyway until one day he thought he saw one. He was near the beacon site so he did the right thing by entering the building, which we never locked in case of emergencies, and telephoned for a ride back to the airport. I kept a

good lookout on the drive there and back but didn't see any bears. When the Inuit heard Swarn's story they went out looking and also found no sign. No matter, that was the last morning Swarn went jogging. Beginning the next morning I was awakened by a series of 'Whish – Thump' sounds coming through the wall from his room, followed shortly by 'Thump – Thump', 'Whap – Whup', and lastly 'Whip – Whup.' Swarn had rigged up a rope and pulley system to his bedroom closet door and had begun a regimen of 30-minute morning aerobic exercises. For the remainder of the shipping season Swarn was my alarm clock and I was never late for breakfast!

The time it took to get freight shipped into northern communities was often long and frustrating, Swarn's television set being the perfect example. Swarn had ordered a Heathkit colour television set delivered to Coral in kit form. He wanted the satisfaction of assembling it himself and it would be a great way for him to pass the time when not working or exercising. It did not matter that there was no television to watch in Coral Harbour; he would ship it back to Thunder Bay when his time was up and enjoy it there. He had ordered their largest set that came with something like a 90 centimetre picture tube and floor-standing console cabinet. It was being shipped in three large cartons. After he had been at Coral about a month, he started sending telegrams enquiring as to the whereabouts of his Heathkit.

He finally tracked it down in Winnipeg where it was waiting its turn to get on the Via Rail train to Churchill. After a couple more weeks and more telegrams Swarn was finally able to report that his television set had arrived in Churchill, only two hours away via our weekly Transair flight! Swarn met the flight each week and each week he was disappointed as mail, produce, and higher-priority seasonal freight kept bumping his Heathkit. His tour of duty came to an end in September. When the last ship had sailed out of Hudson Bay and still no television Swarn left instructions with us to forward it on to Thunder Bay when it eventually showed up. It did arrive, ironically on the same day Swarn left, and then it began the return journey chasing him back to Thunder Bay. I reached out to Swarn when I began writing this book, but he did not say whether or not the television saga had a happy ending, although he is still going strong and running marathons!

The Motor Vessel *Salerno*

Once a year Coral Harbour got a sealift originating from Montreal. This annual resupply brought a year's worth of non-perishable goods including fuel, oil, building materials, vehicles, canned food, dry goods, textiles and other commodities, even vehicles, into the community. Coral Harbour didn't have a dock, so one fine day in August the MV *Salerno* sailed into the bay across the peninsula from the hamlet and dropped anchor off Snafu Beach, not far from our navaid beacon site. She was a general cargo ship of 1,600 tons, Scottish built by Henry Robb of Leith in 1965 for the Ellerman-Wilson Line, and operating under contract to the Canadian government.

Unloading the landing craft on Snafu Beach.

She lost no time in lowering a military surplus landing craft over the side, using that and a large forklift to barge our supplies onto the beach ten tons at a time. Every truck on Southampton Island was pressed into service to haul pallet loads of goods off the beach to where they needed to go.

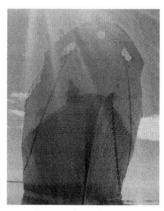

Approaching *Salerno* in the landing craft.

Salerno had been at anchor about 24 hours when a message was received by our marine radio asking if they had anyone who could maybe fix a radio. They said maybe they did, which was how I came to be standing on the stony beach with my bag of tools, watching the sun go around while waiting to get my feet wet when the landing craft had finished unloading. After bobbing out to the ship and climbing a rope ladder to the main deck I was met by the captain. This gentleman was British and had been tramping around the world for more years that I had been alive. He was built like a pear, and had about as much élan. His wardrobe was patriotic and consisted of blue work pants held up by red 'police' suspenders over a white turtleneck sweater. His sparse white hair was crowned with a white peaked sailor hat with "Captain" stitched on in blue thread. Being the man in charge, he decided the first item of business was to ensconce ourselves in his cabin and have a drink. On British ships this meant gin. I sat across from him on his cabin's settee while he poured two generous measures of Beefeater, then in Maritime fashion we toasted "Wives and sweethearts, may they never meet!" It took a couple of glasses before he got around to explaining his problem:

"Your Coast Guard in Montreal said we had to have a special radio for Hudson Bay, so they installed one on my bridge. The guy tried to explain it to me but he only talked French so I just nodded and said 'Wee-wee' a lot. We were only able to hear Iqaluit once we anchored there, but I thought it was supposed to be a long-range set. We couldn't work your station either until we got close...."

"Okay, let's go up to the bridge and have a look."

"Hang on a minute, empty your glass and then we'll go up. There's plenty of time."

Once the gin bottle was empty, we agreed I should visit the bridge. I was a bit unsteady by then although the captain still had his sea legs. I was hoping the radio problem

Canadian Marconi XH-14 High Frequency receiver like Salerno's and used throughout the ANS and Coast Guard for long-range communications. Accessed through Used.ca.

was something I could handle with my limited knowledge and basic tool kit. When we arrived on the bridge I smiled because this was going to be a home run. The receiver was identical to the ones we were using on shore, and if I couldn't find the problem on board I had a shed load of spares back at the airport. In Montreal the Coast Guard tech had installed a transformer beside the radio that converted ship's power to radio power to run the set. I could see right away that it was connected backwards. After rewiring for about five minutes I checked it out and was able to communicate not only with our local marine radio but both Churchill and Iqaluit, each many hundreds of kilometres away.

This demonstration suitably impressed the captain so he led me back to his cabin where he showed his gratitude with a steak dinner laid on by his steward and a second bottle of gin. I thought it impolite to refuse even though gin was not my favourite libation. After all, ship and crew were guests in our waters and I should be properly hospitable. Hospitality extended to the bottom of that bottle whereupon it was time to head back to the beach. I was proud of my ability to hold the gin and noticed that I now had sea legs just like the captain as we both rolled port and starboard along the decks. I put our seaman-like gaits down to the motion of the ship, never mind that she was at anchor in a flat calm sea.

Ellerman-Wilson Line embossed wine glass like the one I drank from on Salerno. Accessed through eBay vendor thepurserslocker.

As we were leaving his cabin, he invited me to take the two glasses we had been toasting each other with. I thanked him very much since they were embossed with 'Ellerman-Wilson Line' and would be memorable souvenirs of my time on board. He then asked, almost apologetically, if I could take some liquor off his hands. I demurred, knowing that gin was not a big seller in our bar, but he told me:

"I went ashore in Montreal to buy some Canadian booze that everyone said was really good and brought half a case aboard. I tried it but can't stand it, not a bit like the good stuff we get at home. I hesitate to unload it on you but I know you lads don't have much chance to get liquor, you've fixed my radio and it would be a favour taking it off my hands."

Now I began thinking that someone in Montreal had played a joke on the captain by recommending Blatz or some such swill as our Canadian top seller, but he opened his closet and pulled out six 40-ounce bottles of Canadian Club rye whisky! I assured the captain that the boys back at the airport would bear him no ill will while doing their best to choke down his gifts!

I managed to stay upright as I rocked and rolled down to the main deck with a pillow case of CC and my tool bag in one hand and the two glasses in the other. The walking problem became insurmountable once I had swung one leg over the rail and tried to climb no-handed down the rope ladder. Something had to go in a hurry before I went overboard. I regret to this day it was the two glasses. The boys back at the airport commiserated with me while toasting my loss with the captain's CC, unanimously agreeing that my decision had been the correct one.

Despite *Salerno*'s captain's comments we had no difficulty at all keeping our bar well stocked with all required and requested drinks courtesy of the RCMP. This cozy arrangement was possible due to a far-sighted airport manager who offered their members free meals and accommodations in our VIP barracks whenever they visited. All they had to do in return for these favours was go shopping for us back in Iqaluit. At that time there was neither detachment nor accommodations in the hamlet so they were happy to perform this service in the spirit of intergovernmental agency cooperation. Each month on their regular visit from Iqaluit they unloaded our previous booze order and left with a cheque and completed liquor commission form for the next month. This arrangement also helped our relations with the dry hamlet since our liquor did not arrive in plain sight on commercial flights.

Snafu Beach

Snafu Beach got its name from the military at some time back in the day. For those who don't know, snafu stands for Situation Normal, All Fouled Up … except Fouled was usually replaced by another well-known expletive. The foul-ups that undoubtedly earned the beach its name continued. Some of the Inuit pitched tents there during the sealift and a beach village sprang up during the summer. Most Inuit didn't know how to swim, at least not then, but they sure tried hard when a pallet load of Coke went into the drink from the forklift.

Airport manager Bill Duffield with schoolteacher Vicki Bielka.

When *Salerno* had finished unloading and sailed away to her next port of call a small tanker, also under Canadian government charter, anchored in her place off Snafu Beach to deliver our bulk fuels for the coming year. A flexible pipe was floated ashore and our new airport manager who had replaced Marv, Bill Duffield, connected it to our permanent line that ran above ground from Snafu to our bulk storage tanks at the airport. The tanker started pumping but there was no fluid coming out the airport end, so Bill got one of his mechanics to drive along the line on his motorcycle and see what was going on. He discovered a break in the line not far from the beach with heating oil burbling out into a depression in the tundra! Pumping was immediately stopped and the airport fuel truck was pressed into service to suck up most of the spill. The fuel had been somewhat contained because of the depression and permafrost and it was fortunate that the environmental damage was not worse. Pumping resumed two days later without further incident after the line had been repaired, and what oil we couldn't recover was later burned off.

Roll Out the Barrels

Hundreds of empty oil barrels had been gathered and stacked at Snafu. The plan was to load them aboard ship and take them south for recycling, but unfortunately they had not been properly cleansed. No one knew for certain what different kinds of fluids the barrels had once held so the ships' captains rightly refused this dangerous, unknown and potentially flammable or explosive cargo. There are many thousands of empty oil barrels scattered across the Arctic besides the ones gathered at Snafu Beach. We repurposed some at Coral Harbour by cutting off their ends and welding them together to make road culverts and similar pipes. Fred Lang won a suggestion award for welding barrels together into large squares about 6 metres on a side. They were then painted in the ubiquitous orange and white checkerboard pattern and erected as distance markers for FSS visibility reporting. In 1969 a competition was held for a Territorial flag.

Most of the submissions featured polar bears, Inukshuks, or the Territorial coat of arms, but there was a large number of write-in votes in favour of a flag depicting an oil barrel on an ice floe. Sporadic efforts have been made over the last few decades to recycle or otherwise properly dispose of waste barrels across the Arctic so the ones on Snafu Beach could be gone by now, but barrel disposal is still an expensive and vexatious problem in the Arctic.

Nature's Hard Lesson

All too soon winter arrived with a typical Arctic blast, the daylight hours shortened appreciably and quickly, and everyone made preparations to hunker down for the next nine months. The ships all scuttled off to warmer waters and the marine radio station signed off for another year.

One of our specialists who was newly arrived from the south had purchased a Skidoo from one of the departing teachers so he could come and go as he pleased in his off hours. One day near dusk he left the airport to visit his sweetie in the hamlet despite advice not to go as the weather was deteriorating. The visibility was not bad when he started so he thought he could make the trip by following our new power line. The wind had started to pick up as he left and there was drifting snow. He had only gone about half a mile when the wind started to howl and the blizzard came down hard. Snow blew into his carb air intake, which plugged it and stopped his motor. Now he was in real trouble. He was unprepared to make a shelter and wait out the storm, then matters went from serious to critical when he lost one of his gauntlets trying to get his machine restarted. He was cold, scared, and starting to panic when he began walking back to the airport. Why he didn't tuck his unprotected hand inside his parka will never be known, but he was lucky enough to follow the new power poles and arrive alive. When he finally got indoors his hand was frozen solid into the colour and consistency of candle wax. We couldn't get him to the nursing station and they couldn't get to us, nor could an emergency medevac flight land due to the storm, which blew for 36 hours. We had only basic first aid kits with no anesthetics so the best we could do for him was keep him in bed with the hand wrapped in Polysporin-soaked gauze, and feed him fistfuls of Tylenol washed down with copious amounts of rum. Ian took charge and followed the directions from the head nurse in the hamlet as best he could. The pain must have been excruciating. As soon as the weather permitted, he was evacuated to Churchill on an emergency flight and then to hospital in Winnipeg where his fingers were amputated. His experience was an object lesson to the rest of us to respect the environment we were living in.

Happy New Year, Dear John

My Christmas present from Val in 1974 was a 'dear John' letter. Our letters were becoming fewer and shorter so I was not really surprised she called off the engagement, especially given my extended stay away from her. If truth be told I agreed with her decision and felt a bit relieved that I would be starting a new chapter from a new beginning once I returned home.

A week after Christmas on New Year's Eve I was hanging around the FSS having a beer with the specialist on duty, keeping him company talking about past celebrations and how our friends down south would be ringing in 1975. Everyone else was in the bar partying with friends from the hamlet but having just broken up with Val I was not in a mood for crowds or jocularity. No airplanes were flying and all the radios were dead quiet until an almighty crash of static erupted from the short-wave receiver we used to talk between communities.

There was a long pause, then an unmistakable "BRAAPP!!" on the same frequency followed by:

"Master Corporal Jones here in Hall Beach wishing everyone a Happy New Year!"

"BBLTTPHPPT! Davey from Chesterfield Inlet with New Year's greetings!"

And the great Short-Wave Farting Contest was on with more contributors from Baker Lake, Churchill, and Iqaluit. Even Resolute Bay blew everyone listening a loud raspberry along with ourselves and one or two others. When the air (waves) had cleared that was the end of the story, at least until a few weeks later when the stations involved all received a snotty-gram from Communications Canada headquarters concerning correct and proper radio procedures. It seems our Holiday Hijinks extended to a public-spirited guardian of morality somewhere down south who happened to own a short-wave receiver.

My bushed look, drinking with Norm Frost in his room.

It was now January 1975 and my extension was half over. I was beginning to realize that Ian was right. I did need to return to Winnipeg, get my head back on straight and continue my career beyond Grand Mother Ducks, vacuum tubes, and short-wave radios. Ian was soon to be replaced by my last TSM, Bill Webster. Bill and I had worked together briefly in Winnipeg and had become friends. He was accompanied to Coral Harbour by many boxes of radio-controlled model airplane kits along with the necessary building supplies. He spent a great deal of his time in his room assembling airplanes and surfaced only when he could not avoid official business. Naturally our friendship blossomed and Bill even got one of the planes in the air before my time was up!

A rare photo of Bill Webster at his TSM desk!

Fire!

Shortly after Bill arrived the electrolyser in the hydrogen shed, which made the gas to inflate the upper air balloons, failed in the middle of the night and started a fire. We airport residents had never received any fire-fighting training or conducted any fire drills beyond evacuation to the remote transmitter site, from which emergency communications could be maintained with Churchill. Our fire-fighting apparatus consisted of handheld fire extinguishers. We did have a dedicated 'fire bomb' snow bus that was painted yellow and towed two cylinders of dry chemical on a trailer. It was intended to put out aircraft fires but I'm not certain that even the airport manager was versed in its use. Until the night of the fire I never saw it leave its garage, and we didn't waste the dry chemical on what was clearly a lost cause. We responded as best we could but by the time we got there with what pitiful apparatus we had the building was fully involved, so we confined our efforts to keeping the fire away from the GMD building next door. Fortunately, our other buildings were metal clad so we were able to put out the embers that were blowing onto them without further incident. We retreated to the warmth of the upper air office and watched the shed burning out the window until someone reminded us there was a great big kettle of hydrogen in the middle of the blaze, then we all backed away from the glass! Fortunately, the hydrogen tank vented as it was designed to do and did not explode. I don't think our slow response to the fire would have made any difference to the outcome. The specialist reported the electrolyser failure as soon as he noticed that the lights had gone out on his monitor but the upper air supervisor did not investigate until visible flames were observed from the FSS. The upper air program was able to resume about a week later when a battery of large helium tanks and a replacement balloon shed arrived in pieces via Transair's Argosy. Coral Harbour now has a completely new upper air station but they still use helium to fill their balloons.

Mikitok, a Friend

Mikitok Bruce, 1975.

One of the finest people I met on my first day in Coral was Mikitok Bruce, who was employed by the airport manager as a cook's helper and janitor. He told me that because we shared a name we also shared a bond. Mikitok said the Sallurmiut people had lived at Salliq before time out of mind. His grandparents used to visit the Sallurmiut before they too moved here to Salliq. He said the Sallurmiut were always friendly and ready to share what they had, but in the early 20th century whalers brought disease that almost wiped them out. Mikitok was disturbed that the Inuit and their lifestyle are all changing so much. Mikitok was a firm believer in teaching Inuit traditions and preserving the

Inuit way of life. He was taught to hunt by his father and grandfather and was a good provider to his family and community. Mikitok had a foot in each culture and was the first Inuk to receive a long service award from the federal government, but his Inuit life and traditions always came first. He had a lively sense of humour and it was a rare visitor who did not find his feet tied to his chair while getting up from the table after lunch!

Mikitok demonstrating how to build an igloo.

I was privileged to be invited to go seal hunting with Mikitok on one of my Saturdays off in early 1975. Although very cold, the skies were clear and the days were getting noticeably longer. He picked me up at dawn dressed in his traditional caribou skins, and I layered on all my warmest clothes including the long johns Ma had packed for me, the only time I ever wore them! Despite my best efforts the superiority of the Inuit clothing was borne out by the time he returned me to the airport some eight hours later.

I got on his Skidoo behind him and off we went, towing a komatik sled on which was a box holding hunting equipment, spear, rifle, and his favourite dog. After travelling a few kilometres out onto the sea ice we stopped and started walking back and forth following the dog, myself tagging along observing and trying to stay warm. After about 20 minutes the dog started getting excited and began pawing at the snow. Mikitok grinned and said: "seal."

The seal's breathing hole was through the ice but under the snow cover and would have been impossible to find without the dog. Leaving his spear to mark the spot, Mikitok took the dog back to the komatik about 100 metres away and made it comfortable. Its work was done for the day. Mikitok returned to the hole carrying his box of supplies and used the spear to carefully probe through the snow cover, making only a small hole about one centimetre across. He explained:

"Seal hide under snow. He has many holes; we wait for him to come here."

"How long does that take?"

"Maybe one hour, maybe all day. We wait."

He laid a sealskin pad beside the hole and knelt on it to keep his feet and knees off the snow. He took two forked sticks from his box and stuck them into the snow in front of himself then laid his spear across them. Lastly Mikitok took a bird's wishbone from the box and, after plucking a few strands of hair from the fur trim of his parka hood, licked the wishbone ends and froze the hairs loosely across the gap. This assembly was placed over his small spear hole.

"We leave snow so seal not see light. When seal comes hair moves. Then we catch seal."

We had to stay perfectly still so the seal wouldn't hear the snow creaking if we moved around. This was serious business because whether or not Mikitok caught a seal would determine if his family would be fed. I couldn't stay still enough and was banished to the komatik with the dog. The two of us shared jerky and thermos coffee as we watched Mikitok remain immobile over the seal hole. The dog soon went to sleep. I soon got cold.

We waited for about an hour and a half although it seemed much longer. Suddenly I perked up as I watched Mikitok slowly pick up his spear and rise to his feet without making a sound. He drove the spear down through the snow and immediately a violent thrashing ensued. He had caught a seal!

I ran over and looked down into the hole from which the snow cover had been knocked away. The spear had gone deep and done its work. The seal was dead and the water in the hole was now a vivid crimson. The spearhead detached inside the seal and hooked the animal to the spear's line as it was designed to do. Mikitok was now pulling on the rope as he tried to haul the beast out of the hole. We each grabbed a flipper and soon had a 50-kilogram ring seal on the ice. Mikitok was grinning from ear to ear. The seal was enough to feed his family for several days. Besides cooking the meat, his wife Tuinnaq would make mukluks from the skin, oil from the blubber, and implements from the bones. Nothing would go to waste and there would be fine dining tonight at Mikitok's house.

The Inuit Seal Spear

I am impressed by the engineering that went into designing the specialized Inuit seal spear by a so-called primitive

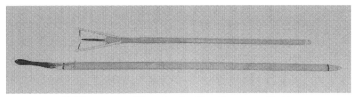

Fishing spear, with a standard hunting spear that is
97 cm long. These are functional models.

culture, so I will digress from my story to explain it in more detail. The spears shown in the photographs are a set of miniatures made for me by a Coral Harbour artisan in 1975. They are constructed from wood, bone, ivory, black baleen, and sinew. The long ones measure 97 centimetres and spears in a similar scale would have been made for boys as young as two. Even at that age they would begin learning the skills necessary to sustain themselves and their families. The first picture, on the previous page, shows a standard hunting spear and a fishing spear; similar spears can be found in many cultures.

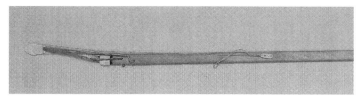

An Inuit seal spear, also a 97-cm-long functional model.

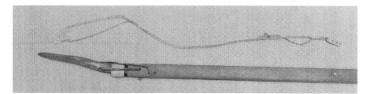

Seal spear with the detachable head removed to show detail.

The two pictures above show the seal spear. The head of the seal spear is detachable and would be tied to a line. When the seal is speared the spear head comes off and remains hooked inside the animal while the shaft goes deep inside to kill the seal. The spear is then withdrawn, the hooked spear head keeps the seal from sinking and is used to help haul the seal out of its hole and onto the ice.

Surveying Our Domain

One of my taxi service duties involved taking the upper air observers to perform snow and ice surveys. They would carry out the surveys while I watched out for polar bears. Ice surveys just meant going for a pleasant drive on a nice day out onto the sea ice for a couple of kilometres, to where an oil barrel with a flagpole had been placed as a marker. A hole was drilled through the ice and the thickness was measured, then hot cocoa and rum was passed around from a thermos.

To carry out a snow survey we drove halfway along the airport runway to where a line of 10 markers each 100 metres apart stuck up out of the snow. They were off to one side and leading away towards a hill. On this occasion a rookie, junior even to myself and fresh out of Met Observer's School in Toronto, was along for his first survey. The depth of snow was measured at each marker and a core sample taken for the edification of persons more interested in snow than I was. I have only one word for snow, the Inuit have dozens. The core samples were measured then placed in plastic bags and weighed, which enabled the density of the different snow layers to be calculated. At the end of the day our rookie asked what he should do with all the bags of melted snow. This was too good an opening to pass up, so our new upper air supervisor, Brock Goalen, told him to package them in a cardboard box and mail them to the attention of his buddy, the Regional Director of Environment Canada in Winnipeg. He told the rookie observer that they kept a warehouse full of these bags from all over the region as a permanent part of the climatological record of Canada. He swallowed this malarkey hook, line and sinker, packed the box, and mailed it off to this senior bureaucrat. Brock's buddy was not amused when a soggy box of leaky water bags arrived, postage due, to soil his desk. Brock's only comment to the resultant flurry of teletype messages as he grinned

Upper air observers Dennis and Dave prepare to survey the ice, which measured 1.8 metres thick.

from ear to ear, was: "Some people just don't appreciate northern humour!"

The VanDoos visit

For several years Coral Harbour had hosted different units of the Canadian Army for a week-long winter exercise and this year was no exception. In March, when the days were 12 hours long but the temperatures were still not much above minus 20, two C-130 Hercules transports descended onto our runway and disgorged the Royal 22nd Regiment, the famous VanDoos, with all their winter gear.

The VanDoos arriving at Coral Harbour.

They were met by the local unit of the Rangers who are a part of the Canadian Armed Forces Reserves working in remote and isolated regions of Canada. The Rangers regularly train alongside regular CAF units. The VanDoos loaded up their sleds, then led by the Rangers, they vanished into the northern ice fog.

A small detachment set up headquarters in one of our spare barrack rooms. The rest of the unit was about 30 kilometres north living in igloos that they had been taught to make themselves, or hollowed-out snow piles called quinzees if they hadn't mastered Igloo 101. On the second day of the exercise the headquarters was augmented by one U.S. Army major from South Carolina who was with the Royal 22nd on an exchange mission. He had made it through one night in an igloo and had had enough. I couldn't blame him. Our soldiers were some of the toughest anywhere. These troops were learning from the Rangers how to survive and manoeuvre in extreme weather. They could live and work very well out of doors in those conditions, as well as fight. We talked to the U.S. major the next evening in our bar and found out that one of our men had gone to South Carolina as the reciprocal of the exchange. We certainly rubbed it in as to who got the better part of that deal! At the end of the exercise, we hosted the regiment in our rec club, stepping aside and turning the place over to them for the evening. They drank the pallet load of beer they had brought and sang martial songs denigrating other branches of the forces well into the wee hours. Even the U.S. major joined in.

They departed the next day, leaving behind many empties and a classy plaque to hang on our wall to thank us for our hospitality. Even better, they left behind all their surplus rations, some spare winter clothing, and empty ammunition boxes. Wood is a very scarce and expensive commodity in the Arctic, so the ammo boxes which had previously held mortar rounds were used all over Coral Harbour for a great many rustic furniture projects. The rations, each stamped 'Keep Fit to Fight,' were rated the best in NATO and were stockpiled into our vehicles, remote sites, and barrack rooms in case of emergencies, or in case we desired some variety from Norm's menu! The military extreme weather clothing was better than our own issue so I put the jingle boots aside for the rest of my time in Coral and wore military mukluks.

Steel Balls

One of my last duties involving the Grand Mother Duck before my tour expired was to help Brock verify that it accurately tracked the balloons. This involved mounting a theodolite on a post fastened into the ground to follow the balloon in the theodolite's telescope as it ascended.

Comparisons between where the GMD said the balloon was and where the theodolite actually pointed to were made every half minute. I should mention that there was about a metre of snow on the ground at the time, and Brock had had one of his observers dig a narrow moat around the post so he could stand upright while tracking the balloon through the theodolite's eyepiece.

Launching a weather balloon. The radiosonde dangles below. Accessed 2021.

When all was ready Brock prepared the balloon and radiosonde package. Once outside, Brock held the radiosonde high so it would not be dragged along the ground as the balloon began rising. His head was up watching the balloon and his hands were outstretched holding the radiosonde as he trotted across the snow with his legs striding out manfully. He was watching what he was doing, not where he was going, which normally would not be a problem except for the theodolite post with the carefully calibrated instrument mounted on top. He nailed it dead centre and because of the depth of snow it caught him square in the goolies. He face-planted onto the far side, clearing the little moat in the process. It was a bravura performance and if I kept score, I would have given Brock nine out of 10 for artistic impression. He managed to keep his arm up and the radiosonde out of the snow. The balloon launch was successful but it left Brock groaning in severe pain. Things would have been much worse had he not been wearing two pairs of long johns, jeans, and two pairs of insulated wind pants. Alas, Brock broke the theodolite off its mount during his attempted vault, which negated the whole exercise as the balloon and radiosonde floated up and away. This caused another flurry of teletype messages between Brock and his superiors as he tried to explain in delicate prose why the GMD was still not calibrated and a new theodolite was needed. I took Brock to the nursing station to get checked out and soon after he became known around town as the man with steel balls. For some time after that the local girls eyed him furtively and giggled behind their hands whenever he came to the hamlet.

A Short Layover

Fred Lang was on his second tour of duty in Coral Harbour. His first was in the 1960s when he met and married an Inuit woman. He and JoAnne also lived in the hamlet with their four young kids who attended Coral Harbour's elementary school. While Bob Harron commuted to the airport with the Inuit staff in their bomb, Fred used his personal Skidoo or motorcycle because of his shift work.

JoAnne had made Fred a full set of caribou skin clothing that was much lighter and warmer than any parka we knew. He also carried a .357 magnum revolver around his waist, à la John Wayne, complete with leather holster and ammo belt with silver bullets, in case he met a polar bear on his commute. He was quite the sight, arriving on his sled for the midnight shift looking like an overweight reindeer with a six shooter on his hip. I think now I must have been there long enough to become fully bushed because I thought this was a perfectly normal and reasonable way of commuting.

One wintry day a Lambair flight diverted into Coral due to weather. The local agent transported the three or four passengers into the hamlet where he had found accommodations for them, and we hosted the pilots and flight attendant in our VIP accommodations. After dinner they settled into our bar and were still there swapping stories with us, and winning the "mine's bigger than yours" line-shoot competition, when Fred arrived a half-hour before his midnight shift was to begin. The door flew open letting in the Great White North, behind which was silhouetted a snow-covered apparition that even I, who had been expecting it, thought at first was a bear. The apparition stomped into the bar, shook off the snow and threw back the hood of his skins to reveal a bearded red face surrounded by frost. Icicles hung from his nose, eyebrows, and beard.

The flight crew stopped talking and gaped as the caribou gauntlets came off and were tossed onto the bar, frost flying off in a misty spray. Reaching down with his right hand, Fred drew his .357. The two pilots sucked in their breath while flight attendant Nora gave out a mousy little screech and tried to disappear behind the larger pilot. Fred spun the revolver's cylinder, then popped it open and set each of the six silver bullets upright in a row along the bar.

"Whisky!" he shouted, and at that the crew came unstuck from their stools and ran out the door, not to be seen until they were ready to depart the next day. Fred's performance had, unbeknownst to him, won the line-shooting competition for our side hands down.

Fred inspired me to ask Bill if I could carry our official government-issued military surplus .303 rifle in my truck, just in case I too might meet up with a bear. Wanting the rifle in my truck was another sign of my 'bushiness' because the truck itself was ample protection from bears and I was certainly not allowed to hunt them. Even though bears were the reason we had the rifle, it was normally locked away in the TSM's office. We never considered taking it out much less driving around with it. I don't think it was ever cleaned in the 18 months I was there. For sure it was never fired and I did not get permission to carry it. The bureaucrats treated us like Barney Fife, the deputy Sheriff from the old Andy Griffith tv show, by issuing the rifle to the TSM but the bullets to the airport manager. Thinking back, perhaps that was not a bad thing.

An Extended Layover

I was really lucky to have met and even flown with some of the last pioneer bush pilots during my time in the North. While in Coral I met Bonner Scott, later to become the chief pilot for Calm Air but in 1975 he was flying around Southampton Island in a turbo Beaver counting caribou for the game warden. When I returned to the North later in my career, I also met Jack Lamb, Max Ward who founded Wardair, and retired bush pilot Arnold Morberg. I flew with Kenn Borek and 'Buffalo Joe' McBryan out of Resolute Bay and Yellowknife. These men helped my latent love of aviation to come alive.

Jack and the other Lamb brothers were operating Lambair at the time and we would see their aircraft come through Coral while on freight or charter runs to points further north. One afternoon a Lambair DC-3 freighter stopped at Coral for fuel while enroute to Churchill, normally a routine event taking 30 or 40 minutes. The weather was starting to blow up a bit and the pilots were anxious to get home before it really turned nasty. After fuelling they started the engines only to have the left one puke its oil over the cowlings and landing gear. Not being good for further flight, they shut it down, got out a step ladder, and began poking around under the cowlings while muttering Neanderthal phrases. It soon became clear that repairing the oil leak was well outside any resources we might be able to provide so they put the canvas covers on the plane, sent off a teletype to their Churchill base and settled down with us for the night. That night was the start of a two-day blizzard so it was on day three of their enforced layover before Lambair was able to fly in another DC-3 with a spare engine and a mechanic.

It took the rest of that day and all of the next for the mechanic to change the engine, assisted by the airport manager and his heavy equipment operators. We had no hangar so they worked outdoors on the apron with no shelter under absolutely brutal conditions of wind and cold. Besides hand tools all they had to work with was a fork lift, ratchet straps, and more Neanderthal phrases. There were many breaks in the airport manager's truck to defrost fingers and noses before the new engine was installed, the propeller and cowlings put back on, and the airplane dug out of the snow that had drifted around it. It took another couple of hours that evening to warm each engine using our only Herman Nelson portable heater before preheated oil was poured into the tanks and both engines were started. No sooner was the DC-3 airborne when the right engine blew a cylinder. So the 30-minute fuel stop passed into day 5.

The silver lining was that a replacement cylinder and other required parts could be taken off the first defective engine inside our warm maintenance garage. The bad news was that the great outdoors was continuing cold and breezy and there still wasn't any shelter. The airport staff tried rigging a canvas tent onto the forks of the lift, but with minimal success. It was the evening of day six before the bad cylinder was changed. The aircraft was ready to have the engines preheated again the morning of day seven.

This time everything went smoothly and both engines were growling normally. Everyone was on board and eager to see Coral Harbour disappear into the distance. The pilots applied power and turned the aircraft on the ramp when there came a ferocious 'Thump-Crump' from the plane's rear. The left elevator and stabilizer had crunched into the concrete-filled bollard that protected our fuel pumps from just such errant airplanes.

There was nothing for it but for the crew to park the plane, send yet another teletype to Churchill requesting spare tail feathers, have some drinks and launder their only set of clothes one more time before going to bed. They were not in good humour and made the pilot walk by himself the 400 metres back to barracks. They were still very tense the next morning when Lambair flew in with the spare parts and a second mechanic. The stranded crew all had very hangdog looks as they watched that plane depart while they were still stuck on the ground.

"The way our luck is running we'll be here another week trying to change the stabilizer. We'll change the elevator and just straighten the worst of the bent stab. If 'Crash' and 'Bang' up front don't break anything else we'll get out of here in time for supper in Churchill tonight."

For the third time in nine days, they preheated the engines, fired them up, and headed for the runway. They departed straight out for Churchill and did not look back. Until the day I left and likely for many months thereafter Lambair arranged their flight itineraries to avoid Coral Harbour like the plague

Leaving

My 18 months in Coral Harbour were nearly done and I had fallen into the habits of other bushed short-timers. I stared for hours at the unchanging weather map willing that stubborn low-pressure system to move away. I slacked off on routine maintenance while trusting the ancient radios to continue working for just a few more days with minimal TLC and tube changes, while spending too much time in the bar counting down the days to departure and saying goodbyes.

Post blizzard snow clearing in front of the FSS. The wind packed the snow dense enough to support the Caterpillar tractor!

My replacement, Alex Petlikau, arrived a week before I left so he had time with me to learn his way around, be introduced to friends in the hamlet, and see what was what with the equipment he was taking over. This normal handover procedure was denied me when I arrived; circumstances then dictated that my predecessor had left a month before I stepped off the airplane.

I did get to play one last practical joke on my unsuspecting replacement, albeit unintentionally. I was taking Alex on his first trip into the village using our bomb. It was spring again in Coral and once more the rushing meltwater had washed out the bridges. I was not confident taking the rotting sea ice route without a guide so I decided to go by land and ford the rivers. A feature of these vehicles was an escape hatch in the roof just behind the driver and the person riding shotgun. Alex stood between the two front seats with his head and shoulders sticking out the hatch, rubbernecking and taking pictures with his new and expensive 35-mm SLR camera. We came down a small hill and around a bend and my travelogue switched to the river in front of us:

"... Alex, the bridge is washed out from the breakup, so we'll go down the bank and ford the river to the right. Don't try going left of the bridge because there are big rocks, and if you go too far right there's a deep hole you want to avoid...."

He was still out the hatch, clicking away at the river and damaged bridge as I hit the water without slackening speed. The water was moving fast but was less than a metre deep, and the resulting bow wave surged up the rounded Beetle-like nose of the Bombardier and cascaded down the hatch, thoroughly soaking Coral Harbour's newest photographer and his equipment.

I couldn't stop laughing as he fell back into the passenger seat, hair plastered and clothing soaked, spluttering and spitting up river water. He swore I had done that on purpose and called me every foul name in the book as we motored up the far bank and back onto the roadway, which made me only laugh louder because it was totally unintentional. I had only been through there before with the truck and I had no idea the water would surge up the Bombardier's nose like it did.

At the end of the day all was forgiven. The next day was my last. The low-pressure system obligingly moved east and Transair was on time. I spent that night in Churchill where I was able to phone home long distance for the first time in 18 months, and the next afternoon I had an emotional reunion at Winnipeg airport with my parents. I moved back into their house until I could arrange my own place, sleeping in my old room, which had been left unchanged since I left. I arrived home with caribou roasts, Arctic char steaks, a trunk load of Inuit carvings, and very fond memories of the people I had met and the experiences we had shared. I was to return to the Arctic many times over the next 30 years, visiting every community in what became Canada's third territory, Nunavut, never with regret.

WINNIPEG REDUX

On my return to Winnipeg, I reported to my old manager John Skitcko and arranged that I would start work in the navaids group in a month. During that four-week interlude I slept in a lot, enjoyed Ma's home cooking and the beautiful warm spring weather, and reintegrated myself into southern civilization. You miss the mundane things when they are not around, like grass and trees. I visited a barber and got my first professional haircut in a long while. I saw my dentist for an overdue checkup, found out I had two cavities needing attention, and got a date with his nurse. I caught up on television shows I had missed, and enjoyed seeing entire movies without the intermissions while changing film reels.

Val did not want the old Hillman so I got a ride out to Anola and retrieved it. I did not go into their house but she came outside to return my engagement ring, which was nice of her because I had not asked for it back. We didn't have much to say to each other and our conversation was awkward; I had an easier time talking to her dad in the front yard. I felt he was sincere when he said he was sorry things had not worked out between us. During my time in Coral Harbour, he had sent me local newspapers that were enjoyed and appreciated by everyone on the airport, and I would miss him. A few months later I was on another training course in Scarborough where I pawned the ring in a shop on Yonge St.

I sold the Hillman then bought a new Volvo sedan. It was a huge ego boost to pay cash for an expensive new car! I paid a visit to Red River College to say hello to some of my old profs, who asked me to step into a class and say a few words to the students who were about to graduate. I stumbled through an impromptu speech about working for Transport Canada and answered a few questions about Arctic life. I guess I couldn't have scared the potential recruits that badly because a short while later Vince Warszycki, who was to become my best man at my wedding, accepted their job offer!

I stopped drinking when I moved back home except for a social beer now and then, and I felt much better about myself for doing that. I looked up some of my friends from college and high school but we had all moved on in different directions so it was time I looked forward and did the same.

The supervisors and techs I had worked with and learned from a year and a half ago were all still there including Cliff Somers, my new old boss. I slid easily into the routine maintenance activities except this time I was assigned shift work on the same rotation as the other techs. I enjoyed the evening shift best because when it was finished my colleagues and I had time to grab a beer before last call if we were so inclined. I could get a decent night's sleep while still having a good part of the next day for myself before reporting for my next shift at 4 p.m. The evening and midnight shifts were not assigned much work beyond routine maintenance or repairs that the day shift hadn't been able to complete. The later shifts were there first and foremost as a rapid response if one of the navaids or radars failed. As such there was a fair bit of free time, and I got quite good at playing euchre and bridge along with the other techs when I was not studying training manuals or tinkering with my electronic hobby projects.

Wayne Hamel

Wayne was one of our senior radar techs who also played a part in seeing that our collective agreement was applied equitably and fairly in his roles as shop steward and the union's unit chairman. He was given an acting promotion to radar supervisor to cover for Don Strath while Don was away on vacation. During that time he applied for leave on an upcoming Friday to attend a family event. John Skitcko denied the leave, saying the radar group needed a supervisor on duty to oversee the work. A supervisor's occasional absence often went uncovered so Wayne complained, John put his foot down, and Wayne did not get his day off.

It turned out that when Wayne came into work on that particular Friday John had decided to take that same day off for himself. Wayne was incensed and filled out a grievance form stating his request for the day off had been unreasonably denied. Part 2 of that form required acceptance by the union before forwarding it on to management, so Wayne, being a shop steward, duly filled out and signed that part as well. Part 3 of the grievance form

Wayne Hamel. Practical joker and friend, he always stood up for the underdog. Winnipeg Free Press photo.

was management's response so Wayne, now wearing the hat of acting supervisor, accepted his own grievance on management's behalf. He filled out their response section allowing that he had been aggrieved and granting himself the day off as corrective action. Then he went home.

When Skitcko saw the paperwork on Monday and realized what had happened he hit the roof and came down screaming, but he was flummoxed and had no idea what to do about it, and neither did anyone else in the organization. This had never happened before in the civil service and likely never will again. After that incident John and Wayne circled each other like two bulls in a cow pasture. Even after the matter died down it only finally went away when one of them retired.

Wayne also liked to play the occasional practical joke. For example JK, one of our techs, rode a moped to work and parked it in a small open area at the base of our ANS operations building. One day as I was crossing this area to report for my evening shift the emergency exit door at the side opened and Wayne beckoned me over. "Hold the door and let me back in…."

Wayne's prank had been well planned. As I held the door he ran over to the moped with a chain and padlock and secured it to the bicycle rack where it was parked. He ran back in and we headed up the inside stairs to the landing above, where we could look out a window and watch the fun. In due course JK came out. He was tall and thin and reminded me somewhat of Ichabod Crane. He took life seriously and was a safety-conscious individual, so he not only had a motorcycle helmet and gloves, but goggles, a leather jacket, and bicycle clips on his pants legs above his safety boots. He pulled on the gloves, adjusted the helmet and goggles, pulled the moped back from the rack, and discovered the locked chain. JK knew he was being pranked and looked around trying to spot us. Then he tried the door we had used, but of course it was locked from the inside. As soon as he had re-entered the building through the main door we rushed back down the stairs and Wayne ran out and removed the lock and chain. Back at the upstairs window, we watched as

JK came out carrying a hacksaw! Seeing the chain removed, he hopped around from one foot to the other, shaking his fist and no doubt cursing our ancestry. Getting no result, he went back into the building to return the saw. We repeated our performance and relocked the moped. JK was getting into the spirit of things because he repeated his part in our comedy; finding the moped chained up with no one in sight and the emergency exit still locked, he again stormed up and down, railing away at all and sundry!

Again he ran back into the building, but being sneaky he waited inside the door for us to reveal ourselves. From the second-floor window we could spot him waiting and remained hidden. After a minute or so he went back to the interior of the building and Wayne ran out to once more remove the chain! Back in our aerie we watched out the window thinking this could go on all night, or at least until our dinner time, when JK reappeared, this time with a commissionaire! Finding the moped free to proceed, the commissionaire ripped a strip off JK for interrupting his business for what he saw as a joke JK was trying to play on him. The commissionaire stomped back to his lair and JK finally started on his way home. Wayne was done for the day but I was just starting my shift and the rocket I received for reporting late to work was worth it!

Tommy Sees a Ghost

Tommy couldn't play cards with us on evenings or nights because he was the only technologist who had a full slate of regular work assigned on those shifts. He was what was once known as a Maintenance Liaison Officer (MLO). These technologists were nearing the end of their careers and usually applied to become MLOs to improve their pensions. Tommy and his fellow MLOs sat at a standard government-issued desk that was situated right in the middle of the ATC operations centre floor surrounded by controllers diligently monitoring radar screens. His desk was illuminated by a fluorescent light, so the poor MLO couldn't even so much as scratch an itch without the whole centre becoming privy to his most personal bad habits. MLOs were like the old Maytag repairman; they had nothing to do until that rare event when something broke. Whenever a controller had a problem they informed the MLO who would run downstairs to find a technologist to repair it.

Thin best describes Tommy. His build was thin, with thinning brown hair combed straight back, a thin wispy moustache, and long thin arms and legs. He dressed for work in polyester checked pants with thin striped ties. He finished off his wardrobe with brown patent leather shoes that he never changed despite the fact they squeaked on the floor tiles. Tommy didn't like to see us playing cards at work. Other MLOs would tell the ATC supervisor to phone them in the techs' lounge if there was a problem and then join in our game if they had some free time. Not Tommy. He would prowl around the centre behind each controller in turn, asking them if anything was wrong, anything at all. This annoyed the controllers, especially the squeaky shoes as he came and went, but they couldn't tell him to go play cards so after he had badgered them for a while they would give in and help Tommy invent a problem. We knew Tommy's game but of course we had to investigate each problem as it was reported.

One could usually find something to complain about on a radar screen if one looked long and hard enough. These were black-and-white television screen displays with a rotating sweep that lit up the target blips as the radar beam passed over them. They were hard to watch for hours at a time and the vigil was made worse whenever a controller heard Tommy's squeaky shoes approaching. Sooner or later one of the Scope Dopes would crack:

"Is everything okay at your position?"

"Sure Tommy, just like half an hour ago when you were by."

"Well that's good.... How are the radios?"

"Five by five Tommy. Tommy, I have to talk to this guy...."

Tommy's shoes squeaked as he fidgeted while the controller communicated with an aircraft.

"What about the focus on the screen?"

"Are you still here? The focus is fine Tommy."

"Looks a little off to me...."

"You know what Tommy, now that you mention it, there is the odd ghost showing up behind the targets, not all the time mind you, just once in a while."

That was enough for Tommy. He squeaked away to the tech's lounge with a serious look on his face, ready to command us to slay the evil radar ghosts. Meanwhile, while Tommy was annoying the controllers we had just settled down for a few rubbers of bridge following our dinners. Tommy did not interrupt our bidding:

"Damn, I hear Tommy's shoes coming. I open one spade."

"Maybe he just wants to use the microwave. Two clubs."

"I doubt it; he was down earlier and heated something up. Two spades."

"Sorry to disturb your card game boys but the arrival sector has reported ghosting on their radar!"

"All the time or just once in a while? Pass."

"It has been getting worse; when I started everything was fine."

"So what's it like now? Four spades."

"Getting worse. You need to look at it right away."

Wayne Hamel was the radar tech on duty and it was his game of four spades that Tommy had interrupted.

"Okay Tommy. Go back to the centre and we'll call you from the equipment room. Come on LeCren, I'll show you how to align a radar display. You guys leave the cards and we'll be back in 10 minutes."

On our way upstairs Wayne explained that radar ghosts were false images of a target that sometimes appeared behind the real image. They could be a serious problem since the controllers could become confused between the target and the ghost. He added that they originated from the radar site equipment so everyone in the centre would be complaining, not just the arrival sector controller, if this was a real problem.

We now stood in the equipment room in front of the rack housing the electronics for the arrival sector's radar screen in the operations room next door. Wayne plugged in a portable maintenance display that let us see what the controller was seeing. Sure enough, the targets were clear without any sign of ghost images. Then he leaned on the side of the rack, picked up the phone, and spoke to the arrival controller where Tommy was standing by.

"Good evening arrival, this is Wayne in the equipment room. I understand you are seeing ghosts on your display?"

The Scope Dope had reported a problem so now he had to follow through. "I think I see one coming and going behind that Air Canada target at 10 o'clock."

The target was clear as a bell, as we could tell from our maintenance display. Wayne, without taking his hand from his pocket or moving off the side of the rack, now said "I'm adjusting the anti-ghost control. How's that now?"

"Ooh, that seems to be worse."

"Okay, let me try this way ... how is it now?"

"Cleared right up. Thanks Wayne!"

As we put the maintenance display away, I asked Wayne how we got away with pretending to adjust a non-existent control. He explained that the Scope Dopes had no clue how the equipment operated and as long as the Radio Knob gave a plausible explanation they were happy. Tommy had talked them into seeing a problem that wasn't there in the first place, so he was happy to have put us to work and would say nothing more. In fact, Wayne could probably convince Tommy there really was such a thing as an anti-ghost control. The rest of the evening passed without incident and Wayne made his four-spade contract.

MLOs are gone today, replaced by Technical Systems Coordinators who have a much more active role in equipment maintenance. A fortress of consoles containing at least a dozen computer displays has replaced the lonely office desk. From this bunker in the corner of the ATC operations centre a team of technologists monitors all essential electronic systems and takes corrective action to restore many faults using computer software even before advising their colleagues in Maintenance. Evening shifts are also busier. During this time the ATC system has less traffic to control so that is when many systems now receive routine maintenance and software upgrading. Even the ghosts are gone, killed forever when the analog radar systems were replaced with state-of-the-art digital processing.

Modern-day Nav Canada Area Control Centre at Winnipeg. Technologists man the Technical Systems Centre equipment in the foreground, having replaced the single MLO at his office desk. Controllers are at their consoles behind. . *Canadian Aviator Magazine,* March 27, 2021. Photo courtesy Nav Canada.

Merit Awards?

Like many corporations and businesses Transport Canada gave out awards for merit, long service, suggestions, and other worthwhile things. We Radio Knobs sometimes handed out awards for noteworthy actions that did not fall into those laudable categories.

Bob Creighton, who had replaced Cliff as the navaids supervisor, had won a promotion to Telecom Station Manager at Kenora, which is a resort town just inside the Ontario/ Manitoba border. Bob was looking forward to relaxing in the pastoral environment among the cottages and lakes of the

Great North Woods until his retirement. He also had a decent-sized boat that was perfect for Lake of the Woods. While rummaging through an old storage room a few days before he left he came across a small dry chemical fire extinguisher with a broken handle. Bob thought this would be perfect for his boat so he resolved to pack it with his office effects for shipment to his new digs. Bob figured he could fix the handle, which just left one question: Was the extinguisher full or empty? Bob clamped it into a vise in our electronics workshop, found a hammer, and tapped the broken end of the handle. Nothing. Bob tapped harder and was rewarded with a spit of dry chemical out of the nozzle. Wanting to make sure, he gave it a wallop…. The broken handle jammed open and a spray of dry chemical powder began filling the entire shop!

He tried to minimize the damage by taking the extinguisher out of the vice, thinking to stuff it under his shirt and run it outside, but he dropped it. The extinguisher now did a credible imitation of a tear gas bomb by propelling itself around the floor spewing powder in all directions! Bob looked like the Pillsbury Dough Boy as he ran out the door covered in white powder! He was there until midnight vacuuming the floor, benches, walls, windows, and even the ceiling tiles, as well as wiping down every tool in the place. Meanwhile, we spirited the now empty extinguisher away. I took it home and mounted it on an old wooden base from one of my model airplanes. The next morning my colleagues added a suitable plaque and couriered it off to Kenora. As his staff was showing Bob into his new office he was greeted with the 'Bob Creighton Fire Fighter Award' hanging above his desk.

Winnipeg's control tower had radar displays that the controllers used when low visibility would not let them see the runways or airplanes flying near the airport. These displays were a smaller version of those in the operations centre and mounted almost flat into the tower consoles. They tended to collect dust and periodically one of us techs would be summoned to flourish wet wipes and rags to clean the screens. On one beautiful summer evening our radar tech was off on a more pressing errand when the controller felt the imperative need to complain about the dust on his screen. Not wanting to wait for us, our Scope Dope decided to give the screen a generous spritz of Windex and a wipe with a paper towel. These screens were cathode-ray tubes just like old television sets, with something like 18,000 volts on their anode terminals. The Windex ran down around the side of the screen and onto the anode. The resulting shock wave sounded like a small bomb going off as our Dope was tossed across the tower and finished up unconscious on the floor a couple of metres away. Fortunately he was still breathing, but he sustained a concussion from hitting his head as he went down. He was awake when the ambulance crew arrived and took him to the hospital for overnight observation. A couple of days later we Radio Knobs hung a framed memorandum in the controller's lunchroom outlining the proper procedure for getting qualified personnel to clean controller equipment in general and radar screens in particular. We headed it 'The Crispy Critter Award.'

I mentioned earlier the driving habits of some of our technologists. PH believed that our employer deserved every productive minute and that time spent dawdling to and from the airport sites was time wasted. Then again maybe he just liked to drive fast? One frosty morning the maintenance crews hadn't yet gotten around to cleaning the aircraft parking apron when PH made his usual entrance. He sensed he might be going a tad too fast so he tapped the brakes and immediately lost control on the icy surface! The car did a couple of donuts while sliding across the apron heading for two aircraft parked at their gates! PH and his passenger were incredibly lucky as their car passed under the wing of a YS-11 and slid to a stop under its tail! The aircraft they were headed for at the next gate was a Fairchild Metroliner that sits much lower to the ground.... The consequences had PH hit either airplane would have been most severe! As soon as our wannabe stock-car racers could breathe again they both rolled down their windows to let the smell out and crept back to their original parking spot while ignoring the controller trying to reach them on the radio. PH spent the rest of the day hiding from the bosses and when he was finally called up on the carpet he received both barrels of John Skitcko's fury along with a formal letter of reprimand. That the punishment was not worse was only due to the efforts of Wayne and the fact that the only damage was to PH's underpants. We prepared a suitable memo for circulation around our office, subject headed 'The PH Driving Award.'

Kingston Calling

Just a few months after starting work back in Winnipeg I was sent off on a course to learn all about Tactical Air Navigation. Tacan, as it is known, was a military system maintained by Transport Canada technologists wherever it was installed at civilian facilities across the country. Tacan was usually installed into the same sites as our civilian Omni-Ranges because a portion of the Tacan signal could be used by civilian aircraft to determine their distance from the site. Pilots using the signals from both the Omni-Range and Tacan systems could determine their precise distance and bearing from the combined site, which is known as a VorTac.

VorTac site located at Upper Table Rock, Jackson County, Oregon, USA. The Tacan antenna sits atop the Omni-Range's cone-shaped antenna. Photo courtesy Zab Milenko, Wikimedia Commons.

The course was held at Canadian Forces Base Kingston located in the Thousand Islands area of Ontario, and was taught by military instructors to a mix of military and civilian students. We civvies stayed in Kingston hotels like the Holiday Inn where we had excellent views over Lake Ontario and daily maid service, while the military students stayed in barracks on the base where they had a view of the base parade ground and daily room inspections to ensure they had made their beds properly.

The course was 12 weeks long so we had plenty of time to get to know and appreciate the social life of the city. This featured the co-ed students from Queen's University who we hung out with in the local bars listening to such bands as Major Hoople's Boarding House. They had just released their hit song "I'm Running After You" and were playing to packed houses. We had no trouble attracting the co-eds because one of our number knew someone associated with the band, so we were always able to score a table near the stage!

With a course that long we were allowed to return home every third weekend. I was still single and living at home so I stayed in Kingston on these third weekends to visit my aunt and uncle in Ottawa and to explore the Thousand Islands and other attractions. One of the other attractions I wanted to explore was named Colleen. She was a waitress in the Holiday Inn restaurant so we saw quite a bit of her during her working hours. She was from Saskatchewan and a bit homesick. She liked having a Prairie boy around to talk with so we enjoyed time together on her weekends off going for walks and taking the ferry across to Wolfe Island for picnics.

There was a lot to learn on the course. The Tacan system was designed by a committee of military contractor engineers with unlimited budgets so it was unnecessarily complex and used over 600 vacuum tubes. It even used an obscure circuit called a Phantastron Delay. Not even our military instructors with their decades of experience could explain how it worked.

Sergeant Brost: "The signal goes into the Phantastron on this pin and comes out here on this pin 50 microseconds later. That is all."

As it turned out the three military students on the course were all different ranks, and they of course had to observe military discipline including the paying of compliments, which meant marching to and from class, parading each morning, and saluting anyone having more stripes or braid. One day it was raining hard and a puddle had formed in a corner of the classroom. A major stuck his head in the door, saw the puddle and turned to our instructor:

"Lieutenant, clean that spill up."

Our instructor turned to our senior military student: "Master Sergeant, clean that up."

The Master Sgt. looked to his right and said "Sergeant, clean that up."

The Sergeant then said to our junior military student: "Corporal, clean that mess up."

By now everyone in the classroom was grinning from ear to ear at this demonstration of rank. The corporal turned but saw only three civilian faces beaming back at him, so he got up and left the room to the chuckles from we who were not part of their caste system, but he had the last laugh. Instead of watching him clean up the water we watched the private who he had ordered into our class with a mop and bucket!

The complexity of the Tacan meant that we studied hard as a group the night before each of the five course examinations. After our three months in Kingston, we all passed the course. I had received the highest class standing and was asked to report to the senior officer of the school, who was the same major who had begun the military rank demonstration. He asked me if I would consider transferring to the school as a civilian instructor. This was a very high compliment indeed and one which I considered carefully. I had really come to appreciate Kingston and the surrounding area; it would be a beautiful part of the country to live and work in, but I turned down the offer. Being employed as a civilian instructor meant I would be working as an independent contractor and I would lose my civil service benefits. I would be instructing only on this older tube-based system instead of more modern solid-state electronics, and the contract would end if the military found more of their personnel to instruct or the instruction on that particular Tacan system ceased altogether. If there had been some other way such as a temporary secondment from Transport Canada I would have accepted the offer and reported to Kingston, but this was not able to be worked out. I have no regrets about how my career unfolded and years later I would find myself teaching for a brief time not too far away, but I sometimes wonder how things might have gone had I taken that very different turn.

Onward and Upward

About this time Bob Stampe took over as navaids supervisor from Bob Creighton. Bob was another in the string of competent and personable supervisors I had the pleasure to work with, although our time together was to be short. He had spent time at Churchill in northern Manitoba while I was in Coral Harbour but our paths never crossed until he came to Winnipeg.

Shortly after Bob arrived he and I drove out to St. Andrews airport north of Winnipeg to perform routine maintenance on their navaid beacon. In reality, our main purpose in making the trip was to check out Point West Flying School. The flying bug had bitten both of us so we each took our introductory flight lessons that day and signed up together for the private pilot ground school course.

The joy and freedom of drilling holes through the skies piloting your own airplane has to be experienced to be understood. My instructor, Dan Reeves, believed in teaching more than required by the private pilot syllabus. He did this for the very sensible reason that as soon as I was flying solo I would likely get into situations from which I would have a hard time extricating myself without Dan on board. I started my flight

Bob Stampe, ca. 1976.
Robert Stampe photo.

training in the fall when the farmers in those days made a

practice of burning the stubble off their fields. Dan took full advantage of the poor visibility created by the smoke to give me actual instrument flight time rather than starting out only flying visually. I had six hours in my logbook before I even saw a horizon out the windshield! By the time Dan considered me ready for my flight test he had also introduced me to basic aerobatics beyond the required stall recovery, including full spins, chandelles and lazy eights. Our favourite navigation exercises were map reading away from the prairie grid road system north or east into the Canadian Shield, over to Dryden or Red Lake and back. Along the way we practised engine failure and forced landing procedures that permitted us to legally fly low over the Crocus Grove nudist colony! Bob and I both passed our flight tests; I give credit to Dan for doing as well as I did. Dan now owns Winnipeg Aviation flight training school and dabbles in airshow aerobatics.

Slip Sliding Away

Not too long after getting my private pilot's licence I decided to add a night flying endorsement so I wouldn't have to land just because the sun was going down. I was nearing the end of that course and building time in my logbook by practising solo circuits at St. Andrews airport one starry winter's evening. The circuits were going well so I decided to add a little navigation practice to my itinerary by flying over to the Lac du Bonnet airstrip, doing a couple of circuits there, then flying back and calling it a night. I announced my intentions to the tower controller who wished me a good night and said he was shutting down and heading home. I enjoyed the solitude of the 20-minute flight to Lac du Bonnet and when I activated the radio-controlled runway lights they came on just a few kilometres directly ahead of me. There is no air traffic control at Lac du Bonnet so after broadcasting to anyone who might be up and about that I would be doing circuits on runway 18 I went ahead and set up for my landing.

As soon as I touched down the aircraft started shimmying! I couldn't take off again because I had lost directional control on what I now realized was an ice-covered runway! If I had added power the torque would have spun me around and sent me off the side. I shut off the engine as I was no longer a pilot but just a passenger along for the ride. The airplane did a donut each time the wheels contacted the snow along the side of the runway, which eventually slowed the aircraft and we came to a stop after about a 600-metre sleigh ride. I confirmed the runway was ice-covered by stepping down off the wing and promptly falling on my ass!

It was getting pretty late and there didn't appear to be anyone else around. There was no way I was going to be able to take off on the ice-covered asphalt but I noticed the airport manager had cleared the snow about 4 metres back from the runway lights, making patchy snow and grass-covered lanes along each side of the runway. I walked back up the nearest lane and figured it had enough grip for me to use it as a runway to take off. The lane was crusty from the ice but it broke under my feet and the snow was only about five centimetres deep. There were no drifts or other obstructions that would catch the low wings of the Piper Cherokee. I had forgotten to reset the radio-controlled runway lights so of course they timed out at the far end of my walk leaving me in the pitch dark. I fumbled my way back to the airplane, only falling down once more. I got the tow bar from the baggage compartment, fell on my ass again, managed to pull the airplane so both main wheels were just on the snow, fell on my ass a fourth time, then got in and started the engine. The aircraft moved ahead and did not start yawing when I added power, so I lined up on the snow lane and set up for a soft field takeoff. This technique horses the airplane off the ground in a short distance at a low speed, the airplane then rides on a cushion of air between the wing and the ground until gaining enough speed to climb away safely.

The takeoff and flight back to St. Andrews was uneventful and the only thing bruised besides my ass was my ego. This was a good lesson in calling ahead to get the latest conditions before visiting a strange airport!

Wedding Sirens

I purchased my first house in the Winnipeg suburb of Charleswood the spring after returning from my Tacan course. Soon after moving in I was coerced into going on a blind date by my match-making neighbour Judy. Both Jovanna and I were dating other people at the time and did not want to go out together but Judy was insistent. We finally spoke on the phone and agreed I would take her flying over the city. The idea was to have a good time without much interaction or conversation due to the noise level in the small Piper airplane. Our date would keep Judy happy then we could go our separate ways. A few months later we were planning the wedding, which took place in September 1977, beginning over 35 years of married life together!

Jovanna and I on honeymoon in London.... Most tourists take pictures feeding pigeons in Trafalgar Square; somehow, we ended up with live monkeys!

One evening after we newlyweds had settled into my house, I used an official vehicle to sneak home for supper during a quiet shift. I did not want to be late so I was going a bit fast coming off the St. James Bridge. I saw the cherries light up behind me.... Aw shit! The last thing I needed; a speeding ticket in a government car on private business! When the cop asked me where I was going in a hurry, I had a brainwave:

"Why were you going 65 in a 50 zone?"

"I'm responding to an airport navigation aid that is off the air. It's part of a precision guidance system for landing airplanes and must be back in service as soon as possible!"

"The airport is in the other direction.... Where exactly is this guidance system?"

"Corner of Loudon and Howe in Charleswood...."

"Follow me, son...."

The cop turned on his lights and music and I followed him as if we were speeding down a runway. We went down Elmhurst Road right past my front door on the way to the Instrument Landing System's marker beacon site! I grabbed the site keys from the vehicle, squeezed through the gate without opening it, got into the site and hoped the cop would leave. No such luck. He followed me into the building so I flipped switches to turn the marker onto standby then right back to main. Various lights flashed orange then green and I announced that everything was back to normal. Just then Air Canada added the icing to the cake as one of their DC-9 jetliners screamed overhead on its landing path to runway 36!

"Thank you very much for your assistance, Officer!"

"Well done, son. Next time if you're in a hurry like that, call ahead to us."

"Thank you, Officer; I will pass that on to my supervisor with appreciation!"

Jovanna had heard the siren and was looking out the window as we sped past. Recognizing the car I was driving, she was wondering why I needed a police escort to be late for dinner!

Fun With Viscounts

Vince Warszycki had followed me into Transport Canada from Red River College and we had become good friends by this time. Like me a couple of years ago he was learning what he could while waiting for his Ground Meteorological Device course and northern assignment. Air Canada had decommissioned their Viscount airliners in 1974 and several members of this venerable fleet were parked off to one side of a parking ramp at Winnipeg awaiting disposal. Vince and I often drove by them and the opportunity to stop and explore the first of the turboprop airliners up close was too good to pass up. We could not get into the aircraft but we could poke and prod around the exterior. We removed a propeller spinner and checked out the electric motor that varied the propeller's pitch. We investigated the hydraulically

Here's where they put the gas in! Just before receiving a kerosene shower for my curiosity! W. Warszycki photo.

operated landing gear. I had opened the access door for the fuel filler:

"Hey Vince, here's where they put the gas in!"

I pushed on the fuel filler as Vince snapped a picture and was rewarded by a spray of aviation kerosene that caught me full in the face and chest! Vince was laughing too hard to take any follow-up photos of me sputtering and gasping. After a lot of rinsing and washing in the nearest washroom I was fit to resume my duties, and that was the last of our Viscount explorations! Air Canada operated Viscounts for 19 years and their fleet logged well over a million hours of air time. Several airframes were sold to other operators, and the last Viscount flew in Africa in 2009.

Time For a Change

By the late '70s I had attended training courses on some navaid systems but they were still the old steam-powered vacuum tube varieties. Many of the ex-military techs were retiring and more, including Frank Gaudet, had transferred to the Department of Fisheries & Oceans (Fish & Ships) when that organization formed its own electronic maintenance division. Techs who understood vacuum tubes were still in demand in the ANS even as that technology was on its way out, but I felt I was being held back as I saw others less senior than I receive training on the latest equipment. I asked for an Instrument Landing System course and was once more told I would be nominated for training on the old legacy system. Boredom with the unchanging regular maintenance routines was also starting to set in. I wanted new challenges beyond improving my card-playing skills.

That night Jovanna and I discussed my career options. We didn't want to relocate away from our roots to a province that did not recognize her nursing licence, so a transfer to Fish & Ships was off the table. I had on several occasions observed our engineering services technologists installing equipment at various locations, and this work appealed to me. A move to engineering would trade shift work for travel because our region spanned Canada between Thunder Bay and the Alberta border including the Arctic. The engineering techs I spoke to told me the timing of trips could often be managed to minimize the strain that the frequent absences put on families. I would be working with the latest systems so no more vacuum tubes, and a transfer to engineering services would be a promotion, so more money.

Engineering Services was holding a competition to fill four vacancies and I put in my application. Bill Webster, who had returned from Coral Harbour and worked alongside me in navaids, did the same. We both qualified and shortly after were called to report to Transport Canada's Winnipeg regional office where we began our second career paths within the civil service. I was leaving behind a lot of good friends in maintenance. Despite all the joking around and card playing the technologists always were and still are an organization of consummate professionals who always put the safety of the flying public before everything. They maintained their equipment to the highest standards and systems were rarely unserviceable due to breakdown.

NEW CHALLENGES

Winnipeg's Engineering Services was one of six regional organizations across the country dedicated to installing all the electronic systems used by Air Traffic Control (ATC) and the Air Navigation System (ANS). Ours was managed from an office in downtown Winnipeg and the electronics were fabricated and tested at our workshop in Winnipeg's west end. Engineering services was organized into specialty groups like maintenance, employing Professional Engineers who did high-level project planning, particularly antenna designs, and technologists like me who fabricated and installed the systems into locations across our region.

Our office also included telecom specialists who oversaw the cables and commercial services that tied the ANS sites together, riggers who installed and maintained all our towers and antennas, and draftspersons who created and updated all the record drawings used across the region. There was also a group of general labourers at the workshop who carried out much of the fabrication work and assisted us with installations in the field. I was to spend the rest of my career in engineering services except for two diversions into other paths. I would have liked to have travelled further down those career paths but circumstances dictated that they would only be interesting interludes.

I came into engineering services at a very exciting time for ATC and the ANS. Solid-state electronics were now firmly in vogue and the vacuum tube systems were rapidly being decommissioned. Integrated circuits were starting to make an appearance in our latest equipment and the first generation of digital radar displays had begun to replace the old black-and-white television-style monitors. Alongside these new monitors at the controller's workstations was the first computer-controlled communications equipment that seamlessly integrated their radio, hotline, telephone, and miscellaneous systems. Each of these first computers only had 64 kilobytes of memory and took up the better part of an entire equipment rack, but they were cutting edge and hot stuff at the time!

Away from the ATC operations centres, Flight Service Stations (FSSs) were also receiving new communications control systems along with solid-state radios, beacons, ILS, and Omni-Range systems. Existing radars were being modernized and additional radar sites were being installed into Canada's middle latitudes for increased coverage of our domestic airspace. This expanded network of navaids and communications reached far afield into small airports and remote areas where a manned FSS or control tower could not be provided. Modernization promised increased aviation safety in Canada but it would take decades to complete.

A Remote Communications Outlet ca. 1980, providing air navigation services from an FSS to a remote area of Canada.

It was our job to install the equipment that made modernization possible. The adjacent photo shows a typical remote site from the early 1980s. The radios in the middle rack are the first generation of solid-state receivers and transmitters and a solid-state navaid beacon is on the right. A diesel generator for standby power is in the background.

The photo on the right shows a larger remote site a decade later having three times the number of radio frequencies controlled remotely from both an FSS and an ATC operations centre. The last generation of non-digital radio and control equipment is installed along with uninterruptible battery backup power. The diesel is gone and the navaid beacon is a similar version of the one in the previous photo.

A larger RCO site from the 1990s. There are six radio frequencies providing services from both an FSS and ATC operations centre. Battery back-up power has replaced the diesel.

I spent much of my engineering services career installing similar equipment into airport communications sites and remote locations all over Western Canada and the Arctic. As my time in engineering services increased so did my responsibilities as I was assigned more complex projects and eventually won promotion to senior project officer. I received excellent performance reviews and several letters of commendation on the quality and completeness of my projects. These installations were all, of course, team efforts. Much of the credit I received was due to the professional and competent people I worked with, men like Bill Webster, Len Cook, Colin Page, Kim Davis, Vince Warszycki, Steve Highstead, Bill Cinkant-Hill's riggers, Stu Patterson, Andre Sharpe, Robert Dobson, John Schmidt, Don Neighbour, Nick Kozak, Coleman Robinson, and others equally outstanding.

ENGINEERING VIGNETTES

Learning my new job was again by osmosis. New engineering techs were fobbed off to whichever technologist needed an extra set of hands until our bosses felt we were competent enough to be turned loose on our own.

Don Parker on the beacon antenna tuning unit stand at Norway House. Note the missing fence picket!

My first job came right away, assisting Don Parker at Norway House at the top end of Lake Winnipeg. He needed a second set of hands to help lift an outdoor antenna tuner onto its stand at their airport's navaid beacon site. This trip provided me with an education into what was sometimes done to address a lack of pre-planning. The new tuner did not fit onto the existing stand that sat next to the beacon's antenna so Don just walked over to the white wooden fence surrounding the site, pulled off a couple of pickets, and nailed them onto the stand to make the new tuner fit.

When we returned to Winnipeg Don's trip report noted that the fence had been vandalized "by locals" and the riggers should repair it on their next regular maintenance trip. Don had asked me to study the record drawings of the beacon facility and make any corrections and updates while there. Besides one or two minor discrepancies I noted that the tuner stand dimensions were given on the drawing so we could easily have brought some pre-painted two-by-fours of the proper lengths with us.

Golf and Darts

Many of the sites we worked at were in small towns with limited services so it was common to pack along a portable BBQ and other amenities to help us better enjoy our off hours. Tailgate dinners or picnics were favourite ways to break the monotony of eating off the same menu for a week in the town's only restaurant. If there was a lake or river nearby then fishing was a great way to relax. In the 1980s and '90s almost every town had a Legion branch and a nine-hole golf course. Many of us took up golf and joined the Legion where we could enjoy a quiet evening playing cards, pool, or darts in an atmosphere that was more convivial than the local hotel bar.

The first time I ever swung a golf club was on the little nine-hole course at Grenfell, Saskatchewan. Bill Webster had brought along his clubs and wanted to play a round. I was going to keep him company, look for lost balls, and kibitz. There was no clubhouse; you just put a donation in the box at the first hole and teed off. Bill handed me his driver and said:

"Here, it will be more fun if you play too. This is a wide-open course so you won't lose too many balls."

"Okay thanks, but I've never done this before so stand back!"

On my first swing the tee went further than the ball. On the second I took another mulligan and a large divot as the ball squibbed off to the right. On my 'Third-Time-Lucky' try the ball actually got some air time! Mind you it did hook off to the right about a hundred yards before getting lost in a wheat field. I had fun once I figured out to take easier swings and not try spanking the ball, then I managed to zigzag down the fairways most of the time. For the next year or so I used borrowed or rented clubs to golf with my travelling partners. I wasn't good enough to be bothered keeping score but as long as I found more balls than I lost I was happy.

Lorne Fehr, who was the telecom area manager in Saskatoon, was an avid golfer who was upgrading his clubs. He offered me his old set of Spaldings including the bag for a bottle of Scotch. I'm not much of a Scotch drinker but I bought him a bottle that I judged to be a good brand based on the liquor store price. I duffed around with the Spaldings for the next 15 years, never taking the game seriously but taking some lessons from club pros and slowly improving to where I started keeping score. I was getting good exercise playing once a week or so with friends and neighbours when I was not on the road. Lorne's old clubs gave me good service and I hope he considered the Scotch I bought him a fair trade.

I did better at darts. Len Cook taught Kim Davis and I to throw in the Thunder Bay Legion. It wasn't long afterwards that I had a board set up in my basement and was practising with my own set of arrows. Len and Colin were both good players who were competitive in their Legion branch leagues. Darts were easier to pack than golf clubs so we began playing darts in various Legions whenever we were on the road and my game improved to the point where I was holding my own in match play.

I no longer golf but I still place in the top third of my town's local dart league.

Len Cook

Len led a very interesting life. He had worked in the steel mills in Hamilton and while there he played AA baseball. He actually had a tryout with the Mets but, as in the Steve Earle song, "I still hang around 'cause I'm a little bit small." Len came to Transport Canada through the military and during his job interview in Regina was given a tour of their maintenance facility. He spotted a military radio test bench in their workshop. None of the Transport Canada techs had any idea of its capabilities so Len spent the next couple of hours putting it through its paces for them, and his demonstration likely cemented his job offer.

Len was a firm believer in worker's rights and the collective bargaining process. He was our regional chief shop steward, always going out of his way to see fair play and that both sides lived up to our contract. I would be very glad to see him arrive at one of my last installation projects before my retirement!

Len, Steve Highstead, and I occupied three of the four positions at what became our regular Saturday bridge night. The fourth was usually fellow tech Nick Kozak, Steve's brother Ian, or Len's neighbour. These sessions started after dinner and usually went until dawn! Players came and went over time but Steve and I were the regulars and our bridge sessions went on for years!

Illegal Clawbacks

Canada's civil servants are all subject to the same travel directive which, among other things, sets out the per diem amounts you are entitled to claim for meals and incidental expenses when away from home on official business. Using per diems greatly reduces the administrative overhead and paperwork compared to accounting for thousands of individual receipts and ensures everyone is on the same level playing field.

Even though the travel directive treats everyone equally it had been a long-standing policy of engineering management that general labourers and riggers were distinctly lower-class employees. Before I arrived in engineering services they were required to stay in lesser quality motels and had part of their expense allowances clawed back. No one expected to stay in three-star resorts unless you were stuck at Hecla Island, but if technologists were approved for stays in a Super-8 or Comfort Inn then our helpers and riggers were booked into whatever Bates Motel was available without any say in the matter. The travel directive allowed everyone $3 per day for incidental expenses but they had a dollar a day clawed back. This practice might have hearkened back to the military rank and messing system that most of our managers came from but it was illegal on many levels. The riggers and labourers did not belong to the same union that we technologists did, but they filed grievances with their own bargaining agent. These grievances were lost as management and the bureaucracy sought to entrench their discriminatory policy.

Colin Page, a former general labourer and now a technologist, began a letter-writing campaign to Members of Parliament that led to questions to the Minister of Transport in the House of Commons. The actions he initiated finally caused this unlawful policy to be rescinded, but even then management fought to avoid reimbursing the illegally clawed-back allowances. Despite the legal decision and the department having everyone's travel and expense records going back decades, they insisted each employee had to present their copies of expense claims as proof of loss. Those who no longer had their records were denied reimbursement. The foul odour from this unrest still permeated the air when Bill, Steve Highstead, and I arrived in Engineering's Control Systems group.

Colin Page. Green Acres photo.

Colin was born and raised in England, trained as a machinist, and came to Canada in his 20s to work for INCO in their nickel mine at Thompson, Manitoba. At the time I met him he had graduated to an engineering services technologist position working in the navaids group. Colin was one of the most stand-up people I ever worked with and during the remainder of my career I tried as best I could to emulate his principles.

Going Solo

My first solo assignment was installing the control system for Regina's new Instrument Landing System (ILS). Norway House had taught me the value of pre-planning and I did not want to be caught short on my first job, so I booked a day trip to meet the Regina staff, get their approval for what I was planning, and confirm drawing information. When I got back to Winnipeg, I began fabricating my control system into an equipment rack and gathering all the necessary materials I would need. It was then that Steve Highstead approached me to ask if we could combine forces. Steve had joined engineering services from Thunder Bay at about the same time I had and this assignment, also his first solo, was to install the control system for Regina's new Omni-Range

(VOR) system. Regina's Omni-Range was co-located with a Tacan in a VorTac site building, and the two Navaids shared a common control system. Steve was unfamiliar with Tacan but I had been trained on it so helping him interface his new system to it and having two sets of hands on-site assisting each other made sense. Our boss, Peter Goertzen, approved of our teamwork so shortly after that Steve and I freighted our equipment to Regina then flew out a few days later.

Regina was a busy place that summer. Other teams of engineering technologists were on-site at the same time we were to install the new ILS and Omni-Range systems that we were connecting our control systems to. There were also riggers, regional office maintenance specialists, and quality assurance staff on-site. Between all these crews we were borrowing most of the station's vehicle fleet to get around to the various sites and our downtown hotels. One was a nearly new Chevy Suburban outfitted with a fancy light bar on the roof. On the first day in Regina the installation team that borrowed the Suburban drove it into the underground hotel parkade and promptly schmeared the light bar off on the low ceiling! The telecom area manager, Murray Koschuk, was less than pleased and decreed that we would have to use rented cars henceforth, no more tying up his station's fleet! We were happy with this new arrangement because the rented cars were cleaner, nicer, and came with stereo systems. Don Parker was there as the quality assurance representative so of course the car he rented for himself was a fire-engine red Camaro convertible. When his boss found out the next day, he had to give it up and car pool in compact domestic sedans with the rest of us hoi polloi.

A couple of weeks later as the projects were winding down a Transport Canada flight-check aircraft flew out to verify the new navaids were within specifications. The flight checks lasted into the early evening so when the aircraft landed the crew just helped themselves to a set of vehicle keys and headed to their hotel. They chose the newly repaired Suburban that now sported an even fancier light bar, and drove it into the same hotel parkade with the same results! This time Murray tore a strip off the flight-check crew, sent the repair bill to their office, and reiterated his ban on outside persons using station vehicles, this time in writing!

The equipment installations went well. The Regina staff was pleased with engineering's work and singled out Steve and I for having consulted with them first, which was something not always done in those days. Regina was a great confidence booster for both of us and resulted in a friendship that endures today. During my time in engineering I worked on many different installations with several different partners at almost every site in our region. I always enjoyed the work and felt I had joined the Varsity team!

A Death in the Family

On December 6, 1978, I had just arrived at Lynn Lake in northern Manitoba as part of a crew that included Colin Page and Len Cook. We worked the afternoon of our arrival then checked into the hotel and met in the bar. We were just starting our first beer when an RCMP constable approached and asked if one of us was Bruce LeCren. I identified myself while thinking there was no way this was good news. He told me I should phone home right away so I immediately went to my room to make the call. My brother-in-law Al Wiebe answered the phone at my parent's house and told me my father had suffered a fatal heart attack a couple of hours earlier. He was only 54.

I was struck dumb, my mind went completely blank and I couldn't think of anything to say beyond "I'll get home as fast as possible, but it might take a day or two to get a flight." I

honestly can't recall any more of the conversation we might have had and I do not recall speaking then to Ma or Jovanna, who had all gathered together. I returned to the bar and told the crew what had happened then went back to my room and lay on the bed. I started thinking about all the family times we had had together and things that were said and left unsaid.... I was dry-eyed but in shock.

Denis LeCren. Taken too soon like many of my friends and colleagues.

I don't know how long I lay there or what time the phone rang, but it was either Len or Colin telling me to get my stuff together and there would be a ride outside to take me to the airport right away. The guys had made some calls and a Lambair Twin Otter was waiting to take me to Thompson where I had a seat on Transair's evening flight to Winnipeg. I can't recall anything about the flight to Thompson except someone must have pulled a string because Lambair removed some freight to make a seat available for me. These were the kind of men and indeed the kind of friends that I was fortunate enough to be working with. I can't thank them enough for their efforts to get me home. Everyone was surprised when I came through the door that night and my brother arrived from Regina about the same time so the family was all together as we sat up late talking. The next few days remain blurry as we went through the logistics of planning a funeral. We buried my dad five days later on my birthday.

A Trio of Summer Students

Summers were our busiest seasons and we hired engineering students from university as summer help. If they worked out the first year they were usually invited back each summer until they had finished their degrees. Besides opening gates and carrying tool boxes they learned some of our work's practical side such as electronic assembly and testing, which was not always emphasized in their university classes.

On one occasion I was helping Colin Page install a radio direction finder into the FSS at Dauphin, Manitoba. The specialists used this aviation safety device to direct lost pilots to the Dauphin airport. We took a brand-new summer student with us and on the drive to Dauphin Colin and I found out this was Dave's first trip away from Winnipeg. Everything was new and exciting for him! Upon arrival we checked into the Dauphin Motel, a two-storey cinder block structure with the outside passages and iron stairs typical of any small-town motel anywhere. Colin and I were waiting in the car when Dave stuck his head over the second-floor railing and said:

"There's a paper strip over the toilet bowl in my room ... is there one in yours?"

Colin thought fast: "That means your toilet is broken. Don't use it. Go to the office and they'll give you another room!"

Dave hauled his gear out of his room and down the stairs to the office while we sat in the car grinning from ear to ear. Eventually he came out and hauled his stuff back up to the second floor then along to his new room. A few seconds later he re-emerged:

"Hey guys, this one is broken too!"

Another year and another summer drive across the dusty Prairies with another new student helper, this time accompanied by Bill Webster. Like Dave, 'Big Bird' was city born and raised. He was tagged with that nickname by Don Parker because he was over six feet tall with an unruly mop of blond hair, and gangly like his Sesame Street namesake. We drove past several herds of cows grazing in the fields....

"So Big Bird, have you ever been cow tipping?"

"What's that?"

"Kind of a rural rite of passage. You walk up beside the cow then push it over. That's one reason all the farmers have bucket loaders or fork lifts, for standing up cows that have tipped over; it's great fun!"

After some more back and forth with straight faces Bill and I had convinced Big Bird to try tipping a cow. We would take pictures with his camera so he could show his friends back in Winnipeg. We pulled over at the next pasture and Big Bird got out, went over the fence without too much trouble, then approached the most docile looking bovine in sight. The steer turned its head and watched Big Bird curiously as he patted its rump, then he laid on a football-style blocking move. The steer bellowed and stepped back as Big Bird lined up for a second attempt, slipped and went down in a fresh patty, then realized he was being pranked. I doubt he passed the pictures around when he got back home!

Andre was a maintenance technologist who had done his Arctic tour then went back to school to get his Engineering degree. During that time he was hired by us as a summer student. One summer he was in Churchill with several engineering techs including Don Parker. Everyone had gathered in Andre's hotel room before heading to dinner and the Legion. Andre was homesteading in the bathroom when Don thought it would be a good idea to take his picture sitting on the throne. Don got his camera ready and prepared to rush the door, but Andre heard them and braced his legs against it. Don pushed harder to no avail, so he took a step back and put his shoulder into it. The door sprung open and Andre was pushed back into the toilet tank causing it to break away from the bowl! Andre was trying to stand up with his pants down and the bowl between

Andre Sharpe—A# as he liked to sign himself, one of our better engineers. *Winnipeg Free Press* photo.

his knees, with water spraying up from the broken bog soaking him and everything in the room!

Everyone was laughing so hard they forgot to take the picture! It cost Don $80 for a new toilet and he tried to claim it on his expense account as "site sanitary appliance." His boss actually approved it thinking it referred to the chemical toilet at our remote site, but the bean counters in accounting knew a turd when they smelled it and denied the claim. Andre went on to a career in engineering services as one of the best Professional Engineers I worked with. As a result of his practical background his designs were functional and easily installed and maintained.

Bring Your Airplane to Work

Larry Stenberg was a maintenance specialist in our regional office who loved flying his own aircraft. He had convinced his boss to allow him to use it on his work trips if he could show a benefit to the department. Most of the flying I was doing was taking friends on sightseeing flights around Winnipeg or up to the big lake, including some to Crocus Grove. Recreational flying was expensive so I thought I would try the same thing with my boss Peter. I obtained approval from the Canadian Transport Commission to fly a rented aircraft on my employer's business, which was a requirement then to protect commercial operators from illegal charter activity.

My first opportunity was a solo project involving a small amount of work relocating master control switches at Brandon, Regina, and Saskatoon control towers. Normally this would entail a four-day road trip involving several hours of overtime. I made the case to Peter that by renting an aircraft I could complete the work in three days with no overtime; the only risk might be delays due to weather, which I could plan around. The travel directive did not speak to the use of private aircraft but Peter was forward thinking and, after talking with Larry's boss, said we would try it out. He agreed to reimburse me the travel directive's "employer requested" mileage rate for use of a private vehicle up to the cost of the rental. This was generous on his part and a better deal than Larry was getting from his boss!

Piper Warrior PA-28-151 C-GEUH, my favourite
ride at Point West Aviation. Photo courtesy
Tomas Milosch, Planespotters.net.

I determined that next week's weather should be suitable so on Monday I took home the tools and materials I would need. When Tuesday dawned bright and sunny I loaded up Point West's Piper Warrior and flew off to Brandon. By noon I had departed Brandon for Regina and by 4:30 p.m. my work there was done. Rather than stay overnight as planned I took advantage of the long days and good weather to cancel my hotel reservation and proceed onward to Saskatoon. By Wednesday noon I was ready to head back to St. Andrews, Winnipeg's satellite airport from where I had started. My old boss Bob Stampe was now the maintenance supervisor in Saskatoon, so he and I got caught up then we flew a few circuits together before I left. Along the way home I dropped into Yorkton where Ian Muir was now the TSM. After some more catching up over coffees we made a flip over the town so we could buzz Ian's house.

I arrived back home that evening with all the work done and walked into Peter's office the next morning a day earlier than planned. I had completed the job ahead of schedule with no deficiencies and at a cost saving to the department compared to road travel. I was out of pocket about five dollars per hour of flying time which were cheap hours in my log book! I did not claim any overtime because I could have taken the full three days and not incurred any, and I wanted this to be a win for everyone.

Several other wins followed this positive first step over the next few years:

Bill Webster and I flew to Dauphin to inspect the FSS prior to a major rework on their consoles, a one-day trip instead of two by road.

Kenora FSS was responsible for flights into and out of the Red Lake airport, so they wanted control of Red Lake's airfield lighting added to their existing remote communications capability. I flew to Kenora and installed the lighting control panel in their FSS console, then I ate my box lunch on the way to Red Lake where I had a rented vehicle waiting to get me to the remote communications site. There I installed wiring between the existing control system and the airfield lighting relay panel, tested the new lighting controls with Kenora, and flew home. The project was completed in one 13-hour day as opposed to a three-day road trip.

A fellow tech, Coleman Robinson, was also a private pilot. He and I teamed up to use the rented Warrior to install Transcribed Weather Broadcast Systems into FSSs in Saskatoon, North Battleford, LaRonge, Prince Albert, and Regina. These computerized systems stored recorded weather information then automatically played it back to pilots over the radio and on telephone lines. I was tipping the scales at 90 kilograms then and Coleman was larger so we would be pushing the weight limits of the Warrior with tools, baggage, and the full fuel tanks needed for most of the flight legs. To save weight we took only one pared-down tool kit and limited ourselves to seven kilograms each of personal baggage. Even so we were a bit heavy and used almost all 3,000 feet of St. Andrews' runway before getting airborne. We returned eight days later after 16 hours of flying time vs. the 12 days we would have taken if we had used a car.

After Steve Highstead had become a supervisor I flew him to Dauphin on another inspection trip prior to closing that facility, then we went on to Brandon control tower where we met with Public Works to inspect major water leaks in their walls.

Peter and Steve were a minority in engineering services when it came to being air minded, and my personal flying on Transport Canada business ended when I left the control systems group, even given the demonstrated time and money savings.

Cable TV Techs

In the early 1980s Winnipeg's cable television company began offering the Superchannel movie service for a monthly subscription fee. The scrambled signal was analyzed by our engineers, who discovered the scrambling to be nothing more than an interference signal that was inserted onto the Superchannel signal by the cable company. Descrambling at that time was considered by many to be a grey area of cable television based on the premise that the cable company was bringing the signal into your television, and if you could decode it there was no-harm-no-foul as long as you did not profit from your activities.

Our engineers designed a simple trap made from a piece of copper pipe with a coil of wire inside. When connected to the television's cable input this tuned out the interfering signal to let the viewer watch Superchannel. We set up a production line at our engineering workshop to make these 'Q-filters': riggers chopped five-centimetre diameter pipes into the correct lengths, techs made the coil and assembled the filter, and engineers fine-tuned each filter assembly. We intended to make filters only for the employees at our shop but it was not too long before we were getting calls from all departments at regional office. The airport technologists also began churning these things out at their workshop. One manager asked us for six filters for himself and his family. This was getting out of hand so we wound down the production line when our stock of pipe was used up.

I installed a Q-filter on my father-in-law's television. One afternoon he was enjoying a free movie when two cable company trucks pulled up on the street outside. The cable employees were just taking a break, but Joe thought he was busted and had visions of his television set being confiscated and himself hauled off to the hoosegow! He slinked out of his couch and crab-walked to the stairs so he wouldn't be seen from the street, hustled down to the basement, and removed the filter from the cable line as fast as he could, hiding it in his basement toilet tank!

Ours wasn't the only electronics shop in Winnipeg manufacturing signal filters and it wasn't very long before the cable company switched to digital scrambling, making our Q-filters obsolete. The game of technology one-upmanship continued. On their quiet evening shifts at the airport our maintenance technologists designed a digital descrambler that fit into a set-top cable box that you could buy for 40 dollars from Radio Shack.

An Evening with Elmer

I was working in Swift Current, Saskatchewan, in the mid-1980s and one evening after dinner I looked up my old TSM Elmer Klatt. He had retired there by that time; he came to the motel where I was staying and drove us out into the Cypress Hills looking for mulies and other critters. We enjoyed a beer on his truck's tailgate while watching the sunset and generally catching up. I told him I still used the flashlight he gave me a decade earlier in Coral Harbour. I am glad we had that time together because he passed away not too long after.

Stu Patterson

Stu was a real character, one of our senior techs who worked in engineering's navaids group with Colin Page and Vince

Warszycki, who had also joined us in engineering services after his time in Maintenance. Stu was an elderly gentleman who was past the normal retirement age but was good at what he did and still enjoyed coming to work. He was a tall lanky drink of water who sported a collection of cuts and scars on his head that made him look like he combed his sparse grey hair with a hand grenade. He was one of those guys who could instinctively see how things worked and was adept at making repairs to unfamiliar pieces of machinery and equipment. Stu hoarded all sorts of surplus materials in his basement, which was laid out with aisles like an army-navy surplus store. He had everything from soup to nuts down there including electronic equipment, car parts, lumber and sheet metal, tools, and even parts of a glider that he was restoring while learning to fly.

Stu was a bit absent minded and often pulled a drawer out from an equipment rack, bent down to get a tool, then stood up and whacked his head on the drawer bottom, hence the scars. If it wasn't drawer bottoms it was tools or hardware dropped by people working over his head, hence the cuts. One of our riggers accidentally dropped a bolt from 15 metres up a tower when Stu was standing underneath. He removed his hard hat to wipe the sweat from his brow at just the wrong time. When he woke up he had collected another knot on his head.

In those days before corporate credit cards we received cash advances for our estimated travel expenses so we would not be out of pocket on the road. Stu would invariably spend his advance money before leaving town. I went on a road trip with him for two weeks one summer installing monitor systems into Omni-Range sites. Stu had already spent his advance as usual so the first place we had to stop at was the liquor store so he could buy a two-four of beer. The second stop we had to make was the nearest KFC where he loaded a large barrel of chicken into the car. Thus provisioned he drove us across the Prairies to our first destination where we passed by the usual Motel 6 and Travelodge motels. I began wondering where Stu had arranged for us to stay because we were coming to the far end of the town. At the last street before the Prairie began again Stu pulled into a little mom-and-pop motel, the kind that had the 'Rooms Available' sign permanently painted on the façade facing the highway. The sheets were clean and Mom and Pop were very friendly, but it lived up to the lines from the Roger Miller classic song "King of the Road": "8 x 12 four-bit room…. No phone no pool no pets … rooms to let 50 cents." What drew Stu to this establishment, and the others like it that we would be staying at over the next two weeks, was not only the low rates but the free breakfasts.

For the next 12 days Stu enjoyed free greasy bacon and egg breakfasts, which were his only hot food of the day. Lunches and dinners were the meals of champions: a bottle of warm beer and a piece of cold chicken each. I still had my advance money so Stu dined alone. Some days I brought him a doggy bag.

Stu's retirement party was another great send-off! Retirement affairs in those days were typically roasts that started at lunchtime and went well into the late evening with a hall being rented and a dinner laid on; nothing less would do to mark the winding down of eventful and colourful careers spanning more than a third of a century! When it was time for the servers to bring out our roast beef dinners one of them placed a warm beer and a cold KFC two-piece meal in front of Stu. His wife gave him a quizzical look as our emcee, Dave LeBlanc a.k.a. "Ace", explained to the crowd that the money collected had been spent in advance and there was not enough left for Stu's dinner!

The Muppet Show

Phil Kor went through WWII as a clandestine radio operator with the Dutch underground. After that experience he travelled the world as a merchant marine radio operator, then held several jobs in the electronics field before eventually coming to Canada in 1959. He was well respected in Transport Canada for his wide range of knowledge tempered by strong

opinions on every subject. He did not suffer fools gladly. His son Bouko went to high school with Bob Crosby and I, and Phil's step-son Frank den Ouden followed him into an electronic technologist career with Transport Canada.

Bert and Ernie were two of our general labourers who were helping Phil install equipment into a remote site somewhere on the Prairies. The two Muppets were

Philip Kor, a life well lived.
Winnipeg Free Press photo.

annoying Phil so he sent them outside to hammer the site's ground rod into the earth. This was a two-and-a-half-metre-long copper rod, so Bert was standing on a stepladder to better swing the sledgehammer. Ernie was afraid Bert would hit his hands, so he clipped two vise-grips together and was using those to hold the rod while standing back as far as he could. Bert couldn't get a good solid swing and Ernie couldn't get a good solid grip, so the rod bounced around without going into the ground every time Bert connected. Phil came outside, observed their cartoon antics for a few moments, then he blew his top and left no doubt who was in charge!

"You Muppets will never get the job done! Do I have to do everything!? I'll show you how!"

"Bert, get off that ladder! Give me that hammer! Stand here and watch me!"

"Ernie, drop those vise-grips! Grab that rod properly with both hands! Not like that, spread your hands apart! Now hold it steady!"

"Both of you pay attention! This is how you hammer a ground rod!"

Saying that, Phil took two steps up onto the ladder, lined up his swing, brought the hammer back over his shoulder ... and nailed Bert square on his cranium! Bert was laid out cold! Phil dropped the hammer and tried to shake him awake while Ernie ran into the building, coming back out with a fire bucket that he had filled with the distilled water kept on-site for our batteries. Bert was waking up when Ernie doused him full in the face from the bucket! Bert sat up spitting out dirty oily water, old cigarette butts, and dead flies!

Phil and Ernie loaded Bert into their car and raced to the nearest hospital. He had a concussion as evidenced by his babbling away like the Swedish Chef, and a large lump on his noggin, but no lasting effects and he needed only three or four stitches on his scalp and some Tylenol 3s for pain. The next day the riggers showed up to work on the site's antenna. They got the rod into the ground in no time using their electric jack hammer.

Corporate Raiders!

I am the first to acknowledge that Canada's civil servants enjoy good pensions and benefits, but 40 years ago our salaries had fallen far behind those in the private sector. Our skills were in demand by technology leaders such as Nortel and Research-In-Motion who, like other big tech companies, were making very attractive offers. Fort McMurray was booming and energy companies were hiring the best talent they could find from across the country. It was getting harder for the ANS to recruit good technologists right out of school and to keep the ones they did hire.

My phone rang one evening at home after dinner and I found myself speaking with Lockheed Aerospace calling from Los Angeles. This was a cold call and to this day I have no idea how their recruiter heard about me or got my home phone number. His pitch was a one-year contract for $50K in U.S. dollars paid into a Saudi bank, which meant tax-free. I would be working for them in Saudi Arabia maintaining airport electronic systems and the offer included paid vacations anywhere in Europe. At the time I was making a lot less than $50K in Canadian dollars and turning more than a third of that over to the feds and province. This offer sounded great to me. Jovanna and I had not started a family yet, so we could sell or rent our house and Jovanna could come with me. She would have a good chance of contract nursing work in a hospital. I saw no down side so I called over to her across the room:

"How would you like an all-expense-paid trip to Los Angeles, for both of us next week?"

"Ooh, sounds great! We can see Hollywood and the Pacific Ocean and go shopping!"

"Yup, and after that, we can spend a year in Saudi making huge dollars and seeing more of Europe!"

"Uh, where?"

"Saudi Arabia.... I'm being offered a one-year contract working there for Lockheed for fifty thousand U.S., and you could probably get a job in their hospitals?!?"

"There's no way I'm going to live in a big sandbox where they beat their wives, make you wear burkas, and kill and eat innocent little baby goats and puppies!"

That ended the conversation. I turned down the opportunity and Jovanna was right about the culture shock. A few of our techs did take Lockheed's offer and found themselves living in a gated compound near Riyadh, paying baksheesh to have a blind eye turned to their concealed booze and minor cultural offences. Their wives had to dress very modestly and were given an escort whenever they ventured out of the compound, minding all sorts of Ps and Qs in the souk. Lockheed lost their contract after a few months and everyone who went over there was laid off and stranded. Some stayed on for a while working for Saudia, their national airline. Eventually they all made their way back to Canada and most were rehired by Transport, but not necessarily at their old jobs or salaries, and some were told they would have to complete another probationary period and Arctic tour.

A fallout from these corporate raids was Transport Canada realizing they were bleeding expensively trained, highly qualified, and hard to replace technologists to private industry. They convinced the Treasury Board, who is the government's bargaining agent, to approach our union with an offer to reopen the salary portion of our collective agreement with the intent to bump up our wages. This was an unprecedented move. Never before or since has the federal government offered more money to any union in the middle of a collective agreement term.

New Blood

Peter Goertzen took over the electronics workshop at Winnipeg's brand-new Air Traffic Control operations centre and Steve Highstead moved up to take over the control systems group in engineering services. Steve became my mentor as well as my friend and helped my career to progress in the years to come. Nearing the end of his own career some 20 years later, Steve said "I only had two bosses I really got along great with and they were both named Peter!"

Not too long after Steve took over several of us were fishing at Duck Bay north of Winnipegosis on the May long weekend. We had three boats strung out in a line when we observed a fourth boat puttering towards us. When it got closer we recognized Steve sitting by himself in the stern. He slowed down and had a look at each boat until he found the one with Len Cook in it. He came alongside and passed over an envelope:

Steve Highstead,
friend and mentor.

"Here's your plane tickets and travel expense advance.... You're leaving Tuesday morning for a training course!"

Len was rather flabbergasted that his boss would drive three hours on a weekend to hunt him down in a boat to send him out of town, but he didn't drop the envelope in the river. Steve pulled out his rod and reel and spent the rest of the weekend fishing with us. He brought beer so all was forgiven.

Stoney Rapids

We were installing a remote communications site for use by Edmonton's controllers onto a hilltop near Stoney Rapids, on Lake Athabaska at the top of Saskatchewan. Stoney's hotel accommodation was expensive and used mainly as a women's shelter at the time, so I checked around and booked the installation crews into a nearby fishing lodge on Black Lake. The cabins were modern, each came with a boat and motor plus the option of either eating at the main lodge or cooking in our cabins, and the cost of our two-week stay for six was thousands less than staying in the town!

View from the Black Lake fishing camp near Stoney Rapids.

One of our riggers asked to be dropped off at the end of each day where the road to the camp joined the main road to town so he could jog the remaining two kilometres to the cabins. On the third day after dropping him off his rigging buddies scooted into the camp, grabbed a bearskin rug off the wall in the lodge, and headed about 100 metres back up the road to where there were some large rocks. They hid behind the rocks and waited for our athlete who soon showed up huffing, puffing, tongue out, and dragging his feet up the dusty road while swatting at bugs. His buddies made bear noises and pushed up the head so it would be seen over the rocks.... Instantly the running rigger recovered reserves of stamina and sprinted the rest of the way into camp! The other riggers showed up shortly thereafter with the rug and beers were had by all, but that was the last day our road warrior asked to be dropped off.

We had to rent private pickup trucks to get to our remote site each day. These were basically relics whose owners had managed to get running so they could earn a few bucks. The road up the hill was very rough and we got shaken up pretty good coming and going. Halfway up to the site on our second day, the old Ford let us know it had had enough of our abuse by emitting smoke and flames from the defroster vents. We beat the flames out with an old blanket from the back seat but the wiring was melted and the truck was done. Bill Webster and I walked the last kilometre to the site accompanied by every flying insect in creation. In the Great North Woods, if it has six legs and flies it sucks blood. Between the deer flies, horse flies, black flies, No-See-Ums, and mosquitoes, we were each down a pint by the time we got indoors.

The site building was a new Atco trailer with everything required to be operational and self-sufficient built into it back in Winnipeg. Once the building arrived by barge from across the lake it was taken up the hill to the site on a flat-deck semi. The truck needed to be pulled by one Caterpillar tractor and pushed by another to make it. Once sited, the local power authority refused to connect us to the grid because we had baseboard heaters in the building. Who knew that in Stoney Rapids homes were heated by burning wood and permanently wired electric heaters were not permitted? Until we resolved this problem we had to keep the door open to let in some light because there were no windows. This also let in the aforementioned flies and mosquitoes, so one of us was designated 'fly-swatter' while the others worked.

Kim Davis rigged up temporary power for us by running a generator that he plugged into the building's exterior outlet using a 'widow-maker' cord. A widow-maker has a male plug on both ends of the cord. The shock hazard should be obvious so don't try this at home, but it worked to back-feed power from the generator into the building circuits. That let us turn on the lights and A/C and close the door. Kim then unwired the baseboard heaters and terminated their circuits with surface mounted wall plugs. Then he made a cord for each heater so we could plug them in. This arrangement was considered acceptable to the power company which left us shaking our heads, but our building was finally connected to permanent power.

Something's Fishy

Prince Albert maintenance techs Kerry Bullock, Brian Hackl and I, evening fishing at Stoney Rapids. Note my bug jacket!

The fishing camp at Stoney worked out great for the guys. They told me they appreciated being able to unwind and relax at the end of each day. If fishing wasn't your thing then the camp had canoes we could borrow and the central lodge had a small library and board games. You could relax by the fireplace by yourself or with the other guests, who were all from the United States. They had laid out thousands of dollars to go fly-in fishing while we were being paid for the same privilege!

I made similar arrangements the next year when we went into Sioux Lookout, Ontario. As Bill Webster and I drove into that fishing camp we were greeted by Bill Howe sitting on the front porch of one of the cabins. Bill was the new FSS manager, who was staying at the camp with his family while waiting for their new home to be ready. Great minds think alike!

After those successes I thought I would try it again in La Ronge, Saskatchewan, where we were building a brand-new FSS co-located with a new air terminal building. This would be a bit unorthodox because there was no fishing camp nearby, but there were houseboat rentals. I got the team together and said it was up to them where they stayed, but the houseboat would be an option that could work if they wanted to use it. The houseboat slept eight and they would be a crew of four. There was a bay just on the far side of the airport runway where the boat could be beached. The guys could either drive or walk to work each day, go fishing each night, and explore the lake on weekends. The total cost was less than hotel accommodations and they could either buy groceries and cook on the boat or eat in local restaurants. My only caveats were that all of the crew had to buy in to be cost-effective and everyone had to get along. I did not want anyone moving into the hotel mid-trip or coming home in a body bag because of arguments on the boat! The guys talked it over and said they would go for the houseboat.

Steve approved my requisition for the houseboat rental supported by the higher cost of alternative accommodations.

The new combined air terminal and FSS building at LaRonge.

There was, however, a dinosaur living up in accounting who took exception, saying the travel directive did not cover this and he could not approve the techs enjoying themselves after hours at government expense. He would only go along if we declared the houseboat to be government accommodations, which meant the guys would receive reduced travel expense allowances. I refused to set this precedent so the houseboat idea fell through, although the guys did manage some time on the lake while they were there!

The same dinosaur who screwed us on the houseboat deal also sent everyone in the regional office regular reminders insisting that every financial requisition had to be properly coded to accurately describe all purchases. He said this was supposed to allow the bean counters to track how many of each kind of beans we were buying and correlate them against our approved project plans and budgets. Steve did not believe these apparatchiks really paid attention to the materials and supplies we bought because we never received any feedback about our budgets, so he decided to run a test. Referring to the financial manual, he started coding every petty cash voucher, purchase order, and requisition that crossed his desk as 'fish.' Over several months our section bought, on paper, tons of fish! The dinosaur never caught on thus torpedoing his story about auditing items vs. budgets. Steve's prank also proved that stodgy and unimaginative bureaucracy was ingrained into our corner of the civil service, feeding off themselves in a perpetual cycle of civility and servitude!

Skyward

I started chartering aircraft for many of our northern trips because it was cheaper, more convenient, and more direct than the commercial air services flying into the small isolated communities where we had to work. One of my favourite charter companies was Skyward based out of Rankin Inlet.

We developed a very good working relationship and I made many trips to points north with them, getting to know their base manager Kathleen Henderson and our usual pilot Kyle Ronan very well. We usually flew their Cessna 208 Caravan, which did not need a co-pilot. Since I was doing the

Cessna 208B Grand Caravan, owned by Skyward Aviation. Photo courtesy Airliners.net.

chartering I got to ride shotgun and Kyle always let me fly once we were airborne. We were flying into Repulse Bay on the Arctic Circle on a beautiful winter day, cold but 'severely clear' and you could see forever. The flight was uneventful and when we had the community in sight Kyle said:

"You can fly it down; I have the levers."

Wow! I set up the descent using the trim tab and made an easy turn onto final. The Caravan almost aimed itself at the runway threshold and I greased it on, one of the best landings I ever made! After gassing up we continued to our final destination at Hall Beach where fog was reported rolling in off the ocean. Kyle and I discussed going back to Repulse but since the Hall Beach weather office was closer to the shoreline than the runway we thought we would have a look and then decide. As we got closer we could see the fog hanging over the airport like a shroud but a little way inland the fog ended abruptly and we could see everything below us. We were almost on top of the airport when I saw the runway approach cones just to the right and the end of the strip sticking out of the fog bank. I pointed this out to Kyle who immediately executed a descending 360-degree turn and touched us down smoothly at the end of the 500 feet of visible runway. We taxied through the fog to the apron and when we checked in with the weather office their observers told us they thought there was no way we were going to make it in. They were reporting sky obscured and 50 feet visibility, which is one of the recipes for "No flying today!" They actually drove to the end of the runway to make sure we were not bullshitting about it being in the clear!

Taloyoak, formerly Spence Bay, air terminal and CARS building, ca.1990. The buildings in Winnipeg region were built to the same standard design.

On another occasion Skyward flew me and a maintenance tech to Spence Bay, Pelly Bay, and Gjoa Haven, where we had work to do at their Community Aerodrome Radio Stations. These 'CARS' stations were staffed by local Inuit who had been trained in weather observation and radio communications. Besides local employment they provided weather reports and flight services that were invaluable to the safety of the flying public. A trip to these three stations would have taken more than a week using commercial airlines with their indirect and infrequent schedules, but with Skyward we accomplished the trip in a single day!

One of the last trips I made with Skyward was also the only time I was really afraid we might die in an airplane. We were heading back into Hall Beach from Rankin Inlet. This time Kyle was not flying so I rode shotgun but kept my hands to myself. Skyward's chief pilot flew us on this occasion. He was an elderly gentleman who didn't say much, which was a good thing because he had a severe case of halitosis! The weather was not good. There was minimal turbulence but Hall Beach was reporting low ceilings and poor visibility in sleet with icing conditions. We both doubted we would be able to land at Hall Beach but our pilot said he would try an approach and if it didn't work we would go to Repulse Bay for the night. This was a normal procedure and fine with me. We had to approach the Hall Beach runway from over the ocean and there were two navaids to choose from that could assist us.

Fox-Main Dew line station, Hall Beach, Nunavut, Canada, showing the huge radar antennas. The beacon is just off to the left, and the airport buildings and runway are just visible at the top of the picture. Photo courtesy of Spiegel online, January 2012.

Hall Beach was equipped with an Omni-Range and I think most pilots would have elected to try that approach, which is more precise than the beacon and lets you line up and approach the runway more or less directly. Our pilot elected to try the less precise beacon approach where you use your instruments to angle towards the runway and make a final right-hand turn to get lined up. As we descended onto the approach path we entered the clouds and sleet, and the aircraft immediately started to pick up ice on the wings and fuselage. We descended lower and I began seeing bits of the ground directly below us, but there was zero forward visibility and the icing was getting heavier despite the de-icing system being turned on. Pilots have to time each leg of a beacon approach as part of the procedure and make accurate turns to line up with the runway. I don't know if his timing was off but our pilot did not make the final right-hand turn towards the runway. Instead, he continued straight on towards the beacon whose antenna was a 150-foot-tall steel tower. At 30 feet above sea level this meant the top of the tower was only about 40 feet below our altimeter reading of 220 feet. The Caravan only had pressure altimeters, which work exactly like an aneroid barometer. They take a second or two to respond to changes in air pressure so 40 feet was a small margin for error and made me very nervous. Then I saw the beacon antenna tower flash by just to the right and maybe 30 feet below our wing. I called that out to the pilot and carefully noted our altimeter reading since we had definitely descended below the minimum safe altitude that was published on his approach chart. He then began a left turn back over the ocean to try again. This increased my fear because we were still at a low level and there were some giant military radar antennas off in that direction that we couldn't see through the clag. He was the pilot-in-command of the aircraft but I was paying him not to kill us and he was not instilling me with a lot of confidence. I suggested to him that since the beacon approach did not work out did he want to try the VOR approach where we would be further from the large obstructions and more in line with the runway? He nodded but once back over the ocean he set up again for another beacon approach. I didn't like this one bit. The hairs on the back of my neck were standing up and I was starting to sweat.

Was he out of practice with VOR approaches? Was he unfamiliar with Hall Beach? Was his instrument flying not current? How will Jovanna and the boys make out if we crash into the tower or a radar antenna? How will they get the call?

Here we went again, heading straight for the beacon antenna tower at less than the safe minimum altitude and gathering more ice on the airframe, with the runway out of sight to the right and the radar and beacon antennas somewhere ahead and to the left. If he was a bit off course in that direction or descended any further below minimums we could be toast. I knew of two other aircraft that had hit the tops of beacon towers because their pilots had flown too low while trying approaches in bad weather. In both accidents there were no survivors and both times our maintenance techs had been among the first to arrive at the crash sites, responding to the failed beacons. This was not a scenario I would wish on anybody and I certainly did not want to arrive at the crash site in the accident aircraft! Slamming into this tower was a strong possibility that was definitely at the forefront of my mind!

Again I advised him when I saw the coastline pass directly below and again he missed the final turn to the runway, but with zero forward visibility we had no hope of seeing it anyway. We were heading straight for the tower below the minimum safe altitude. I was trying to look through a hole in the windshield ice for the red light on top of the beacon antenna that would be coming straight at us. The altimeter was wavering between 220 and 210 feet above sea level, and pilot-in-command be damned, if it went any lower I was pulling back on the controls! We near-missed the tower a second time as I saw the red obstruction light zooming past just to the right and just below the wing. If we were in a hover I could have opened my door and changed the light bulb, we were that close! That was enough excitement for one day so we climbed out and headed for Repulse Bay. The weather there was good and it had improved at Hall Beach the next day so the rest of the trip was uneventful. Our overnight stay at Repulse was relaxing with a great pork chop dinner at the hotel in the proprietor's company. Repulse is noted for its carvers and sure enough after we had eaten, two of them stopped by with some nice renditions of caribou and various birds; I bought three to add to my collection! Despite the happy ending to the day I did not sleep well that night. I kept seeing that red light atop the beacon tower straight ahead out the windshield and coming fast.

I no longer have that dream and I never again experienced that level of fear and trepidation while flying, not even when dodging thunder storms in a chartered Piper Seneca at night near Thunder Bay, or hitting an air pocket over Lake Winnipeg flying with Calm Air. I made a few more trips with Skyward but never told Kathleen my real reason for requesting that only Kyle pilot us, in fact I told no one of this experience until I wrote these words. I still have good memories of Skyward, Kathleen, and Kyle and I still wear my Skyward merch occasionally. Unfortunately, Skyward ceased operations in 2005. Despite that one Hall Beach flight they were a good company to charter with.

Thunder Bay

Cliff House in the old Thunder Bay equipment room during our renovation project. Cliff later advanced to the regional office as a maintenance specialist.

My first opportunity to head up a major project came when Peter asked me to take the lead on a complete overhaul and modernization of the Thunder Bay communications and control systems involving both the control tower and FSS. We were a crew of four technologists plus general labourers and riggers. Cliff House was temporarily assigned from the Thunder Bay staff to our Winnipeg workshop so Maintenance could be fully involved in the scope of work and fabrication. We were a total of 12 weeks on-site in three-week blocks, each separated by a week back in Winnipeg. We became well known at the local Legion where Len Cook was responsible for the reactivation of their dart club, and where Kim Davis and I were responsible for eating their entire supply of hot dogs in an impromptu contest. The waitress who handed us the hotdogs one after the other must have been impressed by Kim because he married her just a few weeks later. Kim left engineering services to work for a private Winnipeg company and eventually ended up moving his new family back to Thunder Bay.

We spent a lot of lunch hours at the Thunder Bay Flying Club where Kim discovered that hitting the coin-operated shuffleboard machine in just the right spot earned us free games. The manager didn't mind because business was slow and we were spending money in his bar. I got checked out on their Cessna 172s and took some of the techs and other new friends for local sightseeing trips, flying them up

Kim Davis, a colleague on many projects. Photo taken during our Uranium City trip in 1982.

to Lake Nipigon or along the north shore of Lake Superior in the evenings or on our weekend days off.

One day one of Transport Canada's Citation jet aircraft stopped in and before I could say hello the pilot ran past me out of the flying club with his hands full of all the drip trays he could carry. "Can't talk now, my airplane is turning to Corn Flakes!" I never found out what the fault was but the plane was leaking both blue stuff and brown stuff out of each wing....

There was another charter operation in Thunder Bay that had a Piper Aztec. Since I didn't want to spend all my free time in the Legion, I approached the owner about maybe adding a multi-engine endorsement to my private pilot licence. After seeing the operation up close I was not too impressed by the hangar or the Aztec, which was in oily pieces all over the hangar floor. I said I would think about it. He was very anxious for my business and said he could have the Aztec ready to go the next day and he would include an IFR (Instrument Flight Rules) rating at the same time. I ended up declining his offer after one of our Air Regulation pilots warned me about some of his sketchier practices. A few months later I learned he had died in his Aztec during flight in adverse weather.

We were staying in the Airlane Hotel and one night Kim and I had to work past midnight to connect up a new operating position console in the FSS. We got back to our rooms about two in the morning but were not tired, so we ordered a pizza, opened some beers, and found a soft porn movie on late-night tv. We decided Len should not be sleeping through all this fun so we called his room, woke him up and told him we were stymied by the wiring in the console we were installing and needed his expertise right away! Then we called the front desk and told the night clerk that a sleepy dude in a green parka would be getting off the elevator and to send him up to my room. Sure enough a few minutes later we watched Len through the peephole drag his ass to the elevator. Shortly after that he came back in through my now open door, sat down, and helped himself to a beer and a slice. When his beer was empty he grabbed two more and left with all the rest of the pizza!

Thunder Bay was the first time we tried co-locating multiple transmitters and receivers in the same site using only one antenna. If successful we would see considerable savings by not having a separate receiver site and fewer antenna towers to maintain. Our engineers contracted with Sinclair Radio Labs to design the system, which we duly installed along with our brand-new Garrett radio equipment.

Unfortunately, Sinclair's design did not interact as expected with the Garrett receivers and Bob Thingstad, one of our engineers, worked hard with them to effect a redesign. His work was finally successful after several attempts although we ended up needing separate receiver and transmitter antenna systems. This was a good example of cooperation between engineers, engineering and maintenance technologists, and contractors. The lessons we learned at Thunder Bay were applied to our other stations where the new Garrett equipment was being installed.

Uranium City

One of the saddest projects I ever had to implement was with Kim Davis in 1982 at Uranium City. We arrived early in that year only a week after the mine had announced it would be closing that summer. The populace was shocked and stunned because only a short time before the closure announcement the mine management was telling people they were there for the long haul and Uranium City would be a great place to start a business. Many families had invested their life savings into their homes and businesses and were left with no choice except to walk away and start over, sometimes with just the clothes on their backs. At the time of closure Uranium City had almost enough residents to achieve formal city status but after the mine shut down the population shrank quickly to less than 100 persons. Every day we were there we saw more houses being boarded up and more people headed to unknown futures on the southbound planes. They all looked dazed and reminded me of John Steinbeck's description of the dispossessed.

The airport was built in the 1950s to support Eldorado Mining. It was taken over by Transport Canada in the '70s and later devolved to the Saskatchewan government. Kim and I were installing yet another remote communications outlet (RCO); this one would be controlled from Edmonton's ATC operations centre. We felt like we were helping to drive nails into the town's coffin even though the project had been planned to

Me with the Uranium City remote communications rack Kim and I installed.

enhance aviation services in the area well before anyone was aware of the closure. A few months later a team of my colleagues arrived to close the FSS, leaving only a local advisory radio frequency besides our remote communications facility. Today this small airport is the community's largest employer.

Chopper Up!

One of our sites where we applied the lessons learned at Thunder Bay was the Regina control tower where our engineers again designed a co-located radio communications system. This time their design was built around a dual antenna on one long pole about 10 metres tall and weighing over 60 kilos. The riggers sized the antenna pole to slide over an existing steel pipe on top of the control tower, which had been built into the building's structure years ago specifically to hold radio antennas. There was no way to manhandle an antenna that size onto the pipe and a crane was out of the question, so the riggers chartered a helicopter to lift the antenna and set it in place. The pilot and riggers talked through the operation, briefing each other on safety procedures and what to do to release the antenna if anything went wrong. For safety reasons the controllers closed the tower and descended to their lunch room on the floor below. Everything went off without a hitch. The riggers guided the antenna pole over the end of the pipe, the helicopter descended, the antenna slid the final 60 centimetres down the pipe and fetched up with a mighty 'WHRANG' at the bottom. The controllers in the lunchroom felt the building shake and thought we had dropped either the antenna or the helicopter!

Everything was working nicely and the 10-metre-tall antenna looked very impressive on top of the control tower swaying in the breeze. And swaying, swaying, back and forth, back and forth … until a few months later the supporting steel pipe fatigued and snapped in half! The antenna toppled over the side of the control tower, the cables parted, and the whole thing went straight down like an arrow into the roof of the air terminal building three storeys below! It speared partway through the roof into the departures level concourse where fortunately there were no passengers present at the time to observe this intrusion into their space! We did not use a second helicopter to extract it, and our engineer's replacement design used multiple smaller and lighter antennas.

Chopper Up, Part 2

Some years after that incident our radar section decided to airlift an electronics building into a remote site near Big Trout Lake in northern Ontario. This was one of the new digital radar sites being added to extend radar coverage into Canada's middle latitudes. The only option to an airlift was the winter road and if you have ever watched *Ice Road Truckers* you will appreciate that we considered the risk of damage to the building and the sensitive electronics inside too great to take. The heavy-lift chopper was well on the way to Big Trout with our building slung below when a mechanical fault occurred. The crew prudently set the building down onto a frozen lake and limped off to Thunder Bay to effect repairs.

A couple of days later they were back in the air to recover our building and complete the delivery. The building was painted white (no more orange checkerboards) and had had some snow fall on it during the time it was resting on the ice, which was also snow covered. The chopper crew had a hard time finding the right lake because many of the thousands in that area look the same, much less the building. It took two days of searching over similar-looking lakes but at least they found our building and completed their delivery before the spring breakup!

Thompson

Bernie Voroney and I were sent to Thompson, Manitoba, to convert the ATC control tower into a new FSS operating position. These conversions were happening at many locations that had both a tower and an FSS and where the level of air traffic did not justify an ATC presence. We had contract electricians from the local nickel mine on-site to rewire the control tower's cab lighting. This involved 16 electrical cables and eight dimmer controls. Zappo and Sparky had cut off all the cables without bothering to label where they came from. Sparky had turned one of the eight power feeds back on at the downstairs electrical panel, and Zappo was upstairs in the cab trying to identify which of the cables was now live. He didn't have a voltmeter for some strange reason, and when I climbed the stairs I observed him sitting on the floor with all

16 cables in his lap, touching each 'hot' wire to ground while muttering to himself....

Zst.... "No, that's not it...."

Zst.... "No, that's not it...."

Zst, **PAF!!** "Okay Sparky, that's the one!!"

I backed down the stairs thinking we might have a new winner of the 'Crispy Critter Award.'

Bernie and I had several hundred kilos of surplus equipment to dispose of in the local landfill. All this scrap was on the fourth floor of the tower just below the cab. Transport Canada always tried to build control towers no higher than five storeys; otherwise, they would be mandated to install an expensive elevator, which was thought of as another unnecessary employee luxury. This meant that Bernie and I would have to carry

Former Thompson control tower, converted into a flight service station. Gil Parent photo.

everything down four flights of stairs by hand, undoubtedly damaging both the walls and ourselves as we went. It was also a very hot day, there was no air conditioning in the stairwell, and we were not looking forward to breaking that kind of sweat while fighting off the bugs. There had to be a better way! We could carry the surplus equipment out onto the fourth-floor fire escape landing, and just toss it all over the railing!

Jim Daher, the tower manager, was sitting in his office on the second floor below us when the first of the old tape recorders came hurtling past his window. He looked up, startled and not sure what if anything he had seen. Puzzled, Jim had just lowered his gaze back to his work when an equipment rack came whizzing past! Now he came charging up the stairs to see what we were up to just in time to see another rack go over the railing! I explained what was going on and he entered into the spirit of things by personally tossing over the old office chairs and the digital clock, which made an impressive landing as the drop-leaf digits exploded in all directions!

We blew off some steam, which made us feel better but we still had to load the junk into a truck to be hauled away. Mind you, we used the airport manager's loader for that, so it wasn't too bad.

Former Thompson control tower with the new FSS consoles installed. Gil Parent photo.

The big day arrived when Flight Services took over tower operations from ATC. Jim was up in the cab and he had invited the mayor, airport manager, and local media to attend the event. He made a speech, mugged for the cameras, and called Pacific Western on final approach. This was the final transmission as a control tower.

"Pacific Western, Thompson Tower is now officially closed, stand by to contact the new FSS tower position!"

Saying that, he put down the old ATC microphone and picked up the new one plugged into the FSS equipment....

"Pacific Western, welcome to the new Thompson FSS tower cab operation...."

Silence on the airwaves....

"Pacific Western, do you read Thompson FSS...?"

More silence....

Heads swivelled to the back of the cab where we had been standing but Bernie and I were already tearing down the stairs and over to the old FSS located in the nearby airport terminal building.

Thompson's old Flight Service Station located in the air terminal.
It is a mix of equipment dating from the '60s to the '90s, typical of
many Transport Canada stations at that time. Gil Parent photo.

We had just tested all the equipment so we knew we did not have an equipment failure. I did suspect that one of the maintenance techs might have left some test switches in the wrong position after our equipment briefing, and that had prevented control of the radios from being transferred to the tower cab. As soon as we entered the equipment room we saw this was the case and immediately set them correctly. It was then that we noticed a certain maintenance tech running for the parking lot, and he did not return to work until we had left the site!

Saskatoon

I always thought Saskatoon was one of the prettier Prairie cities, especially the university and river valley areas, and I still enjoy visiting it although the opportunities to do so are fewer. I was sent there with a general labourer assistant to install a new radar console into their operations centre, which was located in the same building as the control tower. New meant new for Saskatoon; the equipment we were installing was the last of the old tube-type analog displays. Radar modernization would not reach Saskatoon for a few years yet so ATC had to make do with whatever spares and castoffs were available whenever they needed to expand their smaller operations centres.

On the first day we got our equipment and tools unpacked and organized then I went into the ATC manager's office to introduce myself and discuss the project and any concerns he might have for us. Who should I find sitting behind the reception desk as I came through the door but my old friend Colleen, who I had last seen more than a decade earlier in Kingston! After I had my meeting with the manager we went out to lunch and got caught up with each other's personal lives. Colleen had a roommate named Jan, so the two girls along with my assistant and I made a foursome for some of the evenings while we were there. Besides dinners we went to the horse races at Marquis Downs where we cashed enough tickets to pay for our drinks, took a cruise on the Saskatoon

Princess riverboat, and enjoyed the lounge entertainment at Foxy's. It was a pleasant week that flew by very quickly.

During the days the console installation proceeded well and both the radar display and associated radio communications passed all their tests. Both the ATC manager and Lorne Fehr, the telecom area manager for Saskatoon and surrounding work centres, were pleased with our work and said so in writing.

One of the maintenance technologists who worked with us was Bill Smith, a one-of-a-kind jokester who reminded me very much of the late comedian John Candy. Bill's sense of humour knew no bounds and some of his best jokes were played on unsuspecting airline passengers. On one memorable occasion he went into the baggage area of the air terminal and lay down on one of the belts, playing dead and holding a rose in his crossed arms. He got one of the baggage handlers to send him through the curtain and into the public baggage claim area with the passenger's bags that were just coming off a flight. Passengers shrieked, crossed themselves, pointed, and some even took pictures as the 'corpse' passed in review before disappearing back through the other curtain!

On another occasion Bill and I had to travel to North Battleford. Before leaving that city he noticed a garage sale and we stopped to check it out. He bought a floor-standing urinal that was surplus from some business. Bill was going to install it into his basement washroom, figuring it would be an interesting conversation piece and very convenient during poker nights. As we headed back to Saskatoon Bill looked over and grinned wickedly at me as he pulled the station wagon off onto the shoulder of the four-lane highway, turned on all the flashing lights and dropped the tail gate. Then he slid out the urinal, propped it against the gate, and proceeded to test it out right there beside the road! Of course, he waved at all the traffic passing by in either direction, most of whom waved back and honked, and one or two who almost went into the ditch!

There was a second tech in Saskatoon named Bill, only this one was thin and wiry and devoid of humour. Bill Fernuik, aka 'Trapper' Bill, was an outdoorsman who ran a trap line in his off hours. One evening shift he took a load of raw pelts to the tannery using a government station wagon so he would not be out of contact with ATC. The next day several technologists rode in the same vehicle and by the end of their shift they were all infested with fleas and scratching madly. Both they and the vehicle needed to be fumigated and Bill was not too popular around the station for several days afterwards. That car stayed parked until I arrived with my engineering crew about a week later and we did not know its recent history when we used it to go to our hotel and dinner that night. The next day the station techs subjected us to several searching and probing questions about our health and how we were feeling. Of course we were fine, however we were not impressed at being used as Saskatoon's guinea pigs despite the fact we would have done exactly the same thing if the roles had been reversed!

Regina Goes Dark

My brother Mike lived in Regina so implementing projects there was always a great opportunity to visit him and catch up. Besides the earlier tower radio installation already described I was also responsible for replacing the old receivers and transmitters located at Regina airport's remote radio sites, along with Bill Webster and a team of riggers. We were well along with installing the new receivers into their site. The riggers were preparing to trench new buried cables from the building to the antenna towers and I left to see how work was progressing at the transmitter site a few kilometres away across the airport. A second team of riggers was erecting a new antenna tower there. They were using a surveyor's transit to ensure the tower was going up straight and plumb. Eric had a spare moment so he swung the transit around to watch his fellow riggers at the receiver site:

"Bert just cut a cable at the receiver site...."

"How do you know?"

"He is jumping up and down in circles around the trencher and waving his arms. I can see his mouth moving so he must be swearing a blue streak!"

"Ooh ... there's Bill come out of the building ... now he's jumping up and down and waving his arms too!"

I went into the transmitter site building to make some phone calls and discovered that the rigger's trencher had severed both the telecommunications cables serving the receiver site, putting it completely off the air. Air traffic control had standby radio frequencies but some of their lesser-used radios and all of the FSS radios were out of action. I made an emergency trouble call to SaskTel but it would be a while before they could get a lineman to us. Meanwhile I arrived back at the receiver site to find Bert had already dug the cut ends of the cables back out of the trench and Bill was making a length of replacement cable ready to splice across the gap. I sat on the opposite edge of the trench with him and we each took a cable end and began splicing. There were 50 pairs of wires in the two cables so that meant one hundred individual wires and two hundred splices. We worked as fast as we could but we needed to be methodical so as not to make mistakes and cross any wires. We got the temporary splices finished and the site back in service after about an hour just as the lineman showed up. He crimped permanent splice caps over our temporary fixes then weatherproofed our temporary cable so it could be reburied in the ground. The electronic maintenance supervisor, Bob Ridley, took the attitude that 'shit happens' and this was a good opportunity for the Scope Dopes to exercise their standby equipment while we Radio Knobs effected our repairs.

Air Traffic Control was not impressed with the unplanned outage of a major site so I had some explaining to do. The telecom cables we had cut exited the receiver building on the opposite side from the antenna cables and should have been buried in a straight line to the control tower as indicated on our record drawings. In other words, they should have been nowhere near each other. Whoever buried them in the ground many years ago had laid them in a complete circle around the building before they headed off to where they needed to go, and as a result they made an unknown crossing of the antenna cables. That was still no excuse for not hand digging the antenna cable trench. Because I was the senior Radio Knob on the project I had to eat the heaping helpings of crow that ATC were dishing out, and no one has yet to serve crow in a manner I like! We did change procedures for installing future buried cables and eventually we began installing outdoor antenna cables on overhead trays, but this was another lesson in not trusting our older drawings without verification.

Door? What Door?

Towards the end of that trip the Regina maintenance staff put on a fun golf tournament for the technologists and support staff. They also used the occasion to raise some money in support of our union's charity, the Multiple Sclerosis Society of Canada. Bill Webster and I both signed up and we had a great time enjoying one of the local courses for a good cause. After the tournament everyone gathered back at Barry Hlushko's house for steaks and refreshments. Barry was one tech who had spent a lot of time in Resolute Bay, where he used to host Risk tournaments in his barracks room that sometimes lasted for days. His bachelor pad was a nice bungalow in a newer Regina suburb featuring a polar bear rug on the living room hardwood floor in front of an immaculate Harley Davidson Softail bike. The party went late into the evening and I realized I had downed one pop too many when I tried to walk from his patio to the washroom and went straight through his sliding screen door! I didn't even realize I had done it until I walked through it again on the return trip! Both Barry and Bob Ridley said not to worry because it was not the first time that had happened at Barry's parties!

Bob & Shannon

Bob Ridley was another fondly remembered character. He was one of the individuals who had gone overseas with Lockheed then had to make his way home from Libya when that contract went south. Bob ran a happy station with high morale and he always made the effort to see engineering's needs were looked after whenever we were working on his equipment. Bob had helped one of the ATC secretaries through a rough patch in her personal life and later they fell in love and got married. I could see they were meant for each other when I watched them dancing up a storm in Barry's basement on the night of the golf party. He and Shannon tried to elope but someone found out, I think his initials were Ron Taraschuk, and told air traffic control. ATC announced their nuptials to their pilot and the rest of the aviation world over the radio as they flew off to Mexico. The pilot, of course, told everyone on their flight about the elopement. They received first-class service all the way to their destination and deplaned with their airplane's stock of wine bottles in their carry-on baggage!

Broadview & Speedy Creek

Transport Canada has a combined Omni-Range and Tacan (VorTac) site at Broadview which is about 150 kilometres east of Regina. The first time I went there to do work was with my summer student Dave, and we stayed in the Broadview Motel. Our old-fashioned managers would have approved this motel for the riggers. There was no air conditioning or fan so the rooms were hot and stuffy. Opening the small window let in the 24/7 noise from the Trans-Canada Highway and adjacent truck stop. The walls were adorned with religious icons and artwork; I always felt like angels were watching me take a shower. The only place to eat besides the Esso station on the highway was a Chinese restaurant in town that had multiple layers of blue paint covering the windows, the wooden tables, and the seats that were former church pews.

On subsequent visits I knew better and we stayed at Grenfell about 20 kilometres up the highway. On my last visit to Broadview I was accompanied by Ron Schmidtke and Regina's Don Ross. This was late in my career and we were installing new digital radios with battery backup into the site. We had to demonstrate that the radios would run for eight hours on batteries, so Ron had rigged up a timer circuit to pulse the transmitter on and off, simulating normal use by ATC. We did not want to sit there and watch the transmitter hum to itself for eight hours so we told Regina FSS, which was monitoring the system, to call my cell phone if an alarm went off. Then we drove up to Crooked Lake Provincial Park in the Qu'Appelle Valley. We enjoyed the park amenities and nearby Sunset Beach, heading back to our site with about an hour to spare before our batteries were due to run down. My phone remained silent, there were no other issues, and the radios ran well past the mandated eight hours.

Continuing west from Broadview, about the same distance on the other side of Regina, lies the town of Speedy Creek. Summer student Dave was also there with me when we first visited back in the day. Before we left Winnipeg he had sat down with his parents and a road map to show them all the places he would be visiting on his first trip away from home. The next morning he brought the map to work and showed it to me:

"I found almost every place we are going to. Dauphin, Brandon, Yorkton, Lumsden, Broadview, Battleford, even Beechy. But I can't find Speedy Creek?"

I told him to look harder and the penny finally dropped that Swift Current was included on our itinerary!

Brent Kenny was with me on my final visit to Speedy Creek. This was also late in my career and by that time we were working for Nav Canada with Rico Sebastianelli as our boss. We had freighted our materials and supplies, including Brent's heavy toolboxes, by truck. When the trucking company delivered them to us at the site Brent's tools were missing. The shrink wrap covering the goodies on the pallet had been broken open and the tools could not be located anywhere, so we reported them stolen. Brent was going to tell Rico to please ship him some more tools but I stepped in:

"Don't do that, Brent. The guys in the shop will use this opportunity to send you all the worn out castoffs."

"But my tools were all almost brand new! What can I do except borrow yours?"

"Let's not get carried away.... We'll just go shopping and you can use your company credit card to replace them. No problem!"

"What if Rico says 'No' and I have to end up paying for them myself?"

"He won't. If he does ask, I'll tell him the shopping spree was my idea and you needed the tools right away. This is one of those times where it is better to beg forgiveness rather than ask permission. We'll tell Rico after we buy the tools."

We went off to Swift Current's local electrical supplier and Brent loaded up with a very fine set of every conceivable tool he might ever need plus a nifty new box to carry them around in. Of course there were no repercussions and the company got reimbursed from the insurance claim. The reimbursement extended to the shiny new set of Klein Tools BBQ implements that I added to Brent's shopping cart. We used them the same evening to grill our supper on the airport manager's BBQ. They followed me everywhere until I retired and I still use them to flip steaks and burgers today. I consider them the best $20 morale boosting investment that Nav Canada ever made!

Rankin Inlet

Bill Webster and I were sent on a job to Rankin Inlet, up the Hudson Bay coast in Nunavut. The FSS specialists lived in an igloo-shaped four-plex house and Bill and I were checked into the old Siniktarvik Hotel. That building is still there but is now used for storage after the new hotel was built. In the 1980s the old hotel consisted of several rooms with bunk beds. We brought our own sleeping bags because they only changed the sheets on Thursdays no matter how many guests they had each week. Bill and I were invited to spend an evening with the staff where we sampled their homemade apple cider and beer. I woke up in the wee hours with everyone else fast asleep, so I got my parka and boots on and went back to our shared hotel room. Sometime later there was a loud crash and the Arctic blew in through the window followed shortly by Bill. It seems he had lost his key and the outside door was locked so he threw a rock through the window to wake me up and tell me to let him in! Next morning he took a page from Don Parker's book and blamed local vandals!

I returned to Rankin about six or seven years later in charge of a crew replacing the Flight Service Station. This time we stayed in the new Siniktarvik, a two-storey building with fully modern private rooms, a dining room, and bar. The Government of the Northwest Territories (GNWT) had taken over the Arctic airports from Transport Canada and was embarking on a modernization program. The new FSS occupied the second floor of a brand-new air terminal building. Our maintenance technologists regularly travelled up from Winnipeg to look after the electronic equipment, bringing half a dozen large and heavy test equipment cases and tool boxes with them each time. They had a stated requirement for an apparatus to help get this bulky gear up to the second floor. The most cost-effective means was a wheelchair lift on the FSS stairs so I included one in the project plans. The second floor was not a barrier-free zone and there was no need to use the lift for its intended purpose, but no reason why it couldn't be either. The GNWT building inspector said we were not allowed to use the lift for equipment and when I insisted that was its purpose, he refused to certify it. I said that was fine with me and we used it for lifting the equipment. I think at some point when we weren't looking GNWT had it certified because when I last helped our techs use it there was a sticker on it, but it has never carried a wheelchair as far as I know.

The new air terminal building was a showpiece when it opened and included such modern energy saving devices as automatic entry doors and auto-flushing toilets. The doors froze solid after the first blizzard so GNWT constructed a portal to protect them from blowing ice and snow. Eventually they had to be replaced because the sliding doors proved unsuitable in the harsh winter conditions. More perplexing to Jack Lamb, the former owner of Lambair and now Rankin's airport manager, was the water consumption which was way over the predicted estimate. It was soon discovered that children from the village were fascinated by the automatic flush toilets, and had taken to amusing themselves by standing in front of them then backing up to make them flush while laughing hysterically. They never seemed to tire of this game and repeated it over and over! It was easier to disable the auto-flush than it was to educate the children.

This was when I met Max Ward, one of Canada's aviation pioneers. He and his wife were on their way to England when one of their Citation's jet engines stopped turning and burning and they had to divert to Rankin Inlet. Jack Lamb and Max were tripping down memory lane in Jack's office when I knocked on the door to introduce myself. Jovanna and I had flown Wardair on our honeymoon to Europe. We were left stranded when our connecting flight to London from Amsterdam was disrupted by one of Britain's innumerable transportation system strikes. Unfortunately for us Wardair's airport agents in Amsterdam refused to help us in any way. The matter of our unused tickets was never resolved despite several letters passing between Max and myself. Time heals and Max remembered my situation even though it was 20 years prior, and we had a nice talk. Before he left he gave me some bottles of a vintage wine from his private aircraft bar and we parted friends.

It was Thanksgiving weekend and we were in the middle stages of constructing the new FSS. We could not go home to celebrate until our work was done. I wanted to say thank you to the installation crew, including the riggers and Environment Canada technologists who had all worked their butts off to keep to the installation schedule. I approached the staff in the Siniktarvik and arranged a special turkey dinner with all the trimmings including wine and beer. They dressed up an area of the dining room for us with table linen and cutlery. The meal was three course and the chef did his very best for us. Everyone had plenty to eat and drink and I think most of us went to bed that night reminded of things for which we were thankful. Besides my family back in Winnipeg I was very thankful for the professionals I was working with. I didn't know it then but we had less than five years left together before everything would change.

After we had commissioned the new FSS we went home, returning to Rankin in January 1994 to take care of some minor cleanup items. One of the last things we had to do was relocate a satellite dish from the roof of the old FSS building to a special

Rankin Inlet air terminal building and FSS. The Anik satellite dish is visible on the roof. Photo courtesy Wikipedia.

landing on the roof of the new one. The dish was aimed at Telesat's Anik E-1 satellite and was used for downloading weather maps and information for pilots. On the 20ᵗʰ an Environment Canada tech and I got the dish down off the old roof, carried it over to the new building and up the stairs, and bolted it to its new mount. We brought the satellite's receiver up onto the roof and connected it to the antenna, then we began swinging the dish left and right looking for the signal. Back and forth we went but no joy. We tried the spare satellite receiver and still got nothing. It was getting a bit frosty on the roof so we went down to the FSS to warm up and think the problem through. As we came in the FSS door we saw the specialist hopping around like a one-armed paper hanger! There was one long-range radio frequency still in service now that satellites had taken over, and it was the only thing working! That frequency was jammed with pilots, specialists, and even Ham radio operators from communities all over Nunavut, all trying to pass weather, flight plans, aircraft position reports, and other information.

It turns out that during the 30 minutes we had been relocating our antenna both the Anik E1 and E2 satellites had failed, which was why we could not find a signal! All long-distance telephones, telecommunications, internet, television and news feeds, even the bank machines, had all gone dark across Nunavut territory! Our one remaining high-frequency radio was the only long-distance service available for schools, nursing stations, the RCMP, governments, commercial businesses, and aviation who were the intended users. It took several hours for the satellite controllers at Allen Park in southern Ontario to regain partial control of the E1 satellite and five months before full service was restored. We had to remain in Rankin Inlet until we could get our weather service up and running. It became known around town that we were moving a satellite dish when the world went black so of course we were blamed for everything! That one FSS radio frequency made the case that old-school radio still has a place alongside the latest satellite technology. Factions that had wanted to decommission that last long-range radio as being obsolete were silenced and that frequency is still in service today!

My Facilities Engineering boss, Mike Robertson, is on the left. He and I are presenting commemorative watches to the Environment Canada technologists who assisted us with the Rankin Inlet FSS project.

My colleagues and I had spent many months at Rankin Inlet and towards the end of all the projects it was very interesting to see what use had been made of all the surplus scrap we had created. The old terminal/FSS building was saved to become a museum and artist's craft centre. The FSS tape recorder equipment rack had a nice glass door and so became a stereo cabinet in the Siniktarvik's bar. Other equipment racks became pipe and lumber storage racks in the town's warehouses. The beacon had been moved to the remote transmitter site from its previous location at the edge of town, and the old beacon site buildings were repurposed as fishing shacks. The backup diesel generator from that site was taken by barge to Churchill and used for one of our sites there. The steel from the old beacon tower was cut up and used for several projects by the local welding shop and heavy equipment contractors, and the tower's steel guy wires became mooring lines on the harbour's barge dock!

Meliadine Lake

During the time we spent in Rankin Inlet we became friends with some of the local residents. On three separate occasions I was invited to go trout fishing on Meliadine Lake, about an hour's ATV ride northwest of Rankin. The lakeshore cabin there was rustic and consisted of one room with three bunk beds and a wooden table with folding chairs for cooking and eating; the menu, of course, was lake trout! The boat we used was an old 3 metre Lund that had been salvaged from the Rankin Inlet dump, locally known as Canadian Tire. One side of the boat was the original aluminum and the other side a thin sheet of plywood held on with pop rivets and silicone seal. The trout we were catching averaged 2.5 kilograms with bright red meat from the iron content in the water, and were Oh So Tasty! The water was very clear and we could see them swimming six to nine metres deep. All we had to do was present our bait and reel in! The Inuk who owned the cabin had a great recipe for fish chowder so we enjoyed that for lunch, baked trout over an open fire was served for dinner, and trout eggs Benedict for breakfast. My colleague Ron Brehm was a very avid fisherman who I invited to come with me to the fish camp. I know Ron was having the time of his life because he was still on the water when we had to start up the ATVs to return to the town! Today Agnico Eagle operates a gold mine at Meliadine Lake and has constructed an all-weather access road to Rankin Inlet. I hope the fishing is still as good.

Corn??!!

There were six of us at the Meliadine Lake camp the second time I was invited along. That night one of my fellow fishermen had fallen asleep early and the Inuit began chatting amongst themselves, looking over at him and giggling as he lay snoring soundly on top of his sleeping bag in his undershorts. Not knowing Inuktitut, I wondered what was going on when one of them disappeared out behind the cabin, returning in short order with a large turd nestled in some t.p. Then he approached my friend who was lying on his side, pulled the back of his boxer shorts down, and surreptitiously dumped his surprise into the crotch of my buddy's underwear! Then he wiggled the boxers back up and shortly thereafter we all crashed for the night. The next morning the prankster had the coffee on and made sure my friend was the last one awake. He stretched, reached down for his morning scratch, and his eyes bugged out of his head when he realized something wasn't quite right in Man-Land! Standing bow-legged, he grabbed the roll of t.p. and duck-walked out behind the cabin. A minute later, as we were guffawing inside, he shouted out:

"Corn? Corn!? I haven't eaten corn in years!!"

Philip Nukapiak

Philip was the airport foreman and a literal giant among men, standing over six foot three tall and weighing 300 pounds. He was a gentle giant who owned a 7.5-metre Boston Whaler with a centre console and two big outboards. Philip purchased the Whaler new on the East Coast and sailed it himself around the Eastern Seaboard and up the Labrador coast to Iqaluit, then through Hudson Strait and across Hudson Bay to Rankin Inlet; an amazing feat of seamanship that took him months to complete!

Philip took Ron Brehm and I fishing along the shoreline cliffs of Hudson Bay, and although we had a very enjoyable time on the water all we managed to catch were small sculpins which we didn't keep. On another occasion Philip took me and some of the Siniktarvik's employees across to Marble

Island about 75 kilometres offshore. Marble Island is visible from Rankin Inlet and appears bright white from the quartzite stone that laces the island's rocks. There are large colonies of birds and some wildlife on the island but very little vegetation. Two ships commanded by James Knight, the *Discovery* and the *Albany*, were wrecked there in the early 18th century while searching for the Northwest Passage on behalf of the Hudson Bay Company. Although the Inuit tried to help the crews they all died of starvation and scurvy and their remains were not found until 1769 by Samuel Hearne. During the 19th century whalers stopped there and several of their graves are also on the island. Marble Island is a sacred place to the Inuit so when we arrived with Philip we had to disembark into the water and crawl ashore on hands and knees. To do otherwise would, according to legend, cause our deaths exactly one year later.

Marble Island, Nunavut, 2006. Photo courtesy Wikimapia.org.

Philip was one of our go-to guys whenever we needed assistance with any of our projects at Rankin and I was glad to have known him even for a little while. Unfortunately, it was only a year or two later that he was found on the beach beside his beloved Whaler, dead from a heart attack.

Smuggler Alert

Alert is a military base at the top of the world only 817 kilometres from the North Pole. It is the most northerly continuously inhabited place on earth. At the time this anecdote takes place there were about 200 people living there. Besides the military there was an Environment Canada upper air station and a Transport Canada navaid beacon. The single maintenance technologist was assigned from Resolute Bay but from time to time techs, riggers, or other Transport Canada staff needed to visit. They usually got there by hitching a ride on one of the Armed Forces' supply flights that were code named "Boxtop." These Boxtop flights originated from the Canadian Forces air base at Trenton, Ontario, overnighted at the United States Air Force base at Thule, which is in the Danish protectorate of Greenland, then continued on to Alert the next day, weather permitting. It was a common courtesy when travelling into the Arctic to call ahead and offer to bring supplies of a personal nature, so when our techs had to visit Alert they contacted Resolute Bay and got a list of everything from smokes and booze to cameras and stereos. They took along some empty equipment cases and loaded them up with these goodies in Thule where they were purchased for ridiculously low prices in the American Post Exchange store. The next morning everyone got back in the aircraft and after landing in Alert they were back in Canada after visiting Greenland without going through customs or border controls. When their work in Alert was completed a charter flight took our techs and their loot to Resolute Bay, duty and taxes exempt! A few of these trips were made before someone noised it around about the great deals being had. The next time there was a charter arriving from Alert it was met by the Mounties. The guys had to own up and pay the duties and taxes on all their freight and that ended the Alert 'great deal' pipeline.

Dauphin Politics

Transport Canada had decided to close the FSS at Dauphin, Manitoba, in the early '90s and replace it with remote communications services out of Winnipeg. Bill Webster and I were assigned the job and had worked on-site for several weeks to get everything ready. Dauphin's mayor, Inky Mark, was very upset at losing 'his' flight service station. Inky communicated his views to the Liberal Member of Parliament for that riding who in turn leaned on Prime Minister Jean Chretien. With only two hours to go until the changeover the fertilizer hit the ventilator and we were directed to put things back the way they were, forthwith! The FSS staff were called back to Dauphin and had to be put up in hotels and maintained in travel status because they had already sold their homes and relocated to their new assignments. The FSS continued operations, albeit somewhat shakily. The federal government changed at the next election and Inky was no longer Dauphin's mayor so it was not long after that when we returned and quietly closed that facility for good.

Dauphin airport was originally built as part of the British Commonwealth Air Training Plan to train pilots during WWII and was home to #10 Service Flying Training School during that conflict. An interesting footnote to our project was that the FSS had been installed into the original WWII operations building. During demolition the flight status chalkboard from that era was discovered behind the wall panelling with the flight operations from the last day of training in April 1945 still chalked onto it. I believe the board was too fragile to be salvaged so pictures at the Commonwealth Air Museum in Brandon may be all that ended up surviving.

Flood Radio

The Canadian Armed Forces provided assistance during the 1997 Red River flood emergency. This flood was a once-in-a-century event causing mass evacuations and the inundation of farms and even entire communities south of Winnipeg as far as the U.S. border. The city of Fargo in North Dakota was flooded. It was so severe that hundreds of square kilometres of airspace over the flood zone was restricted to just military and other emergency flights. ATC needed dedicated radio frequencies to handle this special air traffic so engineering services stepped up to install two temporary remote communications sites. One went into a Manitoba Telecom microwave facility near Teulon north of Winnipeg, and the second into a CBC television transmitter site near Starbuck west of Winnipeg. Led by Len Cook, our techs fabricated the complete electronics packages from spare parts at our workshop in one day,

Manitoba Remote Sensing Centre image of the 1997 Red River flood, accessed 2021. Photo courtesy Canada Space Agency.

then they trucked all their tools and equipment to the sites, which were near the flooded areas but managing to keep dry. Len's crews installed their equipment into the site buildings while the riggers mounted our antennas onto the Manitoba Telecom and CBC towers. Rob Dobson was our engineer who designed the antenna systems and the resulting radio coverage exceeded expectations. The military provided a boat ride to a cable pedestal in the middle of a flooded field where the telecommunications connections between the Starbuck site and ATC needed to be spliced together. Communications were operational within 36 hours of receiving the request, an achievement which speaks to the dedication and professionalism of our engineering services personnel.

TRAINING DAZE

Until I joined engineering services all formal technical training took place in Ottawa or Toronto. The ab-initio courses for Scope Dopes were up to six months long. Most of our technical training courses were between three and five weeks, and often consisted of two or more modules, so it was costly and inefficient to maintain students in travel status in these major cities. Transport Canada envisioned a self-contained centralized training facility that would serve the entire ANS and other agencies, so they built the Transport Canada Training Institute (TCTI) on the banks of the St. Lawrence River, at the east end of the city of Cornwall approximately equidistant from Ottawa and Montreal.

View from the TCTI dorms over the St. Lawrence River.

Despite being built between a chemical plant and a brassiere factory, it was and still is a beautiful location on an estate large enough for navaids and radars to be installed outdoors. Environment Canada, Fish & Ships, Correctional Services, and others all leased space for their training needs. There was even a Grand Mother Duck in a separate upper air station building with its own hydrogen shed! Besides the training portion of the facility there was dormitory-style accommodation for 600 students, a cafeteria, gymnasium, large central lounge area, and a bar. The head of TCTI liked to brag he was the only manager with his own bar so that is one reason why (according to rumour) Frank Lay, Winnipeg region's director general, named the Frank Lay Lounge in Resolute Bay after himself.

The TCTI dormitory wings, seen from the river side.

Public Works designed and oversaw the building of TCTI. Their team's previous projects of that size were for Corrections Canada so the accommodations have the look and feel of a minimum-security prison. The original design included communal washrooms and showers but that idea was dropped from the plans after vigorous protests from the techs' and controllers' unions. Creating a bathroom in each of the dorm rooms left only enough space for a single bed, a small dresser, and a writing desk with chair. The rooms were arranged in clusters of eight with a small common area that had the cluster's only television set. The planner's thoughts were that the inmates would all gather together in grand bonhomie to watch *Hockey Night in Canada* after an uplifting day of classes and their cafeteria dinner. What actually happened was the inmates gathered all the sofa cushions from several of the common areas and spread them out on the floor in one of them, then threw toga parties that sometimes lasted an entire weekend. The unions complained vociferously about extended periods of cruel and unusual confinement so each room was eventually given a small television mounted on the dresser. The lamp on the writing desk was fitted with only a 40-watt light bulb. Smart students soon learned to bring their own 100-watt bulbs with them so they would have enough light to read their course materials, or to fill out their grievance forms complaining about the food.

The poor-quality food was always the real issue with TCTI. Students were staying in government accommodations so there were no per diem food allowances. You ate their cafeteria food or were out of pocket. The lowest bidder served up the food at a figure around $6 per day per student. The bland high-carb menu repeated each week not counting flatulence. Your room number was ticked off on a list when you got your meal, so even if you wanted more there were no seconds unless you read the proctor's sheet upside down and rhymed off someone else's number who had not eaten yet. There was a 'dessert Nazi' just like on Seinfeld who made sure you took only one bowl of jelly or pudding: "No more for you!"

Experienced students could tell what day of the week it was by following the leftover food chain, for example Sunday dinner could be roast beef. Monday would then be beef stew followed by beef stroganoff on Tuesday, hamburgers on Wednesday, and last but not least, hamburger soup on Thursday. Similar protein reductions were followed for chicken and pork. On one occasion we thought TCTI had butchered a veal elephant because that meat was on the menu every dinner for 10 days straight. Management, of course, had a separate dining room with decent meals, linens and table service.

Hebrews 13:8

The food was tolerable for a week or so, but by the third week of a four-week course the bland offerings were pushing most people's limits. How the air traffic control and flight services students, who were confined there for months, stood it I do not know … some potential controllers may simply have had enough of the swill and abandoned their course for Mom's home cooking. On more than one occasion inmates discovered insects doing the backstroke in their gravy or pasta sauces but all complaints about the food seemed to fall on deaf ears.

On occasions when private companies held conferences at TCTI their attendees had a separate food line with much better offerings than what was being dished up to the inmates. This caused many arguments with the cafeteria staff and a fresh series of complaints and grievances. TCTI's solution was to serve conference attendees their garlic and rosemary grilled lamb chops in the management dining area, out of sight of us peons who were being fed the mystery meat chili.

I was on the last week of a four-week control system course and had had my fill of tasteless pasta. The morning after a particularly vile plate of soggy spaghetti in some kind of nameless sauce served from a tureen that had flies walking all over it, I wrote a one-line memo to management under the subject heading 'Food': 'Hebrews 13:8.' The cafeteria manager stormed into my class and disrupted the lesson, waving my memo and shouting "How dare I complain in this manner and what did this mean!" I told him it would do him good to go look it up, whereupon he threw the memo on the floor, said he would be damned if he would, and stormed out. He must have been a Philistine. By the way, the verse in question reads "Jesus Christ, the same yesterday, and today, and forever." You can look it up in your King James.

The Two-Dollar Bet

FN and I were nearing the end of a month-long digital computer course when we decided we had to get out of TCTI for a decent meal. We planned to grace the best steak house in Cornwall with our presence preceded by martinis after Friday's final lesson. We would each wear the three-piece suits that we had packed for our class graduation picture to add the proper ambience. Class finished early on Friday so FN and I met in the lounge about 3 p.m. wearing our suits and with a pitcher of homemade martinis, shaken, not stirred. We added olives to our glasses and proceeded to raise the tone of TCTI.

By 6 p.m. the pitcher was empty and we had raised the tone by several notches. Everyone else was so impressed by the classy ambience we were creating that they were giving us a wide berth, undoubtedly so not to sully our high tone. We summoned a taxi to the downtown restaurant and were soon shown to the best table near the kitchen door and washrooms. After what was indeed a very fine steak dinner accompanied by a bottle or two of wine, much better than the chicken à la king being served that night to the lesser mortals at TCTI, we returned there to find a concert in progress in the lounge. The entertaining duo named 'Free Beer' had arrived from the East Coast and were banging out some great-sounding down-home tunes to which a large crowd of inmates were moving and shaking. FN and I watched from the fringes with loosened ties and fresh martinis in hand. FN was paying particular attention to a willowy young blonde whose attributes were keeping perfect time with the music.

"Y'know FN, I'd give you a dollar to go up to her and pat her butt...."

"Hell, for $2 I'd kiss it!"

"Here's the $2...."

"Hold my martini and watch this!"

FN got down on all fours in his three-piece suit, dog-walked up behind her, and planted a big wet one on her left cheek! She spun around and dumped her beer on his head, then helped him up and the two of them stood there laughing together. I returned FN's martini to him then went to the bar and bought his new best friend a beer on him. She was teaching him the lyrics to Dick Nolan's "Aunt Martha's Sheep" when I last saw them.

The $6,000 Briefcase

The academic facilities at TCTI were second to none and were anchored by a staff of senior technologists holding professional teaching certificates. We learned on the actual equipment in as realistic a setting as possible. I had just completed a digital tape recorder course and was back in Winnipeg preparing one of these systems for installation. Our workshop testing uncovered a fault with my recording head's channel #42. This would not be an operational issue because we were only using something like the first eight channels, but the recorder's warranty had expired and the $6,000 cost of a replacement head was not justified given that channel 42 would never be used.

That being said, my sensibilities were rankled like Elmer Klatt's were over the transmitter dial because I did not like the deficiency being noted for posterity with nothing being done about it. I phoned one of my instructors back at TCTI and asked if they wanted to trade recorder heads. They would get mine with the built-in fault that would be ideal for training purposes and I would get theirs from the training system so my operational recorder would have zero deficiencies. He said he would do this for me if I would get him a briefcase like mine. During my recorder course he had been admiring my officially issued Samsonite hard-shell 'document security case' with the 'Canada' wordmark embossed on it. He asked where I had gotten it and I told him I simply requisitioned it from Samsonite. My instructor tried the normal channels but his boss would not approve the requisition because if he got my instructor friend one then all the instructors would want a briefcase too. Steve Highstead approved my requisition for a briefcase to be delivered to my instructor's attention at TCTI and I mailed off the defective recording head. In due course a defect-free head arrived back at our Winnipeg workshop. Another bureaucratic end-around resulting in a win-win situation!

Horseshoes Anyone?

The TCTI recreation activities were administered through a contract with the Ottawa YMCA. They looked after the gymnasium and swimming programs, loaned out equipment, and often put on impromptu sports tournaments. One Saturday night two ladies from the Y came through the bar area asking if anyone was up for horseshoes? The horseshoe pits were just outside so several of us loaded up trays of beers and headed out. The horseshoe tournament was a good idea but their timing was off. They were telling a bunch of half-cut inmates it was okay to hurl heavy metal objects in the twilight.

Eventually the inevitable happened and a horseshoe went through a window into one of the dormitory hallways! Of course, everyone scattered and no one admitted to partaking in horseshoes on that or any other night. I think the cost of the window was buried under 'building maintenance' along with the cost of relocating the horseshoe pits.

Martin

Besides the instructing staff, TCTI had a cadre of technologists who both maintained the equipment required for each course and installed it as required into the classrooms and labs. They were all first-rate, but one that really impressed me was Martin Vaillancourt, with whom I would have the distinct pleasure of working in the not-too-distant future! Martin was a carefree and happy-go-lucky individual, a

Martin Vaillancourt, Technologist, world traveller, and friend.

world traveller always up for any adventure whether bicycling alone through the hinterlands of Cuba or teaching himself to sail single-handed while dodging ocean-going ships in the middle of the St. Lawrence Seaway!

One day Martin was tasked with running a communications cable from one lab to another over the top of a classroom through the suspended ceiling space. Class was in session and Martin did not want to wait until the end of the day. He took a good look at the ceiling tile system and figured it would hold him up as long as he kept his weight on the supporting T-bars. Martin set up ladders and removed a ceiling tile from the lab at each end of his cable run. He planned to climb the first ladder, crawl through the ceiling space across the top of the classroom, and finish the job by coming down the second ladder.

With the cable in one hand he climbed the first ladder and put his weight slowly onto the T-bars, which creaked and shifted but managed to hold him up! Thus encouraged he slowly and carefully made his way along the T-bars. The students and instructor in the classroom looked up with a mixture of consternation and amazement as their ceiling began sagging and creaking ominously as Martin crawled above them. They had no idea what was going on up there but prudently backed away from the moving tiles. The creaking and sagging had reached the centre of the classroom above the instructor's desk when Martin made his entrance! One of the bars gave way and he crashed through the ceiling tiles straight down onto the desk, with a surprised look on his face and the cable still in hand! Class resumed once Martin had cleared the debris away, dusted everything off, and coiled up his cable in what was left of the ceiling pending an after-hours return to complete his work!

FAMILY TIME

My years in engineering services were mostly happy times not only because of my colleagues and work variety but down to Jovanna and my three sons without whose support my career would not have been possible. This became especially true later on when my travel increased to over a hundred nights away from home each year.

My eldest son Scott entered the world on April 14, 1981 at almost the same time as the first space shuttle landing. I know that because I was running back and forth between the television in the 'Dad's room' and the delivery room hoping Scott would wait a few more minutes, but as things went I watched the delivery live and the landing on replay. Four years later Sanderson joined him and then Sean after four more.

When Jovanna was pregnant with Sandy we decided that the house in Charleswood no longer met the needs of our growing family. We could not find anything affordable in a neighbourhood we wanted to live in so we decided to custom build, eventually buying about a hectare of bald prairie located in Vermette in the southeast corner of Winnipeg. It turned out that my new next-door neighbour was a custom home builder. We hired him because he was skilled in the energy-efficient techniques we wanted to include and was willing to work with me so I could do much of the work myself. The house included triple-pane windows, a preserved wood basement foundation, double exterior walls, and air-tight construction with controlled ventilation. Common today, these were cutting edge in 1986 and we were able to heat the entire 220-square-metre home with only one 10-kilowatt forced-air electric furnace. Peter Goertzen approved me carrying forward my annual leave so I had six weeks off to install the electrical and HVAC systems myself.

I was camping in the unfinished basement while Jovanna, Scott, and new baby Sandy were living with her parents. My painter and I had worked together all day spraying primer on the walls and a textured finish on the ceilings. It was nearly dark and we were cleaning up when there was a commotion at the front door. Jovanna and Scott stood there with Sandy in her arms and a bag at her feet.

Jovanna announced "I had a fight with my mother and we are moving in NOW!"

There went my build schedule out the window! We got the boys sorted out that night and instead of completing the painting the next day I installed such family necessities as the hot water tank and a toilet. There were no floor coverings, appliances or cabinetry so we enjoyed a month or so of rustic living as these were installed a bit at a time. After I went back to work it took a few more years before we completely finished the rest of the house and the acreage became partially fenced and landscaped.

Jovanna was laid off from the hospital during one of Manitoba's periodic health-care purges so the boys enjoyed having a full-time mom and we did not need day care. I in turn became Cub Scout leader Baloo the Bear and a civilian instructor and treasurer for 176 Air Cadet Squadron. I also volunteered at the boy's school as a director for their fundraising bingo corporation. I joined the Western Canada Aviation Museum and became a restoration shop crew chief. My museum crew of volunteers restored a WWII Yale training aircraft and my boys were old enough to come with me on Saturdays and help out. When the Yale was completed we took it to summer air shows in Manitoba and Saskatchewan along with a ground display of flight simulators and other museum artifacts.

Aviation museum airshow crew with our military
sponsors and Yale trainer, Moose Jaw, 1989.

I was at home enough to do all the cool things with the boys like the Cub Scout and Air Cadet activities, the after-hours museum visits, and helping them make their go-kart track in the backyard. Scott was even old enough to join my museum crew during the last year we attended the Manitoba Airshow. By the time we had Sean I was doing project management work under Mike Robertson who was very flexible with my travel. I did what I could to help with school work, appointments, and managing the boys' social lives but I still missed a few birthdays, anniversaries, and other family events. Besides working office hours I was out of town about every third week so the bulk of the parenting fell squarely on Jovanna's shoulders. I give her full credit for the fact that all my sons turned out to be solid adults and great fathers.

A Septic Situation

The acreages in our development all had septic fields, which the owners had to cover with straw bales each fall so they would not freeze. One spring a neighbour burnt off his bales when the wind was in the wrong direction and the dense smoke carried directly into our house. Jovanna had a severe asthma attack, Scott called 911, and fire and ambulance were dispatched. She was in hospital for a couple of days of observation and my in-laws looked after the boys because I was out of town on another Arctic trip. I was travelling between communities and my boss Mike could not find me until we finally landed back in Yellowknife! I got home the same day Jovanna did and all was well, except she developed a bad allergy to smoke and hay from the experience and needed to carry an inhaler from then on. When I spoke to my neighbour and explained the situation he was more upset about the fire department putting out his hay bales than my wife ending up in Emergency!

Run Forrest, Run!

The travel directive allowed the use of personal vehicles between home and the airport when travelling but the bureaucrats decreed mileage would only be paid in one direction because the employee was not making the round trip. I therefore took the opportunity to stick it to the man and taxied to the airport, which cost Transport Canada $40 each trip compared to the 10 bucks a round trip with my wife would have cost! Coming home was different. After a week on the road I looked forward to home cooking and Jovanna wanted a night out, so she would arrange a babysitter and pick me up from the airport. She got a nice restaurant meal and an evening away from the boys while I was still in travel mode.

I always arranged my taxi rides the evening before departure, but the driver did not show up one Monday morning. After some frantic phone calls a taxi finally appeared at my door with only 30 minutes until wheels up. For an extra tip the driver tore through the Winnipeg traffic like the hounds of hell were chasing us; I threw the cash down on the front seat, grabbed my bag, and wasted no time running to Air Canada's counter.

"I know I'm late and my bag won't make the flight, but can you still get me on?"

"Let's see ... here's your boarding pass. Run!"

Forrest Gump didn't run as fast as I did! I cut to the head of the security line holding my parka open, got a quick wanding and look inside my briefcase, then I ran again to the departure gate only to see the agent closing the doors and the DC-9 aircraft pushing back! Damn ... so close! I stood there with my tongue hanging out and my now useless boarding pass in my hand. The gate agent's phone rang. She raised her eyebrows as she looked over at me and said in a quizzically incredulous voice:

"Hurry! They're putting down the aircraft's airstairs for you, run out the service door on the bridge...."

Then she pinned on her best Colgate smile and gave me a finger wave:

"Have a nice flight!"

Talk about cutting things fine! As I walked down the aisle to my seat I was getting curious looks and more raised eyebrows from every one of my fellow passengers. They must have thought I was some sort of VIP until they saw "Transport

Canada" emblazoned across the back of my parka. Then they no doubt figured I was a government numpty who had slept in then pulled strings to delay the departure and get on board. A pair of little old ladies in the row ahead of me were muttering to each other about Big Shots but I felt more like a Very Ignorant Peon. I didn't know then why I was allowed to board that flight in the unorthodox manner I did but I was relieved to be on board and not losing a day on the job. My bag arrived later on the evening flight.

I found out later a good friend of Jovanna's who worked behind the scenes at Air Canada had seen my name on the passenger manifest and was keeping an eye out for me. Marilyn told us the story later when Jovanna and I were out for dinner with her and her husband; I was slightly disappointed to find out that being a tech did not confer any special status with Air Canada and that it was she who had talked the crew into lowering the airstairs. Marilyn did indeed describe me as a government VIP on essential travel!

The Flood of '97

I earlier related engineering service's outstanding response to the 1997 Red River flood emergency. That river rises every spring and often the highway to the U.S. washes over, communities close their ring dikes, and homes and farms have to sandbag. Winnipeg is protected by 'Duff's Ditch,' aka the Red River Floodway, but in 1997 the river rose to extreme heights causing extensive devastation and coming close to overwhelming the city. Besides the main flood zone in the Red River Valley there was overland flooding from most of the smaller rivers and creeks all over southern Manitoba, and even localized flooding within Winnipeg when some of the river dikes there were topped by the high water. Our neighbourhood in Vermette was put on 24-hour notice to evacuate and we were told to expect about one metre of water over the ground if the dike holding back the La Salle River failed. We sent the boys to stay with their friends or Jovanna's parents and brought everything valuable up from the basement. Some of our neighbours parked semi-trailers in their driveways to store their possessions and moved away for the duration.

Management gave time off to those affected so they could sandbag their properties. One of those was Rob Dobson, our Professional Engineer who designed the flood zone emergency radio system. During the day he designed and helped implement the emergency radio systems and in the evening he sandbagged his home northeast of Winnipeg. We lived within sight of the floodway's berm so Jovanna and I could walk the dogs up to the top of it. The water level was only about two metres below the top on the far side. Standing there was like being on the seashore with nothing but water to be seen in all directions except for the odd tree and rooftop.

This was the occasion of a famous Jean Chretien photo opportunity. As Canada's Prime Minister he was touring the flood zone offering support to emergency workers and those affected. The photo-op was filmed live on the evening news and the organizers had M. Chretien standing in a line of volunteers passing sandbags to protect a home. The talking head finished her lead-in comments and the camera panned to our Prime Minister. On that cue he was passed his first sandbag then he turned to the cameras and said on live national television: "Now what do I do with it?"

In the end the floodway held, we did not have to evacuate and life soon returned to normal as the water receded. We had almost paid off our mortgage and were thinking about refinancing next year to upgrade the house interior and finish the landscaping the way we wanted to, but the flood situation got us thinking about selling out and moving on instead of investing further in the property. Just a few months later work events would overtake the plans we were making and the options we were considering.

NEW OPPORTUNITIES

A few years before the big flood our headquarters decided that the Air Navigation System required a dedicated group within engineering to manage building maintenance and construction contracts. This new group would be called Facilities Engineering and it would interface between the ANS agencies who set operational requirements for our facilities, and Public Works & Government Services Canada whose purview it was to construct and maintain them.

Jim Whyte, the regional director of electronic maintenance, was asked to set up the Winnipeg group and I was seconded to him as the only other employee at the time. Project management became my third career path but unfortunately it was cut short and ended up being an interlude between the different times I spent in engineering. It was probably the most fun I had with my pants on during my entire career!

Jim and I created Winnipeg's facilities engineering group from nothing. We decided how the organization should operate in line with headquarters' direction and we prepared the first operational plans and budgets. Facilities would employ technologists as project managers, which meant that I would be in line for another promotion at some point after we were up and running. Once facilities engineering had been established Jim returned to maintenance and Mike Robertson became its first, and ultimately only, regional manager.

More House Renovations

Even before we were fully open for business we were tasked with renovating staff housing at La Ronge, Baker Lake, and Lynn Lake. These houses had been built from a standard Public Works three-bedroom bungalow design of about 170 square metres and were showing every one of their average 25 year's age. The extensive renovations included kitchens, bathrooms, carpets, fences and decks, windows and doors, driveways, siding, shingles, and sprucing up inside and out. I visited each location and met with the tenants who were definitely ready with their own home renovation and decorating ideas! Ideas were welcome but we could not customize each home. I did commit to making sure their colour choices and carpet selections were respected and their other suggestions would be included in the contracting specifications as minimal acceptable standards. I wrote the specifications for Public Works and after the contracts were awarded I became the point of contact between the tenants and the Public Works project manager at each site. This made good use of my recent experience managing my own home construction and worked well when dealing with the inevitable changes and additions. It was a successful start to the facilities mandate and I learned a lot about what I did not know! Accordingly, I nominated myself for, and attended, several training courses on contract administration and project management.

ATC's 50th

Our office wanted to showcase the technical support given to air traffic control by our technologists and engineers on the occasion of ATC's 50th anniversary in 1989. Management gave me the special assignment of developing ideas for consideration, and I submitted five proposals:

The first was for a Canadian 25 cent commemorative coin that would be produced by the Royal Canadian Mint as legal tender similar to the RCMP commemorative coin of 1973. I envisaged an open design competition with the winner chosen by a panel selected by officials from ATC, Technical Services, and the Mint. After speaking with Mint officials, I estimated $100,000 for the design competition and tooling. Production costs would be borne by the Mint.

Next, I proposed annual scholarships for Electronic Technology and Engineering students. Applicants would be entering post-secondary education from high school and would submit their applications with an essay for consideration. The essays would discuss future ATC technologies or similar topics chosen by a committee that would also award the scholarships. I proposed one $500 scholarship each for a two- and four-year post-secondary program. The cost would be $5,000 per year including committee expenses.

My third proposal was production of an illustrated coffee-table book featuring the technology used in support of ATC. Photographs and articles would be chosen from employee submissions across the region. The books would be given to employees and also made available through Transport Canada, libraries, museums, and direct mail order from the publisher. Friesen Publishing of Altona, Manitoba, met with me and management. They showcased samples of similar books they had published for Parks Canada and other agencies, and we discussed editing and publishing details. The cost of a first print run of 500 copies was estimated at $20,000.

My fourth proposal was creation of an ANS electronics display at the Western Canada Aviation Museum. Now known as the Royal Aviation Museum of Western Canada, they had been recipients in the past of several artifacts donated by Transport

Canada including a complete FSS operating position, radar display console, and navaids beacon. These and other related artifacts were being held in the museum's storage and were not on display. The museum's Board of Directors approved the idea, cleared space for the display, and worked with us to draw up a display plan. Our technologists, some including myself who were already volunteering at the museum, would assemble the display. The costs for this proposal would be mostly associated with the display boards that would accompany the artifacts and was estimated at between $5,000 and $10,000.

The old airport radar systems were in the process of being replaced and my final proposal was to save one of the radar antennas, similar to that shown in the photo that accompanies my story 'Old Hat at the Radar Site,' and mount it in a public park near to the ATC operations centre or the airport. The cost of the plinth to mount the sail was estimated at $30,000.

Unfortunately, there was insufficient time before the end of the 50th anniversary year to design, tool, and strike a commemorative coin, so that proposal was quickly dropped. Management were excited about the others, none of which were particularly expensive, and all were considered for funding. Management particularly favoured the commemorative book and the museum display. I was told by my director general that my suggestions were, to use his word, 'visionary.' Each suggestion could be implemented not just in Winnipeg but by every region across Canada, and all would raise the public profile of the technologists and engineers within the ANS as well as air traffic control itself.

Ottawa denied funding for all ATC commemorative projects. I received a nice letter of condolence from regional management thanking me for my efforts. I do not have too many regrets from my more than 33 years in the ANS but a big one is that not even one technology-related commemoration of this historic anniversary was carried out.

Internal Charters

Facilities needed an inventory of the sites we were now responsible for, especially in the Arctic where GNWT was in the process of taking over ownership and operation of all the airports 'North of 60,' and where discussions were under way to create the new territory of Nunavut from the Eastern and Northern portions of the North West Territories.

This was going to be an expensive and time-consuming project and without actual site visits inaccuracies were bound to creep in. I suggested we combine forces with our aerodrome facilities inspectors to keep costs down. These pilots made annual inspection visits to the airports I was interested in but were otherwise having their flight hours cut back for budgetary reasons. Mike Robertson agreed to offer them a cost-sharing arrangement for our inspection trips. We all got our surveys and inspections completed in a timely manner, our pilots maintained their flying hours and flight proficiency, and I got some amazing views of the Arctic from the right seat of the Twin Otter aircraft. The first trip worked out so well that facilities engineering as well as engineering services continued the practice of using internal charters on other projects whenever it made sense to do so. Jack Ireland and Chuck Frankard flew me on many of these flights. Jack proudly sported a lapel pin from De Havilland Canada, makers of the Twin Otter aircraft, signifying he had 10,000 hours piloting that type. That is almost three and a half years of non-stop eight-hour days flying the Twin Otter. It was on the parking ramp in Resolute Bay where Chuck tutored me in starting and taxiing the Twin Otter.

A memorable incident happened when flying out of Resolute Bay with Chuck as pilot and myself enjoying the view from the right seat. In these high latitudes normal compasses are useless. We were so close to the magnetic North Pole that the magnetic compass just wandered in random circles. The gyro compass pointed to true north but it too became unstable in the polar region and internal friction caused its heading indication to slowly move away from an accurate course. There was no GPS in our aircraft so to overcome the compass limitations we carried an astrocompass mounted above the dashboard between the pilots. This instrument, which I thought was a fascinating device, could be used to accurately

set the gyro compass. You point it more or less north and set your latitude and longitude on it. Then you refer to a very thick book called an almanac to determine the 'hour angle' and 'declination' of some astronomical object you want to line up on, usually the sun, moon, or Venus. Setting these angles onto the astrocompass dials then rotating the compass until the heavenly body you are looking for appears in your sights

Mk.II astrocompass. eBay photo.

gives an accurate heading that you can then use to set the gyro. This procedure is cumbersome, especially in flight, so normally our pilots ignored the astrocompass and set their gyros before taking off simply by lining up with the known runway heading. On this occasion Chuck and I decided to play with the astrocompass in flight. We were both leaning forward into the middle of the cockpit trying to interpret the almanac whilst setting the compass dials, and neither of us noticed that we were both pushing on the control columns. The Twin Otter started descending towards the Arctic Ocean, which was never too far below us in any event, and we didn't realize anything was amiss until the constant speed propellers changed pitch due to our increasing airspeed! We levelled off safely and returned to our visual navigation but the almanac stayed in its holder after that!

Our senior pilot Ron Chercoe used to announce his homecomings by low flying over his house north of Winnipeg and cycling the aircraft propellers. He often flew our venerable old DC-3 and the sound of the two Pratt & Whitney radial engines with props in fine pitch was unmistakable. His wife was alert for this signal, which was her cue to drive to the Transport Canada hangar at the airport to pick him up. One time Ron was piloting the Twin Otter over the sea near Igloolik when a flock of gulls rose in front of us. We heard and felt three or four distinct thumps but no birds struck the windshield and the engines continued their normal operation. We headed straight for Igloolik as a precaution and after landing our safety inspection revealed hits on two of the landing gear wheels and the nose of the aircraft. If the birds had been a couple of metres higher the incident could have been a lot worse.

Kazan River falls, Nunavut. Photo courtesy Nicolas Perrault II, Wikimedia Commons.

We almost always flew around the Arctic at low level in good summer weather so we could sightsee. We departed Baker

Lake one day heading for the Hudson Bay coast and made a slight diversion to land the Twin Otter on an esker near the Kazan River falls. We walked the short distance to the falls carrying our box lunches from the Baker Lake Lodge. We sat at the edge of the waterfall in idyllic surroundings with the breeze keeping the mosquitoes at bay while enjoying the beauty of the summer tundra and the river. As we ate our sandwiches a small herd of caribou crossed the scene in front of us on the far side of the river. God's country!

Standing on the Arctic Circle at Repulse Bay.

Standing on the cairn at the geographic centre of Canada, near Baker Lake.

Repulse Bay sits right on the Arctic Circle but during previous visits I never had the opportunity to have my picture taken at the cairn marking that line of latitude. On these inspection trips I was finally able to get my picture taken not only standing on the Arctic Circle, but also at the big Inukshuk south of Baker Lake that marks the geographical centre of Canada!

The great scenery extended along the coastlines and over the oceans. We saw huge glaciers coming down from the Ellesmere Island ice cap and on another occasion encountered a mammoth iceberg off the west coast of Baffin Island. The berg was over 120 metres tall as measured by the aircraft altimeter, and as we approached for a better look a strong downdraft caused by the air currents around the ice made Jack apply full power to climb away.

Ellesmere Island glaciers
south of Eureka.

120-metre-tall iceberg off the
west coast of Baffin Island.

We had opportunities to experience the rich history of this region. While at Resolute Bay we visited reconstructions of whale bone houses that were used by the Thule people who inhabited the Arctic a thousand years before the Inuit arrived. Imagine a family spending an Arctic winter in one like this!

Thule culture whale bone house, Resolute Bay.

We visited the stone church in Pelly Bay, now known as Kuugaruk. It was built by Fathers Pierre Henri and Franz Van de Velde in 1941, and was later used as a museum. It was razed in 2000 because stones falling from the steeple were becoming a hazard to visitors.

While exploring near the Resolute Bay Omni-Range site we found a friendship cairn left by Chinese visitors several years prior to our visit.

Stone church in Kuugaruk (Pelly Bay), Nunavut.

Leaving Resolute Bay, we flew over the Franklin expedition graves at Beechey Island. Franklin's story is well known. He spent his first winter at Beechey before vanishing into history, leaving behind the graves of three of his men. Only in 2014 was the wreck of the first of his two ships, HMS *Erebus*, discovered off King William Island by Parks Canada. HMS *Terror* was discovered two years later. At the time of our overflight archaeologists were investigating these graves to try and determine the sailor's causes of death.

Chinese friendship marker near Resolute Bay.

Our usual mode of Arctic transport was C-FCSW, one of the last Twin Otter airframes built by De Havilland Canada. In this picture, Jack Ireland is examining the propeller while Chuck Frankard is on the right. Jack could usually be found each morning on top of the wing, sweeping off the night's accumulation of snow and frost. CSW is now flying for a private owner in the Maldives.

Franklin expedition graves, Beechey Island near Resolute Bay.

De Havilland Canada DHC-6 Twin Otter C-FCSW, our usual Arctic transport.
Jack Ireland checks the prop while Chuck Frankard on the right looks on.

Pickle Lake

I used internal charters not only for Arctic trips. In 1990 we
took our corporate Queen Air into Pickle Lake, Ontario, where
I had managed construction of a weather station on the
airport. Part of that project involved trenching a cable along
the south side of the runway to the anemometer tower. An
anemometer measures wind speed and direction and needs
to be distanced from other structures and trees for accurate
readings, so it was about a kilometre away from the weather
station near the far end of the runway. Our local contractor
had opened the trench parallel to the runway and was
preparing to lay the anemometer cables into it when a C-46
cargo plane owned by Air Manitoba, registration C-GTPO,
veered off the runway. There is a steep slope near the south

side of the runway, and the C-46 was heading right for it when its main wheels dropped into my trench and the aircraft

came to an abrupt halt. The landing gear was messed up but the crew and cargo were all in one piece. The open trench saved them from going over the edge of the slope to

Curtiss Commando C-46F, C-GTPO, at Pickle Lake after being removed from my anemometer trench! Photo courtesy Peter Garwood, Flick'r.

certain destruction. The aircraft was repaired and is owned today by Buffalo Air of Yellowknife.

The Pickle Lake building was constructed as a single-wide mobile trailer by a Thunder Bay company and outfitted by Environment Canada technologists. The equipment racks were bolted to the floor but also needed to be braced at their tops so they would not topple over during the truck ride to Pickle Lake. I saw the building before it left Thunder Bay and there seemed to be a lot of odd-shaped two-by-fours bracing the tops of the racks against the walls, but I figured the boys had used up some scrap boards and that more bracing securing the racks was better than not enough. After the building had arrived and was mounted on its foundation the Environment Canada techs carefully removed the bracing lumber and reconstructed their picnic table, which had been purchased as a kit of lumber back in Thunder Bay!

Pickle Lake weather station, taken from Transport Canada's
Queen Air directly over the runway, looking north.

My final trip into Pickle Lake was from Thunder Bay so I used a commercial charter operator who flew me and my Public Works colleagues in a nearly new Piper Seneca aircraft. The flight into Pickle Lake was uneventful but afternoon thunderstorms were developing over Lake Superior and moving north from Thunder Bay. We departed Pickle Lake after dinner as the sun was setting and in the last of the light we could see the storms in a line ahead of us. Our pilot took us up to 23,000 feet, which was near the maximum ceiling of the aircraft. The air was a bit lumpy and the thunderheads were still well above us, but we were above the lower cloud layers and the worst of the turbulence. I was again sitting in the right-hand seat in the cockpit where I could observe the on-board weather radar display. We started to get bounced around pretty good as we penetrated the line of storms and the turbulence became moderately heavy as air traffic control had us descend to lower altitudes on our approach to Thunder Bay. Our pilot was demonstrating a great deal of skill calmly weaving between the cells guided by his radar, and managing to keep the wings level as the turbulence pitched us up and down. I watched the lightning shows pass in review on either side of the aircraft. We left the storms behind and the air smoothed out as the lights from Thunder Bay came into view ahead. Other than the turbulence it was a good flight and we made a normal landing. I felt confidence in our pilot and was never concerned for our safety, unlike my last flight into Hall Beach.

Martina

Transport Canada divested itself of airports in the early 1990s, turning them over to local or provincial authorities to operate and maintain. The biggest devolution, as mentioned earlier, was to the Government of the Northwest Territories (GNWT), which at that time included Nunavut. The GNWT placed over 40 new airport acquisitions under their Minister of Transportation whose personnel found themselves on a steep learning curve because airport runways were, in the words of one of our Public Works managers, "a lot more than a mile of straight road."

I spent a lot of time in facilities engineering managing joint projects with my GNWT counterpart Martina Simons, meeting both at her office in Yellowknife and at several Arctic airport locations. She was born and raised in the North; a petite, very active and outdoorsy lady with a holistic approach to life, but tough and smart as a whip. While in Resolute Bay she read my personal aura with a divining rod, which was an eye-opening experience. She taught me, among other things, the correct usage of the word 'skookum,' which equates very closely to the old Air Force term 'pukka,' both translating as "very good"!

Igloolik air terminal and Community Aerodrome Radio Station, Nunavut. A project jointly managed by Martina and I.

GNWT had embarked on an airport modernization program at the same time that Transport Canada was closing many northern FSS stations, so together Martina and I had a skookum time managing new construction projects at Rankin Inlet, Arviat, and Igloolik.

The airport buildings at Resolute Bay dated from 1948 and were extremely costly to operate and maintain, so they also came on the chopping block. They were demolished in 1998 along with many memories, and the FSS was replaced by

The Community Aerodrome Radio Station (CARS) equipment installed into the new air terminal at Resolute Bay. Gil Parent photo.

a Community Aerodrome Radio Station (CARS) installed into a new terminal building.

Closing Coral Harbour

Another northern FSS whose time had come was Coral Harbour. It was now the 1990s and this hamlet still did not have an air terminal building. The needs of the community and the devolution of airports to GNWT, combined with the high cost of flight service operations and the low air traffic levels, dictated the replacement of the Coral Harbour FSS with a CARS station built as part of a new air terminal building. This would be Coral's first air terminal and had been sorely needed for many years; now it was even more of a necessity because with the closure of the FSS the Transport Canada accommodations facilities would also shut down, leaving no shelter at the airport. There was talk of maintaining the old airport barracks and messing facilities as an airport hotel however the distance from the community and the very high costs of environmental remediation and building code compliance meant that option would not go ahead. All the airport buildings were slated for demolition except for the upper air buildings, power house, and maintenance garage. The FSS building was also spared because it received heritage status from a federal preservation group in Ottawa.

I made two final trips into Coral Harbour during this time. The first trip would only take one day to inspect the nearly completed new air terminal/CARS building. Public Works were sending four representatives who specialized in various building trades so I chartered a King Air aircraft from Calm Air to carry us all there and back from Churchill. The trip was uneventful until we departed Coral on our return flight. The co-pilot came back into the small cabin, turned his pilot hat backwards on his head, and announced:

"Welcome aboard. Since we are leaving Coral Harbour and it is the evening hour, I am now your in-flight steward and the bar is open."

He then pulled a commissary container from behind his seat and opened the lid to reveal a stash of assorted liquor miniatures! Everyone wasted no time in helping themselves and two hours later we were all in a very happy mood as we prepared for touchdown in Churchill. The co-pilot again entered the cabin to give his pre-landing safety speech and retrieve his commissary for stowage. Five radiant faces beamed back at him as he peered into the container. His eyes bugged out and he exclaimed:

"It's all gone! You drank it all! There's only one broken bottle in here! I can't believe you guys drank 48 bottles of booze! That was our entire supply and it was supposed to last all our charter flights for the next three weeks until the end of the month!"

Of course, we had only drunk about half of the bottles and our parka pockets were tinkling merrily as we deplaned!

After that inspection trip our engineering services crew along with Environment Canada techs went in to Coral to install the CARS radios and weather equipment and to remove everything from the old FSS. Coral still retained its strategic location under the international air routes so our crew installed new remote communications equipment controlled from both Winnipeg Flight Service Station and the Edmonton ATC operations centre. Both the CARS and upper air programs were now locally staffed by the Inuit, which provided much-needed skilled employment in the community.

We took advantage of the decision to save the FSS building to have Public Works create emergency accommodations in what was the former electronic equipment room. It was outfitted with furniture from the old barracks, a kitchenette unit from the old dining hall, and there was already an electric 'turd-burner' toilet present in the building. The building was only intended to be used if our people became stranded at the airport but the local hotel operator was furious and complained all the way to the Minister of Transport that we were undermining the local economy. We won our case due to the distance and isolation from the community plus the probability that our techs would become stranded at the airport at some point.

Coral Harbour air terminal and CARS building, Nunavut, June 1995. Photo courtesy Ansgar Walk, Wikimedia Commons.

At the end of all the electronics work I returned to Coral Harbour for the final time to accept the last of the contract work on behalf of Transport Canada. On this trip I was accompanied by Costin Antonescu of Public Works. We used commercial flights because we would need a couple of days on-site. We stayed in the community hotel called 'Leonie's Place,' but I was not made to feel at home and ended up having very little interaction with the people in the hamlet. I drove back and forth to the different sites with Costin and his contractor in their rented truck and did not spend much time in town.

I had said my goodbyes to the people when I left in 1973 and a lot had changed since then, including myself. Most of those I had known and worked with no longer lived in Coral and I had no desire to revisit the past with the few who were left. I wanted to look forward while keeping my memories intact. I took a last sad walk through the old barracks, dining hall, and rec club, thinking about my friends and colleagues and the times we had shared there. Then the buildings had been alive with the voices and energy of people living, working, and playing while coming and going. Now they were dead. They squatted dark, gloomy, damp, and musty, awaiting the coming of their final summer when the wreckers would knock everything down and cart the pieces away for scrap or recycling.

The silver lining was that all the recreation equipment, kitchen fixtures, and furniture had been donated to the community where they would find good uses and help many families and individuals. When I left I did not look back.

On the flight home Calm Air stopped briefly in Chesterfield Inlet. We would only be on the ground about 20 minutes but Costin figured that was long enough to borrow the CARS operator's Skidoo and make a quick visit to town where he needed to give some documents to a contractor he had working there.

"You'll never make it; the flight attendant says 20 minutes tops."

"Calm Air always takes longer than that to get the freight off and on. I'll just drop the papers with my guy and come right back."

"Why not leave them with the CARS operator and your guy can pick them up?"

"Can't; they are legal copies and I have to hand deliver them. I've wasted enough time … see you!"

Off he roared into the night. I told the crew to please take as long as they could and he should be returning in just a few minutes, but they were in a mood to get home and unlike Air Canada they did not want to keep their airstairs down for one late passenger. They had no delays with the freight that night and a very short time had elapsed when we were told to re-board the Hawker 748. The flight attendant said they were going to leave without Costin if he wasn't on board in two minutes. I wasn't going to go look for him and risk getting left behind too so Costin was on his own. The pilots started the engine on the right side away from the airstairs. They were on the intercom telling the flight attendant to raise them and close the cabin door when I saw a Skidoo headlight bouncing across the snow towards us. Costin barely got the machine stopped before he was bounding up the stairs and into his seat accompanied by dirty looks and pithy comments from the crew but he, like me with Air Canada, was just another VIP who made it in the nick of time.

Thunder Bay

The largest project I managed while in facilities was the airport refurbishment at Thunder Bay in 1993–94. The impetus behind the work was the Nordic Winter Games being held in 1995 and as the host city Thunder Bay needed a modern gateway. Our Airports group in the person of Brian Hodgson was in overall charge and responsible for the construction of a new air terminal building. My portion of the work for facilities included constructing a temporary FSS to replace the old one being demolished to make way for the new air terminal, the new permanent FSS located in that air terminal, modernizations at the ATC control tower, and a new building to house the technical maintenance staff.

Airside view of Thunder Bay air terminal, Thunder Bay, Ontario, July 2012. The FSS is on the left. Wikipedia Commons User P199.

Thunder Bay air terminal, Thunder Bay, Ontario, July 2012, showing the swooping roof and ice catchers. Wikipedia Commons User P199.

Airports group had specified a conventional flat roof on the air terminal to save money. We agreed with that decision because it would be easier for us to install the FSS antennas and weather monitoring equipment onto a flat roof. Our consultants on the project were the IKOY group, represented by Jim Yamashita (the 'Y' in IKOY) who came up with a beautiful-looking building with an airfoil-shaped roof. Jim used his arms and hands to emphasize that the roof must "Swoop like an airplane wing!" The only problem with Jim's design was that it was something like $1 million over budget so Airports vetoed it because of the cost. We went back and forth with Jim and his Swooping Roof for what seemed a very long time until Airports convened a final meeting with him to say once and for all that the money was not there and the new terminal would have to have a flat roof. After that meeting Brian and I went to lunch after which we were informed that phone calls had been made, Ottawa had found some money, and today Thunder Bay does have a beautiful terminal with a roof that swoops! The one disadvantage to the Swooping Roof, which we found out during the first winter, was that it shed ice that fell onto the sidewalks and entryways along the terminal entry road. That is why there are large steel structures disguised as part of the light standards along that side of the building, to catch the ice before it falls onto the passengers!

Our electronic maintenance staff had never had a building of their own before! The new Technical Services Building was a single-storey structure located near the centre of the airport, housing our staff and their vehicles and workshops that were displaced when the new terminal went up. The specifications included a central vacuum system for ease of cleaning and to minimize distracting noises. Public Works came to me during construction and said they needed more money because the lowest bid for the central vacuum came in at around $30,000! This was an order of magnitude larger than the budget and absolutely outrageous for a building that size. The Public Works manager I was dealing with agreed with me but said the high bids were because of the 'hiring hall' system of contracting in Thunder Bay. I refused to amend my budget and told Public Works to stop the process and reject all the bids, then I issued a new request for proposal to companies over a wider geographical area. This allowed companies as far away as Winnipeg to bid on the vacuum system. Winnipeg companies did bid on the contract and all came in much lower than the Thunder Bay companies, even allowing for travel costs for their employees, and one of them won the contract to install the central vacuum system. The Thunder Bay mayor and Chamber of Commerce were pissed off but I told them straight out to fix their local contracting system and bid

The Thunder Bay Technical Services Building, Google Maps, Accessed 2021.

accordingly because I was tired of answering for cost overruns due to their business practices.

The Tech Services Building had a sheet-metal roof that wrinkled when it was installed and had to be replaced by the contractor. The old roof panels could not be reused but before they could be disposed of in the landfill they found new homes on several summer cottages back in the woods where wrinkles would not matter!

Back to Engineering Services

I knew the fun in facilities had to be too good to last. Shortly after finishing the Thunder Bay projects our headquarters reorganized us yet again and disbanded facilities engineering. Our Winnipeg group had grown to include Steve Highstead, Roly Rutkauskas from Public Works, Pete Woloshyn from the Airports group, plus Wayne Johnson who was the regional environmental officer. Our Ottawa headquarters took over the management of new construction projects while our other functions and duties devolved back into the electronic maintenance organization. Mike Robertson took over the management of engineering services when their incumbent engineer retired. Steve Highstead went on to work for a senior ATC manager in Ottawa who was the second Peter that Steve enjoyed working for during his career. Roly went back to Public Works where he managed the construction of Winnipeg's Level Four virology lab. Wayne was laid off but I heard, and I hope this is correct, he found work with the Canadian Space Agency. Pete Woloshyn eventually ended up as an electrician at the E d m o n t o n international airport. I went back to my old job in engineering

Rob Dobson getting hands-on in Churchill, tuning parts of his antenna system with a Radio Frequency Network Analyzer.

services but now working for Gary Abraham, a very quiet-spoken engineer who headed up the communications group. I would be working closely with Rob Dobson on many of my future projects. He, like Andre Sharpe, had a technology background before attaining his P. Eng. Degree and his designs were sensible and efficient systems. One of my first projects after returning to engineering services was going to eventually lead me into my fourth and final career path.

Dial Us Up

Transport Canada paid huge bills every month to telecom companies for the dedicated circuits connecting each of our remote sites into manned ANS sites on a 24/7 full-time basis. Many of these circuits received little use so in an effort to reduce costs and provide service that was commensurate with fewer flights into smaller airports, our headquarters purchased dial-up communications equipment that used ordinary telephone lines to talk to pilots. When pilots wanted to talk to the FSS they clicked their microphone four times to activate the dial-up equipment, which automatically called the FSS on the phone.

Not every region was installing dial-up equipment so I was asked to develop a regional training course for it. I received my system training from our life-cycle manager in Ottawa, Jan Brown. She made her manufacturer's materials available to me so I would have a head start in writing my course manuals. I was given training in instructional techniques in Winnipeg after which I had a free hand to prepare the materials and develop the course. The written materials were edited to national standards at the training institute in Cornwall, which also printed and bound the student manuals. Cornwall also maintained the individual student records and issued the course completion certificates.

My main teaching aid was a complete dial-up communications system including the radio receiver and transmitter that I fabricated into a portable equipment rack. I also designed and built test boxes that demonstrated all the features of the system. Duplicate boxes were manufactured for the techs who were to maintain the systems after they were installed.

Remote Dial-Up RCO installation, with new Park Air digital radios in the adjacent rack. The rack-mounted mobile radio simulates aircraft calls to test the system. Ron Schmidtke photo.

Rack of four dial-up RCOs at Winnipeg FSS. Each RCO communicates with a different remote location using its own telephone line. Ron Schmidtke photo.

Over the next few months I took my travelling road show across Western Canada, delivering courses to many technologists who were then qualified to maintain this new equipment. After the initial batch of training was finished headquarters decided to convert the course into a self-study package. Bill Webster had retired by that time but he was pretty whizzy with audio-visual software. He won the contract to produce copies of my dial-up course on CD-ROM. He and I worked together recording video clips and audio tracks to accompany my student manual. Then he collated all the course materials onto compact disc and Ottawa distributed the finished training package to positive reviews across the country.

I enjoyed this first taste of formal instructing. I received positive feedback from both the students and management and a certificate of appreciation for the training courses I put on. I began thinking that I would rather enjoy other teaching opportunities if or when they presented themselves. I would not have too long to wait.

PRIVATIZATION

In the mid-1990s the Minister of Transport set up a committee to investigate the privatization of the Air Navigation System (ANS). During one of the early meetings someone at the table said they needed a temporary name for the proposed new organization, something that the bureaucrats could drop into memoranda and other documents as a place-holder until a proper name could be decided on should the privatization go forward. Someone else at the table suggested 'Nav Canada' since the ANS was commonly referred to within the bureaucracy as 'Nav' and government departments were suffixed 'Canada.' Nav Canada stuck, and the new ANS Corporation was named by bureaucratic accident.

There were good reasons for privatization, money being chief among them as it usually is. Transport Canada was coming to the Treasury Board seeking hundreds of millions of dollars to modernize the ANS whose equipment, particularly the air traffic management equipment used by the controllers at their workstations, was outdated and inefficient. It was not a slam-dunk that they would be given all the cash they were asking for, nor in a timely manner, because Transport had to compete with the other government departments for a share of a shrinking taxpayer-funded pie. What money they were allotted would have to be borrowed and added to the federal government deficit in a time of restraint, so Transport wanted this fiscal albatross off their back.

Privatizing the ANS would be a huge windfall to Canada's treasury. Equipment modernization had already begun but was bogged down in the financial and political quagmires of huge cost overruns, constantly changing requirements, and long delays. Instead of paying out hundreds of millions more for modern equipment, the sale of the ANS assets to a new entity would realize well over a billion dollars to the federal government, while at the same time thousands of expensive civil servants would be removed from their payroll.

Transport Canada was once again having trouble attracting qualified people into the ANS due to a long succession of government wage restraints and salary freezes, salaries that had once again fallen far behind those in the private sector. Privatization would, it was optimistically hoped, help to alleviate that situation.

Transport Canada was also both the operator and the regulator of the ANS so privatization would put operations at arms length and remove that obvious conflict of interest.

The committee hammered out details. If the new owners of the ANS were to pay for its costs then they wanted control of the decision-making as well as the revenue stream that funded the system, therefore they rejected the idea of creating a Crown corporation. The final recommendation was that the new entity, now formally known as Nav Canada, be set up as a non-share, not-for-profit, fully private corporation owned by the users of the ANS. Eliminating shareholder profits from the decision-making process was intended to ensure aviation safety remained first and foremost among their objectives. A majority of the board of directors would be drawn from Nav Canada's stakeholders. The federal airline ticket tax that was funding only a portion of ANS operations would be repealed. In its place Nav Canada would be allowed to charge fees for service sufficient to recover their operating and borrowing costs. As a private corporation Nav Canada would be able to fund the purchase of assets and future capital requirements by issuing corporate bonds or through other publicly traded debt without government involvement.

Of course, there was much more to the decision to privatize than these bare bones but both the political and industry will to proceed was strong. The Civil Air Navigation Services Commercialization Act was passed by Parliament and on November 1, 1996, the ANS was sold to Nav Canada for the sum of $1.5 billion.

Ten seats on the new board were allocated to the founding stakeholder groups: air carriers, general and business aviation, the federal government, and the unions. These 10 directors elected four independent directors having no ties to the stakeholder groups. The 14-member board then appointed a president and CEO who became the 15th board member.

Nav Canada corporate headquarters at 77 Metcalfe St. in Ottawa, a short walk from Transport Canada headquarters. Photo courtesy A. Hunt, Wikimedia.org.

Over 6,300 ANS employees were deemed to have retired from the federal government subject to the provisions of their collective agreements on November 1, 1996. The vast majority became employees of Nav Canada on the same day but there was great uncertainty whether or not the new corporation would keep everyone on staff over the longer term. Quite a few employees decided not to accept Nav's offer of employment, preferring instead to transfer to other federal departments or take their retirement early without any special buyout package. Each new Nav employee had to make several non-revocable decisions concerning their personal work and retirement situations within a short period of time and without understanding Nav Canada's long-term plans. This caused a great deal of water-cooler gossip, speculation, and angst in every office and operational location across the country.

As far as day-to-day operations went the name on the paycheque changed but not much else, at least not at first. Many office processes were streamlined. Head office continued and then expanded the ATC modernization projects. These became much easier undertakings with the backing of the user groups and without the political considerations we had formerly lived with. For example, implementation of one Transport Canada modernized radar site went from costing about $18 million over six years to Nav Canada costs of less than $6 million over six months.

Management employees were no longer represented by their former unions and were given individual contracts of employment without any job security. Despite the initial optimism about Nav Canada being easier to work for most employees remained distrustful of their long-term prospects with our new employer and it wasn't too long before the hammer fell. The board had decided major restructuring was necessary in order to achieve their priority objective of reducing user fees to the aviation industry. Everyone knew there was fat to be trimmed from a former federal bureaucracy and we were all expecting some action in that regard, but the depth of the cuts across the entire company came as a surprise. It was a shock to many employees to be told their services were no longer required or they would need to relocate to another city in order to keep their job, and to see what they had built up over decades suddenly tossed aside.

The airlines and other user groups understandably did not want to pay for levels of service that were seen as excessive or that were underutilized. Most of the remaining northern Flight Service Stations like Baker Lake, Hay River, and Fort Smith were converted to Community Aerodrome Radio Stations. New FSSs in the planning stages were cancelled, like Red Lake and Dryden in Northern Ontario. Many of the remaining smaller control towers such as Brandon and Peace River were converted into FSSs. Weather, pilot briefing, and flight planning services that had been provided from FSSs were taken over by centralized Flight Information Centres. The number of manned electronic maintenance sites was reduced by nearly half, from 75 to 41, and preventive maintenance of equipment was scaled back. Operational training began to be decentralized back into the regions and away from TCTI, which was now renamed the Nav Canada Training Institute (NCTI). Technical training became more reliant on self-study courses and mentorship. Nav Canada began operating NCTI as a conference centre to try and cover its operational costs and the food there did improve somewhat as a result. In Ottawa both Nav Canada's head office and the technical systems centre laboratory were downsized. The three Western Canada regional offices were amalgamated into one. The company wanted to do the same thing with the three Eastern Canada offices, but it was unacceptable not to have a separate office for Quebec so Toronto, Montreal, and Moncton were spared amalgamation. This whole series of restructurings involved layoffs and forced relocations that reverberated throughout the organization and affected every employee. Eventually the company reduced user fees by about a third at the cost of downsizing by a similar amount including 20% of the electronic technologists. In human terms that meant about 2,000 employees were let go.

Winnipeg Regional Office Closure

All Winnipeg regional office employees were summoned to the ballroom of the Westin Hotel one morning in early 1998 to hear our regional director general, Al Sutherland, announce that our office would be closed that summer. Winnipeg's central region would become part of Edmonton's western region. The Winnipeg engineering workshop would close and there was speculation about the future of Winnipeg's ATC operations centre. We were told that only a few operational or technical personnel could expect relocation to Edmonton and all other regional office employees would be laid off.

Well that was a kick in the nuts! We in engineering services were justifiably proud of our high standards and project efficiency. We felt strongly that Nav Canada was lowering the levels of quality and service by shutting us down and dispersing our personnel. The Edmonton office had also been considered for closure and everyone in Winnipeg felt Nav Canada had made the wrong decision. Their personnel had also been called together to hear the news and they breathed a collective sigh of relief at having dodged the closure bullet!

The Vancouver regional office was also amalgamated with Edmonton. Their people went through the same things we did only a few months later. It was eventually decided to keep the Winnipeg ATC operations centre open but the one in Moncton was scaled back and many of their controllers were relocated to Edmonton's ATC operations centre.

Most of us took the rest of that day off to digest the news. I phoned home and told Jovanna, saying that the decision would be on the evening news and that there was a chance we might be offered a relocation to Edmonton but everything was up in the air and nothing was for certain. Before going home, I asked around about employment with the other government agencies I had worked closely with. I talked to the aviation inspectors but my private pilot licence was not enough to qualify me for a position there. Environment Canada and Public Works had no electronic technologist jobs open at that time and neither did the Winnipeg Airport Authority. There were few electronic technology opportunities available in Winnipeg's private sector, and in any case I still had 10 years to go until I could draw my full pension, so I pinned my hopes on either a federal government or Nav Canada job opening up for me somewhere.

My only real option with Nav Canada aside from a relocation to Edmonton would be a transfer to NCTI, but NCTI was in Cornwall and that was an economically depressed area of the country. I had three boys who would soon be leaving high school and their prospects there would be bleak. They would have to move away to attend post-secondary schools and Cornwall itself held very few job prospects. Most of their major industries were struggling and it would not be long before NCTI and Walmart became the two largest employers in the city. On the other hand, the Alberta economy was doing very well and both education opportunities and job prospects were plentiful. I would accept a position at NCTI if that meant keeping my career going until I could qualify for my pension but Jovanna and I were crossing our fingers for an Edmonton opening.

We all received our layoff letters in short order as talks went forward with the Edmonton office to determine who would be offered jobs. Edmonton needed technologists and engineers because of the new responsibilities in their expanded territory. After the Vancouver office was assimilated the western region, formerly just Alberta, the Northwest Territory and the Yukon, spanned all of Canada west of Thunder Bay including all of Nunavut except Baffin Island.

I was fortunate to be one of about two dozen technologists, engineers, telecommunications specialists, and outside plant rigging staff who received an offer to relocate to Edmonton. A couple of senior technologists found employment with Nav Canada in Ottawa but everyone else from the Winnipeg office, about one hundred souls, was laid off. Some of our office staff made a soft landing back into the public service but the majority were left scrambling in Winnipeg's non-too-hot job market.

Once we knew we were relocating to Edmonton both Jovanna and I became excited about our impending move. We had been discussing the possible sale of our acreage ever since the big flood the previous year. Now with our mortgage discharged a company-paid relocation meant we would cash out the full value of our property. We both saw the positive opportunities of a fresh start in a new city and a province that held a lot of promise. The difference in the provincial tax regimes between Manitoba and Alberta meant about a 10% increase in my take-home pay so financially we would be better off right out of the gate. The boys were less enthusiastic because they would be leaving their friends behind, but they were all at ages where they were going to have to change schools and make new friends even if we had stayed in Winnipeg.

RELOCATION

No one in the company had ever managed multiple relocations on this scale before. Nav Canada was following the federal relocation directive but the staff who were administering it were all losing their jobs, so whenever they could bend rules in our favour they did. The Edmonton staff did all they could to make our moves as smooth as possible. My new boss, Rico Sebastianelli, sent us copies of Edmonton newspapers, community information, and real estate guides. We read these avidly to get an idea of what we would be able to afford in what areas before we began exploring on the ground. Rico and others in the Edmonton office were always ready to answer our questions and offer guidance. The Edmonton office arranged welcome gift packages through the Chamber of Commerce to area attractions for us and our families.

Each relocated family was allowed a three-day 'familiarization trip' to Edmonton in addition to the usual five-day house-hunting trip. This gave families an opportunity to scope out Alberta's capital region before committing to the major financial and lifestyle decisions of buying a house. Jovanna and I selected an Edmonton real estate agent who was the sister of Bob Ridley, my colleague from Regina. Maureen spent our fam trip showing us as much as possible between Ardrossan and Devon, Pigeon Lake and the southern Edmonton suburbs. We hadn't totally given up on the idea of acreage living although I did not want to spend my future retirement on a lawn tractor, so we looked at estate lots as well as urban areas. Edmonton's management told us their regional office would be moving from the downtown core to the international airport within two years and their advice to us was "buy accordingly." The more we explored the more we realized that moving into one of the smaller towns near Edmonton would seem to be our best option. A small town would let us enjoy some of the benefits of acreage living but without the property maintenance and upkeep, and I could sell the lawn tractor! We would not have to drive the boys hither and yon every day or evening to activities and events. There would be no further need for them to ride school buses! There would be more opportunities for all of us to make new friends and involve ourselves in new activities. The office relocation to the international airport turned out to be a broken promise, but Edmonton proved to be an easy city to get around in so most of us happily settled into south-side neighbourhoods or nearby communities like Leduc, Devon, and Beaumont.

A couple of days after returning from the fam trip we got a call from Maureen to hustle back because she had found what she described as the 'perfect listing' for us. Jovanna and I began our five-day house-hunting trip by viewing a pretty split-level home on a quiet cul-de-sac in the town of Beaumont, located about a 10-minute drive from both the international airport to the west and Edmonton city limits to the north. That first home we saw was not for us but there was a vacant pie-shaped lot with mature trees a few doors over that was for sale. Maureen introduced us to the builder, Denis Royer, and we liked what we saw in other homes he had built so we signed an offer to purchase a Royer Custom Home built on our selected lot.

We still had a couple of days before our return to Winnipeg so we used the time to register the boys in their new schools and check out our new town. Beaumont had grown up around a Catholic church that was built on top of the only hill in the area. The land for the church was donated by the founding families who emigrated from Quebec in the mid-19th century. The railway bypassed Beaumont so it remained a sleepy little French hamlet of a few hundred people for almost a century. In the 1970s it was 'discovered' by Edmontonians desiring something more bucolic. By the time we moved in it had grown to six thousand people. Beaumont was a young town with new residential development as the major economic activity but it still boasted only one four-way stop intersection, two gas stations, a post office, and a single grocery store. Beaumont's proximity to both Edmonton and Leduc meant it had almost no other shopping and entertainment amenities.

The sale of our Winnipeg acreage fixed our moving date for the end of June. The moving company looked after everything; packing all our possessions, loading the van, and transporting our cars. All we had to do was pack clothes and essentials for the time we would be living in temporary accommodations until our new house was ready, crate the pets, and head for the airport.

The Big Move

Normally we would have had to drive across the dusty summer prairies to Beaumont but Jovanna's asthma and hay allergy meant we were given approval to fly on medical grounds. The five of us were accompanied on the plane by two large dogs and a small flock of budgie birds. The pet lizard died before the move but it was still a menagerie. We had to change planes in Calgary and the flight from there up to Edmonton was in a smaller Dash 8 turboprop. We were concerned about space in the cargo hold for the dog crates, but Canadian Airlines took good care of us and ensured both made it onto our Edmonton flight. We had given them sedatives before leaving Winnipeg but the pills weren't working very well and the entire aircraft was treated to a chorus of howls from behind the rear bulkhead all the way between Calgary and Edmonton! The dog's baying set off the birds, which began squawking from their box stowed under Scott's seat. Our pets entertained the passengers for over an hour. After landing we didn't have to search for the oversize baggage belt because the dogs were still letting everyone in Edmonton's airport know where they were!

The first stop in our rented van was the Club Mead Pet Resort not too far from the airport. The two mutts would share a double kennel and we would take them for walks and visits to their new home in Beaumont every couple of days. The birds were boarded with a local fancier and then it was off to the Campus Tower Suites, which would be our home for the next six weeks until we took possession of our new house! This apartment hotel was on the U of A campus and only became available to us because classes were out for the summer. I was within walking distance of my new office just over the High Level Bridge near the Alberta legislature, while Jovanna and the boys could explore Whyte Avenue, Jasper Avenue, and Edmonton's river valley. We were also able to take advantage of the university's swimming pool and gym on several occasions.

At least four times during our first night in Edmonton we were woken up by sirens going by on the street outside that caused us to wonder what kind of high-crime neighbourhood we had moved into. The next morning we were told by the hotel staff that University Hospital was only a few blocks away. The sirens were ambulances heading to Emergency from all over the city and we needn't worry about our safety!

Our cars arrived a couple of days later so Jovanna was able to explore more of Edmonton with the boys while I was working. On weekends we used the welcome passes that the Edmonton office had arranged for us to take in K-Days, Folklorama, Telus World of Science, the Valley Zoo, and the West Edmonton Mall Waterpark and Fantasyland. We were quickly becoming acclimated and finding Edmonton an easy city to navigate and live in.

When we arrived in Edmonton our Beaumont home was at the drywall stage and we visited regularly to check on the progress of the build. The home was turn-key including a finished basement and with all the landscaping and fencing done. We were able to choose the paint colours, trim, finishes, cabinetry, window coverings, and appliances, which completed the buy-in for Jovanna and the boys. Denis Royer hired Scott and Sandy to paint our new fence, which kept them busy for a few days and earned them some spending money.

When move-in day arrived Jovanna directed the mover's people in the unpacking of all the boxes and filling of the closets and cupboards. The next day we retrieved our birds and the dogs were turned loose into their new backyard. It wasn't all smooth sailing. There was damage to about 10% of our items, which we found was a typical experience for most of the relocated families. The mover's adjusters were good to work with and most of the damage was soon repaired by professional restorers to our satisfaction. The few items that could not be repaired were paid out on a 'replacement cost' basis so at the end of the day we were made whole and were happy with the way things had gone. Overall, the relocation had been a positive experience. We were looking forward to settling in to Beaumont, and I into my new job.

Welcome to Beaumont

Our new home in Beaumont.

The cul-de-sac we moved onto was right at the western edge of Beaumont. At the time we moved in there was a farm just down the road from us. We could hear the coyotes that lived along a nearby creek so we had our rural ambience while living in town. The boys were able to tour their new schools before classes started in September. The schools were nearly new with atriums and modern science and computer labs. Scott and Sandy were pumped to find the high school had welding and automotive programs including a student-maintained race car that was driven regularly at the local drag strip. It won regularly too!

All three boys could walk or bike to their respective schools. Our house backed onto the road leading out of town so I installed a gate into the fence to give direct access to the fields and beyond. We walked the dogs in the fields and the boys could launch their model rockets. During the winter months Scott drove his Skidoo out the back gate, turned right, and was gone across country. One of his new friends rode her horse down the cul-de-sac and hitched it to the trees in the front yard while they visited. Sandy played guitar and found musician friends just a block away where they jammed regularly in their basement. When he got a bit older, he and his friends played at open-mic nights in the local bars.

We soon felt at home at the local Anglican Church, St. Columba's. The congregation was small but active and they soon found out I had experience being a treasurer for charities back in Winnipeg. Before too long I allowed myself to be dragooned into taking on that role for St. Columba's. Besides our new friends in the church community Jovanna connected with several of the Nav Canada wives who banded together because of our relocation. They called themselves the 'Winnipeg Wives' and had social get-togethers semi-regularly. There was one local taxi in Beaumont that was owned and operated by Robin Johnston. He became a buddy since he drove me to and from the airport every time I travelled for work. He invited me onto his dart team and I have been a member of the Beaumont Dart League ever since.

Beer O'Clock

Our cul-de-dac was all new homes so our neighbours were all getting to know each other. On many Fridays after work Duane Cartier rang a bell to announce Beer O'Clock. This was our cue to congregate in the middle of the street or in someone's garage and bring each other up to date on happenings in our worlds over a pop or two. These became impromptu block parties and we brought out BBQs, lawn chairs, even fake palm trees and grass mats while wearing Hawaiian

My Beer O'Clock jacket ... happy times!

shirts and shorts. On Hallowe'en we sat in lawn chairs around Teresa's propane heater in the middle of the street so the trick-or-treaters could get their candies without knocking on all the doors. Jef Gibbs owned a promotions company and had 'Beer O'Clock Cul-de-Sac' jackets made up for us. It was happy times.

BACK TO WORK

We had no sooner gotten squared away in our suite at the Campus Towers when I reported for my first day at work in my new office. I had a very pleasant walk along the university's fraternity row of stately homes, then over the High Level Bridge and up 109th Street to the regional office that was located in what was then the Alberta Treasuries building.

My new boss Rico introduced me around and showed me my workspace. Rico was another interesting character, and although this may sound repetitive he was also a great boss to work for. His hobby was raising chickens on his property north of Edmonton. These were not McChickens but show-quality birds. Rico would bring dozens of eggs into the office for the employees, eggs that were all the

Rico Sebastianelli, a fine judge of chicken flesh! Rico Sebastianelli photo.

colours of the rainbow from the different breeds of hens. Rico was well respected in the hobby and was invited to locations across Canada and into the U.S. to judge poultry shows. Rico gave me a free hand to implement my assigned projects and he was pleased enough with my work that he told me to write up my own performance evaluations and he would just sign them! His one instruction to me was to make sure I let him know what trouble I had created five minutes before his phone rang!

Rico would also be my boss right up to my retirement date, except for the second interlude from engineering that took me down my fourth and final career path. Nav Canada managers were told to make sure their employees sang the company song and danced the company dance but both Rico and his boss Peter Dawson tempered these directives, believing carrots motivated better than sticks. They and other like-minded managers in Nav Canada were walking a fine line because they could be, and some were, escorted out the door at any time for showing too much humanity towards their employees.

Obviously, there were some differences between the way our old and new offices were run but we quickly settled into the new routine. One major difference was Winnipeg did much more contracting out of electronic assembly than Edmonton. Prior to Nav Canada taking over we had lost our general labourer helpers to attrition and fiscal restraint. In Winnipeg we contracted out the assembly of printed wiring boards and similar repetitive work rather than have the higher-paid technologists add that work to their normal duties. Edmonton transferred their assembly work onto the technologists, which meant they were now doing the work of two people; therefore their projects took longer to fabricate and implement.

Our Winnipeg drafting department was a casualty of amalgamation. Edmonton had a small cadre of draftspersons but their drawing process was much different. In Winnipeg our drawings were created and amended by engineering's drafting department. In Edmonton most of the project drawings were created and amended by the technologists or engineers who were doing the design and implementation.

We had to get up to speed on AutoCAD software, and once I became familiar with it I liked this new procedure. Creating preliminary pencil drawings was eliminated as was the intermediate step of submitting corrections to drafting. The maintenance technologists got final project drawings faster and with fewer 'red line' changes.

Early on there was a feeling among some of the Edmonton personnel that 'we won, you lost.' The Edmonton staff had no great interest in learning how Winnipeg had done things and we were expected to conform to Edmonton's procedures. This attitude eased somewhat when Vancouver's personnel started reporting to Edmonton, and at the end of the day Nav Canada created new engineering standards that were mandated across the country so everyone ended up adapting to different procedures and realities.

Chicken George and the Electric Fence

One Saturday after I had been back to work for a few months I fastened a bare copper wire along the top of the backyard fence all the way around three sides of the property. I fed the nearest end of the wire through my den window and connected it to my short-wave radio receiver's antenna terminal. It worked exceptionally well and pulled in signals from countries all around the world. On Monday two days later I was leaving to work out of town. I told Jovanna to expect a visit from Beaumont's by-law officer, who everyone called Chicken George, sometime around the middle of the week.

"What have you done now?"

"Nothing ... but one of our neighbours did not ask me about the copper wire when I put up my radio antenna so I am sure they will complain to the town that I electrified the fence. I figure it will take Chicken George until Wednesday to come ask about it."

Sure enough, on Wednesday morning Jovanna saw George's car parked on the road outside the back fence. He was standing by the fence looking at the wire, waving his fingers near it but apparently afraid to touch it. Of course the dogs were running back and forth inside the fence barking their fool heads off at him. Shortly after he drove around to the front and rang the doorbell.

"Good morning, I'm George Martin, Beaumont's by-law officer. I need to ask you about the wire on your fence."

"Okay ... what would you like to know?"

"What is it? Is it something to do with your dogs in the yard?"

"Nothing to do with the dogs. My husband said you might stop by. We presume the neighbour who didn't ask us what it is thinks they will get a shock from it?"

"Well ... yes ... there was a complaint made about an electric fence. They are afraid they will get electrocuted if they touch it. I thought it might be to stop the dogs from barking?"

"Of course they won't get electrocuted, and you saw for yourself it won't make the dogs stop barking. It is the antenna for my husband's short-wave radio. All the neighbour had to do was knock on the door and ask us."

"What can I say ... neighbours being neighbours, I guess. So it is a radio antenna? Nothing electrical? No shocks?"

"No shocks, perfectly safe to touch, but if it does keep prospective burglars away then that's a bonus!"

Jovanna invited George in to see the radio then he apologized for the intrusion. George was an interesting character. As the by-law officer he responded to complaints of anything that was not criminal-code related. Beaumont did not have a 'Good Neighbour' by-law so the complaints were usually subjective and George got pretty good at mediating disputes between neighbours. When asked, he said he got his nickname from a group of high school girls who thought he reminded them of the character 'Chicken George' from the television mini-series *Roots*. The name stuck and he was known as Chicken George for as long as he worked for Beaumont.

The Thousand Days

When we were privatized eight unions each with their own collective agreements with Treasury Board continued representing their employees who had moved over to Nav Canada. We electronic technologists belonged to the International Brotherhood of Electrical Workers (IBEW) local 2228. For the six years prior to privatization we had worked without any wage increase, like others in the civil service, due to ongoing federal government policies of wage freezes and fiscal restraint. This had caused our salaries to lag far behind the private sector so the anticipated return to collective bargaining in November 1996 was a major reason for our early optimism with our new employer. Our first contract saw only modest increases that matched inflation. That contract expired in 2000 after which a year passed without any response from the company to our union's next contract proposals. IBEW then broke off negotiations in June 2001 and filed for conciliation according to the terms of our collective agreement. The union also filed a bad-faith bargaining complaint with the Canada Industrial Relations Board at the same time. By the middle of 2003 the electronic

technologists working for Nav Canada had been without an effective salary increase for 13 years and without a collective agreement for a thousand days. During that time Nav Canada's executives and CEO were paying themselves very generous salaries and bonuses while making major reductions to user fees.

To mark 1,000 days without a contract, the IBEW asked all members to wear black armbands like this one (most were in English). Nearly 100% of the technologists wore them with pride!

The nearly 50% reduction of manned maintenance sites, reduction of scheduled electronic equipment maintenance, amalgamation of regions and downsizing throughout the organization made it clear to all Nav employees, and as stated by the air traffic controllers' union, the Canadian Air Traffic Controllers Association, that Nav Canada's "predominate financial goal has been to reduce ANS fees for commercial airlines, rather than to operate Nav Canada itself in a prudent manner." Employees belonging to all unions across the company became disillusioned and frustrated by what we saw as the company's refusal to bargain in good faith, and effective denial of our right to strike through stonewalling on the issue of designating essential employees in the event of strike action. By the time the technologists had gone the thousand days without bargaining Nav Canada had become a toxic work environment. The work-related stress placed on employees resulted in steep increases in grievances, disabilities, sick leave, and stress leave, all of which could potentially work against the safety of the ANS. Many employees began recording conversations with managers so they would have a record of threats that might be made against them. Retirement dinners, Christmas parties, and social functions quickly became a thing of the past with managers being walked out the doors, and because few if any were in the mood to socialize in or out of the office even if the company had permitted these events. Employees were no longer allowed to play a game of cards during their unpaid lunch breaks and some managers began timing lunch, coffee, and even washroom breaks. Labour relations had not improved by the time I retired notwithstanding the efforts of Rico, Peter Dawson, and other front-line managers who supported their employees as best they could. I considered us fortunate to be working in engineering services because our projects took us out of the office to work away from much of the toxicity, whereas maintenance technologists did not usually have that luxury.

During the thousand days I became more involved with the IBEW and was carded as a shop steward. I had an overnight stay in hospital with sudden chest pains that I thought might be a heart attack. Fortunately, it was just a scare and my doctor diagnosed work-related stress. He prescribed two weeks off work with a prescription for the antidepressant Wellbutrin. Without naming names he told me that a good number of his patients were Nav Canada employees from the ATC operations centre and many of them were receiving similar diagnoses. These pills had a smiley face on them and many were referring to 'happy pills' during this time. Our chief shop steward, Doug Oates, phoned me every day during the time I was off work to see how I was doing and to keep my spirits up. He was phoning others too and being the shoulder for many workers to lean on must have taken a huge toll on him. The thousand days stretched to over 1,200 before an agreement was finally reached through binding arbitration. A couple of years into the dispute Nav Canada realized we would eventually be awarded a salary increase of some amount either through conciliation or arbitration. Once a new contract was signed they would have to disburse retroactive pay for all of the years we had been without one, so to ease their upcoming fiscal pain they gave each technologist a $1,000 cheque at Christmas. The employees saw this for the partial back pay that it was and not the holiday bonus some managers tried to make it out to be.

Cancer Strikes

In the middle of all the uncertainty and stress at work Jovanna was diagnosed with breast cancer. The support we both received from colleagues, friends and family was sometimes overwhelming but always much appreciated. Rico immediately told me to take whatever time I needed and he was backed up in this by Peter Dawson. By their kindness I was able to work mostly in Edmonton instead of on the road, which allowed me to accompany her to all her appointments throughout her treatments.

She first underwent successful surgery to remove her tumour. Her mom Karen arrived from Winnipeg to stay with us and help see her through that first phase of treatment and recovery. As soon as Jovanna had healed from the surgery she began chemotherapy at the Cross Cancer Institute. The staff at the Cross, particularly the nurses, were amazing and took great care of her. This was another reason to appreciate our move to Edmonton; if you are so unfortunate as to be diagnosed with this disease the Cross is one of the premiere research and treatment centres in the country. Jovanna tolerated the chemo well, even enjoying her outing to try on and select a pair of wigs, which she wore with confidence and even pride in her new looks.

Towards the end of the chemo she became very tired and needed help to move around and perform even simple tasks. I hired a house-cleaning service and the boys and I stepped up to make sure her smallest needs were met with little or no effort on her part. The St. Columba's church family was always there to pray for her, hold her hand, and provide any other support she needed, particularly Reverend Carolyn Pollock who would always sit in the pew with Jovanna every week to deliver her a personal blessing.

Her prognosis was positive after the chemo and we were told she was free of the cancer but radiation was still recommended to make sure any remaining cells were killed and to prevent a recurrence. The radiation probably beat her down more than the chemo but once that series of treatments was completed she bounced back quickly. Her beautiful auburn hair had grown back grey but there were products to deal with that! Everyone who followed her journey, especially her family back in Winnipeg and the boys and I, felt blessed and supported; fortunate that the treatments were successful and she had come through and was considered cured!

Her cancer and my heart scare got us thinking about our mortality. Between those events and the thousand days situation at work we resolved that I would look into early retirement so we could enjoy what would hopefully still be many more years together! My normal retirement date after 35 years of service would be June 25, 2008, it was now 2003 and we started to plan my departure for as soon as we could make the pension numbers work.

Throughout all this time and right up to my final day at Nav Canada there were projects to implement, new places to see and new people to meet, including my final career path which would be, like facilities engineering, another very interesting interlude in my life!

John Travolta's Airplane

Three relocated Moncton air traffic controllers were among my new cul-de-sac neighbours. One evening they all somehow ended up drinking beer in my garage where one of them passed around an aviation magazine. The magazine's classifieds featured an advertisement for a small jet that was for sale in Florida. This jet was a Canadair model CL-41G made in Montreal for the Malaysian Air Force. It was a version of the Tutor jets flown by Canada's famous Snowbirds air demonstration team and was owned by none other than John Travolta! By the time we were on our third beers we had convinced ourselves that the $600,000 asking price was affordable if we each bought a quarter share. We could rent it out to earn money when we were not flying it ourselves, we could fly it in airshows, and we would get Jef to make us customized flight suits so we would look even cooler than Ace McCool! Later that night I talked up our plan with Jovanna. She enjoyed flying with me so gave her blessing to this latest venture as long as I assured her we could afford it and she got a custom flight suit too!

CL-41G jet formerly owned by John Travolta. He ended up donating it to the Embry-Riddle Aeronautical University as pictured here. Photo courtesy Jetphotos.com.

The next day at work I contacted the Florida broker who faxed me the full information package. The airplane was a beauty with a polished pin-striped paint job, recently overhauled and complete with an extensive inventory of spare parts including a spare engine and canopy! I was already dreaming of learning to pilot this airborne hot rod and couldn't wait to meet up with the others back in my garage that evening. When we got together and I was passing around the broker's information I couldn't help but feel they were all somewhat subdued from the day before. It turns out one of their wives had got wind of our plans, she told the other two, and the three ladies promptly scuppered our deal.

WESTERN REGION TRAVELS

For us flatlanders from Winnipeg our expanded territory now included Alberta, the Yukon, the Northwest Territory, and British Columbia. Except for the months caring for Jovanna I spent much of the time following our move either getting to know these new parts of our region or showing some of the Edmonton technologists around my former stomping grounds. I travelled mostly with Stan Loo, Dennis Chan, Kirk Carston, Gil Parent, Ron Schmidtke, Brent Kenney, and Rod Muddle. Like my former Winnipeg compatriots, they were all great to work with and I think we all got along well together. The prairies have their own beauty, but working now in the mountains was a whole new magnificence that brought with it a whole new set of challenges.

The Rabbit-Boiling Psycho

One of my first projects in the expanded region was conversion of both the Hay River and Fort Smith FSSs to CARS stations as part of Nav Canada's service rationalization plan. I would again be working with Martina and her colleagues from Yellowknife, and with Edmonton technologists Stan Loo, Gil Parent, Dennis Chan, and Ron Schmidtke at various times throughout the projects. It was also the first and only time I worked with Kirk Carston. Kirk used to live in these communities and knew many of their people plus, of course, all the watering holes and restaurants. After our first day's work in Fort Smith we took our rented car to his favourite bar.

I drove into the parking lot and was lining up a parking spot when he yelled:

"Quick, drive away! Drive! Leave! NOW! GO-GO-GO!!"

I hit the gas and fish-tailed out of the lot and onto the road, only slowing down when we were a block away. Kirk was looking out the back window.

"Whew, that was close!"

"What, did you see a guy with a gun or a stabbing or something?"

"Worse than that, I saw my ex-wife's car!"

"You had me scream out of there like a maniac because you saw her car?!?"

"You don't understand, I can't let her see me!"

"Why not, you owe her money??"

"No, no, nothing like that. I'm scared of her! She's toys-in-the-attic crazy and if she finds out I'm in town she'll turn into a rabbit-boiling psycho like in *Fatal Attraction*. I'm seriously afraid she'll stalk us everywhere, screaming and causing scenes! I wouldn't put it past her to slash our tires if she spots me in this car!"

Dennis and I concluded there was a bit of history between these two. We suggested we should return to the bar and meet this lady so we could form our own opinions about her, but Kirk was adamant he was getting on the next plane if his ex-wife got any inkling he was back in town. We spent the entire week sneaking around Fort Smith's back roads, backing into parking spots for quick getaways, sitting in dark corners of restaurants and pubs, and Kirk was always back in his hotel room by 7 p.m.

Kirk was first to board the plane home on Friday and he breathed a great sigh of relief as he sank into his seat. We went through the pre-takeoff rituals and I heard the #1 engine of the Fokker F-28 start to spool up. Instead of the normal whoosh and whine of engine ignition the sound peaked, then wound down to dead silence. F-28 engines are started by blowing compressed air through them to spin the turbine fast enough to ignite the fuel. The pilot came on the intercom and informed us that they had had an 'Aw-shit' moment and something had gone wrong with the ignition sequence. There was no air for another try and the air bottles could not be recharged in Fort Smith so we had no option but to deplane and then try to get our hotel rooms back for one more night! We suggested that maybe Kirk's ex could put us up if the hotel was full. That suggestion flew about as well as our broken airliner so we had one more night of bobbing and weaving around town trying to keep out of her way.

Our initials engraved into the Ft. Smith floor trench. Gil Parent photo.

Soon after this adventure Kirk went to work for electronic maintenance in Yellowknife then he left Nav Canada to pursue an interesting career with a variety of employers. He definitely lived life well, just not in Fort Smith!

I made a return trip to Fort Smith to install remote communications back to Edmonton with Ron, Gil, and Rick Staples who was the Yellowknife maintenance manager. A contractor had created a small equipment room for our radio racks; part of his work was to fill in the old cable trench in the floor with concrete. This gave us the chance to memorialize our presence!

Winter Roadies

Vince Warszycki and I flew to Norman Wells where we met Rick Staples and one of his technologists, Moe Baksh. Yellowknife techs maintained the equipment at Fort Good Hope, which is a remote community located on the Mackenzie River west of Great Bear Lake and our final destination. Engineering already had a crew on-site there doing work on their Omni-Range system and Vince and I were

Rick Staples. *Hamilton Spectator* photo.

going to install new remote controls for it. Normally we would fly into Good Hope because there is no road into the community, but this was early spring, the winter ice road was open, and Rick had some freight to deliver so he decided we

Pit stop on the winter road to Fort Good Hope.

would drive. The road was about 150 kilometres long, mostly cross-country rather than on the Mackenzie River ice, and being unmaintained it was also very rough. We set off early and the trip took most of the day because we couldn't travel faster than about 30 kilometres per hour. The days were short so much of the trip was in twilight conditions. We passed one or two broken-down vehicles that attested to the road conditions, each with the remains of a campfire nearby where the former travellers had kept warm during the night and had maybe heated some food. They had already been rescued so we did not stop. We saw no other vehicles or people anywhere along the road and, strangely enough, no animals either. The mountain scenery was amazing but the desolation was as complete as the Arctic tundra.

Part of the winter road to Fort Good Hope, over lake ice.

Scenery along the winter road to Fort Good Hope.

The techs who were already in Good Hope had settled into a small house that operated as a bed and breakfast. It was used by whoever needed accommodations, there being nothing else available in the small community of some 500 people. They were a crew of four, which was double what would normally be assigned to this type of project, but they were mentoring other technologists on how to work on this particular system. There wasn't enough room in the site for all of us so Vince and I followed their directions to find the house. There were no house numbers or street names so we had to get redirected by the locals once or twice. We were on our own for supper so we boiled up something unremarkable on the stove from rations we had in the vehicle, shoehorned ourselves into what space was left in the house, and settled down for the night. It was a restless sleep punctuated by others coming and going while expelling various bodily noises and vapours.

In the morning a very nice elderly Sahtu Dene lady arrived to cook us bacon and eggs for breakfast. She spoke very little English and we did not speak any Dene, but with nods and smiles we conveyed our appreciation with her culinary efforts. After that hearty meal Vince and I shooed the spare bodies out of the Omni-Range site and got the control system installed before lunch. After lunch our new control system passed its tests with no problems and our work in Fort Good Hope was done, however we had to remain the rest of that day and a second night until Rick was ready to depart. The others told us they had been there for a week on the same unvarying diet of bacon and eggs followed by two meals of rations from their stash. This made me think of the road trip with Stu Patterson and had me wishing for cold KFC and warm beer! Vince and I used our free time to explore Fort Good Hope, especially their landfill. Vince collected rusty artifacts which he took home to his wife for display in their backyard. Old cranks, gears, and other mechanical scrap was preferred, as long as there was some artistic merit to the rust and

Vince Warszycki, my best man and still BFF today.

it would fit in their garden. This time Vince found a rusty gear on a shaft; later I saw it planted among the peonies where it actually fit in and looked quite nice!

When we returned to Norman Wells we enjoyed a steak dinner and then some time playing darts in their Legion. Moe was a champion darts player who had played nationally for the Legion. He put on a clinic and I picked up a few useful tips that hopefully would help my own play back in the Beaumont league. Moe told me he wanted to transfer out of Yellowknife and I extolled the benefits of applying to Edmonton. My ulterior motive was, of course, to enlist him onto my own dart team, but he ended up happily moving to the East Coast instead.

Yukon Calling

"I have gazed on naked grandeur where there's nothing else to gaze on." This line, from Robert Service's "The Call of the Wild," came to mind as we flew low along the mountain passes from Whitehorse, more or less following Yukon's Highway #1 west as it meandered beside the Takhini River to Haines Junction, then north past Kluane Lake and up the Kluane River to Beaver Creek near the Alaska border. Along with me were Rico, Stan Loo, a gentleman from Yukon Transportation, and Rick Gorman, one of our engineers. I was in the co-pilot's seat aboard Alkan Air's Piper Navajo, enjoying the mountain vistas and musing about Klondike Sourdough pioneers in between stops at Haines Junction, Burwash Landing, Beaver Creek, and Carmacks. The route we were flying was a very scenic low-level airway often used by tourists and adventurers flying between Alaska and southern Canada. Unfortunately, tourist pilots from the southern latitudes often had little or no training in mountain flying, which requires a special skill set coupled with a large dose of common sense to carry out safely. Their safety was not enhanced by the lack of radio communications and navaids along this sparsely settled route. Most of the airway had no communications coverage at all. Nav Canada and the Yukon government wanted to install a Community Aerodrome Radio Station facility at each of our stops as well as Remote Communication Outlet sites remotely controlled from Whitehorse along the airway. These services would provide both enroute radio coverage as well as local airport condition and weather reports, thereby greatly enhancing the safety of the flying public. At each stop the team deplaned to select a location for the CARS equipment in the airport terminal building. For the RCO sites we were looking for height, preferably mountaintops that were already occupied by a telephone or microwave site. Height translates into radio range, and telephone sites meant that the power and telecom services we would require would already be available. Rick would design the RCO antenna systems to give us the best radio coverage possible along the entire air route.

It was a beautiful summer day and we were kind of dozing off as the airplane snored along smoothly after we had left Carmacks heading back to Whitehorse. I was still sitting next to the pilot where I had the best view along the river valleys and mountain passes. Suddenly both engines coughed once, twice, then quit! No fuel! Both engines were drawing from the left-side tank and had run it dry. The pilot reached up right away for the fuel selector switches on the overhead panel, selecting both engines to the right-side tank while turning on the electric fuel pumps. Both propellers only windmilled for a few seconds before the fuel flowed again and the engines started right up, but that definitely got everyone's hearts racing! I had started looking around outside for a decent forced landing area but saw only mountains to the left and right and river rapids directly below and ahead. Our pilot got on the intercom and fessed up, saying he had not paid attention to the fuel gauges but we had a full tank on the right side that would take us the rest of the way back to Whitehorse with no problem. I turned in my seat and saw only nervous grins and goggle eyes looking back at me while busy hands were tightening seat belts, so I'm not sure how well he sold his explanation!

Stan Loo later returned to Haines Junction and Beaver Creek with Gil Parent to install our RCO equipment into Northwestel

The Horse Camp Hill Northwestel site near Beaver Creek. Paint Mountain is very similar. Gil Parent photo.

Haines Junction RCO equipment installed into the Northwestel site on Paint Mountain. The Horse Camp Hill equipment is identical. Gil Parent photo.

microwave sites on the top of Paint Mountain and Horse Camp Hill, respectively. These sites were only accessible by helicopter so everything including the equipment racks and the technologists was airlifted to landing zones at the top. These airlifts went off without a hitch and the RCO radio coverage exceeded expectations! These were among the last sites to receive analog radio technology. Before too long Nav Canada would be switching to digital communication radios.

Nav Canada's First Digital Radios

Dennis Chan and I flew to Whitehorse where we picked up a car then drove back down the Alaska Highway to Watson Lake. There we would install yet another remote communications site, but this project was special because it was to be the first installation of digital radio equipment by Nav Canada.

Our life-cycle manager for these new Park Air radios was Kevin Kavanagh, who arrived from Ottawa accompanied by maintenance technologists from Whitehorse. They came on-site after our installation was complete and would take part in the acceptance testing. Kevin's presence meant any issues that might come up with his newly written maintenance standards and procedures could be corrected right away on-site. The Park Air transmitters and receivers had never been tested in the field so as we began

Kevin Kavanagh, electronic equipment life-cycle manager. Kevin Kavanagh photo.

everyone crossed their fingers because this was all new and uncharted territory. We eventually got through the tests after some procedural issues, which cost me a couple of beers after work. I had to make up with Kevin for slagging his documentation, but the fact he took the trouble to travel to Watson Lake to observe this first installation and to assist with the testing got him props from me as well as the rest of us there.

These radios were installed into Watson Lake's Omni-Range site. Prior to the acceptance tests Dennis and I had pre-checked all the equipment and found everything to be working except for the antenna system. The radio antenna was mounted on top of the stacked Omni-Range and Distance Measuring Equipment antennas and should have worked, but much of the transmitted energy was being reflected back to the radio equipment instead of being radiated into the ether. This was puzzling because we had done this type of installation before without issues. We tried everything: replacing antenna connectors, removing and reinstalling the cables, putting up the spare antenna, but no joy! Finally, we accidentally discovered that the new antenna performed flawlessly if there was a rigger on a ladder just

Riggers working on the Omni-Range and DME antennas at Resolute Bay's VOR site on Signal Hill. Similar gymnastics at Watson Lake accidentally discovered the method by which we made our communications antenna work there. Photo courtesy Jane George, airports-worldwide.com.

underneath it! We determined from this empirical trial that our digital radio communications antenna needed a shield between it and the navaid antennas below. We couldn't leave the rigger tied to the DME antenna so we tried various other possible solutions. The riggers finally hit on the idea of suspending a copper wire loop below the antenna using extra spreader bars from one of our equipment racks. It worked perfectly and was a great example of teamwork and the innovation that was sometimes required to meet an unforeseen situation. I wrote a memo commending the riggers' initiative but management did not acknowledge their efforts or that their solution had allowed the project to go forward to successful completion. I was told the engineers would come up with a permanent solution to replace the copper wire but as far as I know no further action was taken

Tuning Nav Canada's first digital radios. Kevin Kavanagh photo via Ron Schmidtke.

and the temporary loop is likely still there today, some 20 years later as I write this.

Watson Lake Tourists

The Alaska Highway zigs and zags back and forth across the Yukon/ British Columbia border between Watson Lake and Whitehorse. We saw lots of black bears, but only on the B.C. side. I think they had some sixth sense

Black bear with cubs on the B.C. side of the Alaska Highway.

that told them they were safe from hunting in B.C. but not the Yukon. It was summer in the Yukon and there was a steady stream of motor coaches heading to and from Alaska. The tourists usually spent the night in Watson Lake and as a result we could not find rooms in a single hotel for the duration of our stay. During our 10-day visit we had to move between two hotels three times to dodge in between the tourist bus arrivals!

Watson Lake sign post forest. Beaumont is in there somewhere!

Dennis and I had a weekend off in between installing and testing so we stayed in Watson Lake and checked out the local area. It is like many towns and villages all over Canada that have interesting tourist attractions off the beaten path

Liard River hot spring.

and are worth taking the time to visit. Besides visiting the 'sign post forest' and leaving behind a Beaumont highway sign that I had 'acquired,' we checked out hot springs at Liard River and tried our luck fishing for trout along the north shore of the lake. The water was clear and I saw several fish following my bait, but they were either not hungry or the Watson Lake trout did not like the Meliadine Lake trout lures I was using! Dennis did catch a nice Arctic grayling so the frying pan was put to good use that night!

While there we met several locals who told us the history of their town and the nearby tungsten mine. The mine property held about 15% of the world's reserves of tungsten, most of the rest being controlled by the Chinese. The mine was closed when we arrived but the owners had obtained new financing and markets for their ore. They had a plan to reopen the mine and were paying off creditors in the town; the people we spoke to were very optimistic about the mine's and Watson Lake's futures. I had some underperforming stocks in my RRSP so when I returned home I told my fund manager to sell them and buy Canadian Tungsten when they came out with their Initial Public Offering. He warned me about the high risks associated with mining and other penny stocks but I told him to please go ahead because I had no intention of holding the stock long-term and the funds I was freeing up were not performing, so I considered the risk acceptable. I bought twenty thousand dollars' worth of shares at the IPO price of thirty cents then I watched the stock closely over the next couple of weeks. The price levelled off and I could see nothing in the news to make me think it would go higher, so I sold all the shares at a dollar sixty-five each. This nice profit would offset much of the financial penalty of early retirement and cemented my decision to leave Nav Canada before my full thirty-five years of service would be completed.

Back to Hall Beach

I had made a couple of trips into Hall Beach using charter flights, but this final one was via scheduled airlines travelling through Toronto and Iqaluit. We were going to be there for a few days relocating the CARS and installing new radio equipment into a new equipment room built into the airport terminal. We stuck pretty close to our accommodations at the DEW line site and our work site at the airport because polar

Polar bear checking out the Hall Beach weather station. Photo courtesy Hall Beach weather observers.

bears had been reported wandering in the area. We were told not to go outdoors alone, and to sign ourselves in and out whenever we left the DEW line buildings saying where we were going, who we were with, and when we were expected back. Presumably that information would help the searchers identify the remains if anyone went for a stroll and did not return. There were some active bears, including the one in the photo above who showed a great deal of interest in our weather station; perhaps he just wanted an updated forecast?

We were changing planes in Toronto on our way home from Hall Beach when we saw a fellow passenger place a bag behind a chair and then walk away. Being security conscious, we called security. A few minutes later an RCMP constable showed up, took the bag and plunked it down on the chair, unzipped it and started rummaging around inside. Right away I thought we should have left the area since if there was anything in the bag that could go 'Bang!' it was very likely that this Queen's Cowboy was going to accidentally set it off! It turned out to be nothing, the owner showed up a bit later and had a one-way chat with the RCMP about airport security and unattended baggage; but you never know and I would not hesitate to take the same action in similar circumstances.

Back to Baker Lake

Just before the millennium Baker Lake became the latest of the northern flight service stations to be converted to a Community Aerodrome Radio Station. Len Cook, Steve Highstead, and others from our Winnipeg organization had taken great pride in constructing the FSS into Baker Lake's new air terminal building in the 1980s. At the time it was a prototype of how Winnipeg region would construct future FSSs; now it was up to me and my crew from Edmonton to undo their good work.

Baker Lake air terminal and FSS, now a CARS station. Photo by Paul Gierszewski, accessed 2021, courtesy of Wikipedia.org.

There were seven of us on-site and we were working to a hard deadline that had been set for us by technical operations. There was a lot of last-minute coordination between my crew and airport operations, the airlines, and the GNWT. Our airport operations management had to intervene at one point with GNWT's arctic airports' management because the local airport manager did not want to accept the new radio frequency we were installing into his vehicles. Rod Muddle and Winnipeg tech Neil Kornberger were in charge of that part of the work. Rod was tall and broad in the shoulders so he did not fit well under dashboards or into the odd corners of heavy equipment. To change the dozen or so radios once called for an 'atta-boy'; to persevere through bureaucratic nonsense and redo the work three times went above and beyond! Stan and Vince were there with me as well as Winnipeg techs Cam MacIsaac and Cam Mason. We were all singled out for a job well done by Terry Ferguson, the outgoing FSS manager. He said in writing that if project teams were eligible for a Chairman's Award he would nominate us.

While we were removing the old telephone equipment from the former FSS we chanced upon a Bell Northern line interface module that contained a vacuum tube! Some members of my crew had never seen one before and I drew them a quick schematic to illustrate how this 'electronic valve' operated. I believe we could lay claim to having just decommissioned the last vacuum tube remaining in ANS service!

Terry and I were the last of the Nav Canada personnel to leave Baker Lake. We were flying home via Winnipeg on Calm Air's Hawker 748 when we hit a rough air pocket that caused the airplane to roll past 60 degrees and the port wing to suddenly point almost straight down towards the ice-covered surface of Lake Winnipeg. I was in the window seat and Terry had fallen over on top of me as his laptop computer crashed onto my knees. This incident showed the wisdom of keeping your seat belts fastened in an aircraft because the only person who was tossed about was the flight attendant. She and the contents of her commissary cart were thrown across the unlucky passengers seated a few rows ahead of us. Fortunately, she landed in their laps on a cushion of juice boxes and cookie packets so she was not injured. I remember looking straight down the wing at the surface of the lake in a rather calm and detached manner. I was not thinking at all about an impending impact and I have no idea why I felt no inclination to close my eyes, scream, pray, or do anything similar to what many of my fellow passengers were doing at that moment. Perhaps this was because the incident did not last more than a few seconds and I did not have time to react to incipient fear; I don't know, but the pilots managed to roll the wings level and fly us out of the air pocket after losing a couple of thousand feet of altitude.

Old Crow

The last CARS station I helped to install was in Old Crow at the northern end of the Yukon Territory where the Porcupine and Crow rivers meet. Old Crow is a traditional Gwich'in community whose less than 300 people depend on muskrat trapping and the Porcupine caribou herd for sustenance and survival. It is the only Yukon community not served by road so Stan Loo and I flew in on Air North. When you arrive you really step back in time because this area was not glaciated during the ice age. The land is rich in fossils from mammoth and bison to prehistoric horse and lion. Even western camel fossils have been found here, and many bones show evidence of human activity as far back as 30 millennia.

The equipment installation was routine. Stan and I had it complete in one day. The trip was memorable because of the

Gwich'in people who preserve their culture by passing down traditional knowledge through oral histories. I have heard oral history related by other First Nation cultures, particularly the Inuit, but the following story that was related to us in Old Crow gives weight to the veracity of the people charged with keeping these stories alive.

Joe Kyikavichik, also known as Joe Kaye, related to the paleontologist Richard Harington the Gwich'in story of a giant creature, a 'monster.' The story was told to Richard in the 1960s in the first person as an eyewitness account so it must have been passed down for thousands of years. The monster became stuck in the mud under a bluff between a lake and a river. It used all its strength to get free, and when it did the hole it left behind allowed the lake to drain into the river. Harington decided to investigate and after following the directions related in the oral history found a nearly complete woolly mammoth skeleton buried in the Whitestone River mud right where Joe Kaye's story said the monster would be. These ancient oral histories are ingrained in the Gwich'in culture as deeply as the permafrost.

Three Final Mountains

By the time my third decade with Transport/Nav was coming to a close I had lost count of the number of remote communications sites I had installed. I still enjoyed the variety of work at each site and travelling the country while meeting interesting people but in my mind I had begun paraphrasing Ian Muir's comments to me back in Coral Harbour: this time I was thinking that there was more to life than Remote Communications Outlets! I installed three more on the tops of mountains with my Edmonton colleagues as my career began winding down.

Horn is a semi-remote site at the top of a rocky tor near the coast of Lake Superior not too far from Schreiber, Ontario. It is the easternmost site in our western region and is reached by an unmarked road off the Trans-Canada Highway. Nav Canada had a remote communications outlet there that extended the radio coverage from Thunder Bay FSS along the north shore of the big lake. Like many of these sites on high ground it commanded great views, in this case of Lake Superior and the islands along Superior's north shore. We

Dennis Chan with Gil Parent, two stars on my installation teams! Gil Parent photo.

needed a rigging crew but ours were all busy on other projects so I reached out to a former colleague who also happened to be familiar with the Horn site. Todd Zale was a Transport Canada rigger who left to start his own company, Skyline Tower, when Nav Canada was formed. Todd did a great job for us on short notice, and it was nice to catch up with him over a beer. On the drive back to Thunder Bay Dennis and I visited an amethyst mine where we picked up some souvenir jewellery pieces for our wives.

It was staying connected with people far and wide plus these little diversions that did much to keep our work interesting and morale up.

On Watt Mountain west of High Level, Alberta, stands a GlenTel wireless site that holds the radio repeaters that serve the oil industries in the area. Nav Canada needed radio coverage in northern Alberta so we leased space on their site for a building and antenna tower.

Nav Canada building and antenna tower at GlenTel's Watt Mountain site.
Their building and tower are in the background. Gil Parent photo.

Our building was prefabricated in Edmonton by Gil Parent and Ron Schmidtke and included four equipment racks. Each rack held a different self-contained remotely controlled radio facility. We drove to High Level from Edmonton after our building and tower were installed by contractors. I must have taught my guys well because we stopped in Grande Prairie so Ron could buy a portable BBQ for tailgate lunches at the site and balcony dinners at our motel. Of course I had my Klein BBQ implements, purchased in Swift Current, in my tool box! The track leading to the site was one lane and pretty basic. We had to follow a team of Natural Resources officers who removed several beaver dams ahead of us, allowing their floodwaters that had run over the gravel road to drain away! About a year later Dennis, Vince, and Lionel L'Heureux returned to install new digital radios.

Inside the Watt Mountain site showing a mix of analog and digital radios. Gil Parent photo.

Deanna Cadoret was one of our few female technologists in Nav Canada. All the women I knew in the ANS were very smart and capable. They certainly knew their jobs as well as or better than any man I worked with and asked for no special favours. Deanna drove us up to another mountaintop off the Forestry Trunk Road south of Hinton, Alberta, to the third RCO site. We needed a four-wheel-drive vehicle to make it up what was a cross between a logging track and a goat trail. All our company approved rent-a-car vendor had was a Hummer! Of course, I jumped at the chance to test drive one of these monsters off-road! It was almost too big for the narrow path we had to follow. Deanna was driving and she had to back and fill around a couple of the sharp hairpin bends we encountered, being careful not to put a wheel over the edge because it would have been a long way to the bottom unless a tree stopped our fall! Deanna's husband Peter was also a technologist in engineering services and they both went on to further their careers at NCTI, where I would have the pleasure of working with them again.

THE POLAR BEAR CAPITAL OF THE WORLD

When I first saw Churchill on my way to Coral Harbour it contained about 5,000 residents, but today the army base and rocket range are closed and much of the remaining industry has left. The population now is less than a thousand. That is not to say there is nothing to see or do there because it remains a vibrant and viable community at the northern terminus of the Hudson Bay railroad and Canada's only Arctic seaport on the shores of Hudson Bay. It is also home to more polar bears than people. Normally a quiet town, it is impossible to get a hotel room in Churchill during the fall when thousands of tourists descend on the community to see the bears as they migrate up the coast.

That Would Be Illegal

On a beautiful summer day some colleagues and I were walking across Churchill's aircraft apron. One of our Transport Canada business jets had just arrived and the pilots, who were air cops from Air Regulations in Ottawa, were staring at the right-side engine of their Gulfstream. They saw our ID tags and asked us if we were techs (he didn't call us Radio Knobs then). We said yes then they asked us if we could help them with an electrical problem. He explained that they had lost electrical power from the right-side engine and without it their gyro compass on the co-pilot's side of the cockpit would not work. They were not legal to fly under Instrument Flight Rules (IFR) without two gyro compasses.

"Can you take the engine cowling off and reset the generator circuit breaker inside for us?"

"Yes, but that would be illegal because we are not Aviation Maintenance Engineers."

"But it's only a circuit breaker. All you need to do is reset it."

"Hmm … nope. If the breaker is off it tripped for a reason. We can't say whether or not the generator or the wiring is faulty. If that is the case you could have a serious problem, maybe even end up with an in-flight fire."

I pointed at the magnetic compass hanging over the instrument panel and asked why they couldn't use the pilot's gyro and the magnetic compass….

"The mag compass is not legal for IFR."

"All you fly is IFR, so why bother having a magnetic compass on board?"

"It contains an emergency supply of alcohol for the pilots. Seriously, we need it in case both the gyro compasses fail then we have to revert to flying visually."

"The weather is great so why not fly visually using your one good gyro and the mag compass? Head south until you see the big lake and Winnipeg is at the bottom end."

"Smart-ass Radio Knob…. So you can't help us?"

"If you take the cowls off we could show you how you could reset the breaker."

"That would be illegal; we are not Aviation Maintenance Engineers."

Our disgruntled pilots spent two days enjoying the sights of Churchill and two nights getting beaten at darts in the Churchill Legion before an Aviation Maintenance Engineer could come up from Winnipeg and fix their wounded bird. I often wonder if they were really anxious to get home or if these air cops were just testing us.

The Churchill Legion

There was always something going on at the Churchill Legion. The pool tables and dart boards were usually busy and there were often several card games in progress. It was a centre of the town's social activity and almost the entire population were members. Colin Page, Len Cook and I were there for a week doing work at the Omni-Range site. Every day at 3:30 Colin would announce 'Miller Time' and we would tramp off to the Legion for a beer. We always intended to have just one or two and then go elsewhere for a steak dinner, but people started arriving as we were thinking about leaving so we never seemed to get out of there before closing time. For the entire week I subsisted on beer with pickled eggs and pizza pops, the only food the bar had. Len and Colin just stuck to the wobbly-pops and their stomachs probably thanked them more than mine did!

The Legion was filled to capacity one evening and people were milling around outside in the cold waiting to get in. Eddie Breland, one of our riggers, had just arrived from a working trip further north. He figured we were inside, but they wouldn't let him in through the door so he came around to the side of the building, saw us through the window, and rapped on the glass. Vince got the window open and pulled

Eddie in over the threshold, the last person to be admitted that evening. Unfortunately, the blast of cold air coming in the window alerted the bouncer to his unconventional entry. No sooner was Eddie on his feet than the bouncer took him by the shoulder and marched him right back out the door!

Vince met the crew off a Polish freighter in the Legion one night. This was a great chance for him to practice his Polish, which he hadn't used much in a few years. The crew had been at sea for months and were homesick. Their next port would be somewhere in Europe where they would unload their grain and after that who knew where they would sail to? The sailors ended up back in Vince's hotel room where they made many long-distance telephone calls home to wives and girlfriends in Poland. Vince wasn't keeping track of the time or charges but being a traveller himself he understood the loneliness from being away from loved ones. He was happy to cover the 30 or 40 bucks that showed up on his hotel bill and the sailors' zlotys wouldn't have worked in the Tundra Inn anyway!

Hotels and Motels

Tourism has always been a major industry in Churchill. Besides the 16th century Hudson Bay Company fortress and the fall bear watching there were Beluga whales to see in the estuary and thousands of different avian species brought birdwatchers from around the world. Just before I joined engineering services one of the engineering techs, Doug Dyrland, was staying in the Churchill Motel when he smelled smoke and went into the hallway to check what was going on. Sensing there was a real fire he went back into his room to grab what he could but when he went back to the hallway a few seconds later it was too late to get out that way! Doug ended up going out his second-floor window and into a snowbank, suffering a few scrapes and bruises in the process. The motel was a total loss but fortunately Doug managed to save his project plans even though he lost his shirt!

Besides the Churchill Motel, there was the Churchill Hotel. This establishment boasted one of the few places where you could get a hot lunch back in the day, so we often went there for our midday meals. The chef was a Greek gentleman. Local lore had it he was the ship's cook who came ashore with the rest of his crew when the SS *Ithaca* went aground nearby in the 1960s, got the cook's job at the hotel, and never left. I can't vouch for that story but I do know we stopped ordering soup when he brought our first bowls out to us wearing a stained BVD undershirt over his hairy chest and with his thumbs way down inside the broth! After he dropped our lunches on the table he headed back to his kitchen licking his thumbs clean then wiping them dry on his undershirt!

During my time working in Winnipeg we usually stayed at the Tundra Inn whenever we had a job to do in Churchill. Owned at the time by Pat and Bob Penwarden, this family-run hotel was clean, quiet and we were always well looked after during our stays there. Bob needed a new floor in the Tundra's lobby so when the army base closed he bought the bowling alley lanes for a good price. The hardwood strips were perfect for his floors and you can still see the little dots and arrows that used to line up bowling balls. All the maintenance and engineering techs from Winnipeg were on a first-name basis with the Penwardens. They hired Bill Webster to install their central vacuum system, which he did during the evenings after working at the FSS during the day.

Later on in my career there were fewer places to get meals in Churchill as the population of the town declined. We started staying in the Aurora Inn, an apartment hotel originally built as condominiums. Each suite featured a full kitchen and a second-floor bedroom configured as a loft. They were then and maybe still are the most comfortable places to stay if you needed to be in Churchill for an extended visit. Besides the kitchens we had the use of their outdoor BBQ so quality and variety were never issues with our menus, especially because Vince always packed lots of Montreal Steak Spice!

Long-Range Radios

The final remote communications site I installed in my career was in Churchill and was to be the first in a special application of the new digital Park Air radios. We were trying to achieve extended radio coverage that would enable Automatic Dependent Surveillance of aircraft over large sparsely settled areas of northern Canada, in particular over Hudson Bay and our oceanic airspace where radar coverage was not possible. This system, called ADS-B, was at the experimental stage and Nav Canada was a pioneer of the new technology. In essence it allows the aircraft to communicate its GPS position to the ATC operations centre. Computers can then plot the aircraft's position on a radar display without the need for a radar site. Rob Dobson designed the extended-range antenna system and Kevin Kavanagh came up from Ottawa to see how well it worked.

Dennis Chan and Ron Schmidtke were there too and when we were not testing the system I took the guys along the shore of Hudson Bay to see some of the local attractions such as the old rocket range, 'Miss Piggy' (a Lambair C-46 cargo plane wreck), and the rusted hulk of the SS *Ithaca*. We were looking for bears too and we did spot a couple along the way, close to where some dog teams were tied up. The dog's owner fed the bears so they wouldn't eat his dogs, and by hanging around for the free food these 'tame' bears kept other bears away.

"Miss Piggy." Parks Canada wanted to remove her because they thought her an eyesore, but local opinion prevailed and she remains where she landed years ago. Gil Parent photo.

Polar bear near our Churchill site. Natural Resources officer photo.

We also spotted the sign of one that was too close for comfort. We had stepped out of our remote site to head back to town and right there on the wooden stoop was a fresh ursine footprint that had to be 45 centimetres across! The bear could have been lurking right around the corner of the building, which, of course, had no windows so we could not see to be certain, so we scuttled back inside. Being the senior Radio Knob present I said to Ron:

"Okay Ron, you're junior so you go outside and run around to the driver's door and climb in. We'll stand guard here and distract the bear if it puts in an appearance."

Ron was former military and knew all about rank so without actual stripes on our sleeves there was no way he was going to be ordered anywhere, especially back outside to face the bear. We were all laughing but no one was interested in playing 'rock-paper-scissors' so we called FSS and got them to send a rescue party. In due course the game warden showed up and spotted the bear about 100 metres away.

He got it to move further away with his bang-stick as we all scrambled out of the building and into our truck. Every time after that we always parked so the truck's door was only one step away from the site entry!

We had a couple of foggy days with freezing drizzle just after we had installed the long-range radios and this brought on a lot of static interference. The receivers were banging and crashing like New Years' Eve 1975! Kevin and I couldn't figure where it was coming from but I thought the source might emanate from a private home just up the coast from our site. The family that lived there had a lot of radio antennas and also a windmill for generating electric power. Kevin and I drove up and introduced ourselves and asked if it was possible they were transmitting any radio signals that could account for our interference. They were a bit cool to our enquiry but did invite us in for a cup of coffee. They were not causing our static so our next call was to Manitoba Hydro. We asked them to please investigate their power line for faulty insulators, and they did in fact discover one on their line about half a kilometre from our site that was creating a lot of arcing, and which turned out to be the source of our interference!

The Bears Are Eating Bert!

One fine autumn day Bert Seeman, one of our riggers and not the same Bert who featured in my earlier story "The Muppet Show," got a ride to the remote receiver site from SC, one of Churchill's maintenance techs. Bert's job was to climb the towers and change the light bulbs on top, as well as checking to make sure the hardware and guy wires were all in order. Bert had climbed up the first tower when SC was called away to an urgent job. He told Bert he would be back in about an hour and if Bert was done before then he should just wait in the site building. It did not take SC long to finish his task, but then he joined his cronies for coffee, and before too long coffee turned into a beer in the Legion after work. Along about the time the beer glasses were half empty Bert's rigging cohorts stopped in, having completed their work at other sites, and asked:

"Where's Bert?"

"Bert? Bert! Oh crap, Bert! I forgot all about him! He's still at the receiver site!"

Our Radio Knob almost knocked the table over as he ran for the door while pulling on his parka! SC gum-booted his truck out to the site only to discover Bert was not in the building. He hadn't passed him on the road, so where could he be? By now it was dark, and as he stepped back outside he could hear a faint cry off in the distance. Putting his truck into four-wheel drive, SC proceeded off-road behind the building, his headlights sweeping across the rocky tundra. His heart was racing with worry that Bert might have fallen and was lying on the ground severely injured somewhere nearby! What his headlights uncovered was worse: three polar bears, presumably momma bear and two cubs, sitting at the base of one of the antenna towers, from which were coming the plaintive cries for help!

"O my God! The bears are eating Bert alive!"

Bert was in fact about seven or eight metres up the tower, where he had tied himself off with his rigging harness, and from where he was afraid he would have to spend the night! The bears were looking up at him and showed no inclination to leave. They were being very patient and knew Bert had to come down eventually; he had already been up the tower for about two hours and he was getting cold. What energy he had left he was using to curse at the bears in both English and his native German while throwing spare light bulbs at them from his supply bucket. He had long since run out of spare nuts and bolts!

SC roared up to the tower, revving his motor, flashing all his lights, and honking the horn to frighten the bears away. They did move back from the tower base away from the onrushing vehicle, which allowed Bert to climb down directly into the box of the truck. As they drove off Bert found new reserves of energy and began beating on the cab with his fists while verbally abusing techs in general and this Radio Knob in particular. It was an interesting ride back to the Tundra Inn because SC was afraid to stop and let Bert get into the cab with him. As soon as Bert got down from the box SC sped off out of sight before Bert could show him how he really felt, then he remained hunkered down and out of sight until Bert departed Churchill the next day.

Churchill Flight Service Station

Churchill's original hangar also functioned as an air terminal and FSS among many other things. Today it is a historic site. Photo courtesy Transport Canada.

Churchill's old flight service station was located in a former military control tower that was built onto one corner of the airport hangar. The hangar was built by the military in the 1950s and was taken over by Transport Canada in the 1960s. Besides a hangar for airplanes it was also the air terminal building, air cargo facility, offices for the airport manager, airlines, and electronic maintenance staff, the FSS and marine radio stations and the electronic equipment rooms and workshops that supported them. The marine radio station shut down in 1986 and was taken over first by Thunder Bay and later by Iqaluit using remote communications. By the end of the 20th century the old hangar was no longer performing any of the remaining duties satisfactorily and plans were under way to replace it. A new air terminal was built and Nav Canada constructed a new Flight Service Station. The old hangar is now a historic site, still located across the gravel runway away from the new facilities. If those walls could talk, the tales they could tell!

The new FSS was sited in the airport infield between Churchill's two runways, near nose dock hangars that were formerly used by Strategic Air Command air refuelling tankers and just to the north of the new terminal building. It was designed by Nav Canada's construction services branch in Ottawa as a modular structure. The idea was to prefabricate the FSS in sections in Ottawa then erect it on-site like a modular home. The object was, of course, to save money versus conventional construction methods. My counterpart in the eastern region, Tony LeBar, did the liaison work with construction branch and oversaw installation of the specialist's consoles into the cab sections. The building's design required an insulated basement for the electronic equipment,

Modular FSS at Churchill, a good idea but poorly executed. The white building is the standby diesel generator. Photo by Tim Kalushka courtesy Airport-Data.com

workshop, and storage areas, which posed special challenges because Churchill is in a permafrost zone. If the permafrost was allowed to thaw under and around the basement then the whole building could possibly shift, sink, and even destroy itself.

The concept of a standardized modular FSS was sound; unfortunately, the building's construction at Churchill left much to be desired. It came off the train from Winnipeg in six pieces, two for each of the three levels. Construction branch's contractors set them onto the basement and assembled the modules. The first major issue arose when Manitoba Hydro refused to connect the FSS to the power grid. This was not a simple issue like the baseboard heaters at Stoney Rapids. There were pages of electrical code deficiencies, many of which would not have been made by a junior apprentice and a few that were major safety-related items. Local contractors worked for days to remedy them while the building was powered from its standby diesel generator to allow the work to proceed. I saw the contractor's invoice and it exceeded sixty-five thousand dollars' worth of remedial electrical work completed before we could be connected to the power grid.

Other safety issues came up as soon as we technologists and the FSS specialists started moving in. Unlike other control towers and FSSs the Churchill building did not have an emergency exit from the cab. We were all fearful that if a fire started in the service level below the cab, where the FSS kitchen and storage was, there would be no way out from the cab except through the smoke and flames. Major cracks were discovered in a concrete pillar in the basement that held up the upper levels. We could push a steel ruler more than 30 centimetres up into the pillar and wiggle it around. We feared for the structural integrity of the building.

All the employees working in the building—engineering technologists, maintenance technologists, and FSS—raised these concerns with our managers. We were all told our concerns had been passed on and that construction branch would take care of things "in due course." Meanwhile construction branch was telling us that the structure was sound and the service level under the cab was not a separate storey but part of the cab therefore an emergency exit was not required. We all discussed our situation and we were unanimous that we considered the building unsafe. We also felt, given the history of Nav Canada employee relations, that the company would not take any action to address our concerns. All three employee groups advised their managers and unions that we were withdrawing from work in the FSS because we felt we were in imminent danger.

We all walked out of the building and the next day managers, union representatives including Len Cook from IBEW, and Occupational Health and Safety inspectors all descended on Churchill. The inspectors determined that our concerns were valid and serious but did not constitute imminent danger so we all returned to work. The inspectors went through the building and uncovered a slew of building code deficiencies including the fact that the building had not been fastened to the basement foundation! We were unaware of this and this discovery alone validated our decision to walk away from the building. A strong Arctic gale could have blown the FSS off the basement, possibly causing injury or loss of life. Nav Canada was ordered to repair the cracked concrete pillar in the basement, attach the structure to the foundation, and remediate other building code safety deficiencies, but the specialists did not get their emergency exit.

Shortly before we walked away from the building the temperatures in Churchill tanked and all the windows in the

FSS cab iced up so the specialists could not see out! The HVAC system could not cope with the winter environment. There had been other prior issues with the HVAC system, but this was serious because the specialists required a view of the Churchill airspace as well as the airport runways, taxiways, and aprons. At the end of the day the HVAC system needed to be totally rebuilt with properly sized and insulated ductwork and proper ventilation and humidity control.

I know that some managers supported our actions but without a union behind them they couldn't say or do much without putting their own jobs at risk. Many others thought we were just shit disturbing. I was made aware of one mid-level manager who was looking for any excuse to fire us! It was clear to all of us on site that Nav Canada's only concern was how cheaply they could build an FSS. I remain confident we took appropriate action because of what the inspectors uncovered, and bringing them in was the only way that legitimate safety concerns were found and addressed.

Nav Canada has never built another modular FSS.

TEACHING TIME

Technologists traditionally entered engineering services from the maintenance ranks after typically three or more years' experience plus formal training on some equipment. Nav Canada wanted to hire directly into engineering services from the private sector or colleges. The company needed to satisfy the regulator, Transport Canada, that technologists coming into engineering services would be properly trained and qualified to install Air Navigation System electronic equipment. Learning by osmosis was no longer going to be sufficient.

Nav Canada's answer was to develop an engineering competency program. Technologists would earn certification to become qualified to install equipment on their own and to manage equipment installation projects. Experienced technologists already in engineering services would be grandfathered into the program. Training courses would demonstrate competency on specific equipment. The actual certificates were wallet sized so we could carry them with us and produce them upon request by any Transport Canada inspector who happened to come onto one of our job sites.

My old friend Steve Highstead was now the manager of technical training for Nav Canada. He was tasked by the competency program developers to get the training courses up and running. I readily agreed to work for Steve when he asked me if I would develop and present these classroom courses. This would be an opportunity to exercise and improve my training skills while being in on the ground floor of a new and exciting program in Nav Canada. It would also be a break from installing communications sites onto remote mountaintops. Teaching would be my fourth and final career path. Unfortunately, I only got to dip my toes into the teaching waters, but it took me into retirement and even a little ways beyond. The instructional techniques course that I had taken back in Winnipeg was a good foundation for formal teaching, but for the competency program I needed a higher qualification. I enrolled in NCTI's instructor training program, which was recognized by Conestoga College, an affiliate of Brock University. In 2005 I received my college certificate as a Technical Instructor in Adult Training after two years of part-time study and course work.

Teaching the Basics

Basic Installation Competency, or BIC, was the first component of engineering competency and was earned by demonstrating all-round knowledge and abilities relating to equipment fabrication and installation techniques. Developing the BIC course was Nav Canada's priority for the new hires that were now coming into engineering services and my first task was to explore the training possibilities at NCTI. Environment Canada used to have a presence there including a complete upper air station. The buildings were now used for storage but were in very good condition and Steve offered them for my training venue if I thought they could work. The old GMD building was three levels and set up as a classroom on the second floor. This would be perfect for the lecture portions of the new course and the first floor would do double duty as a workshop setup and simulated equipment room. The dome where the Grand Mother Duck used to live would become simulated remote sites. All the course objectives could be met by having participants pair up, each to build a complete and working remote communications outlet system. This concept not coincidentally played to my own strengths and the participants would have the satisfaction of seeing their efforts result in something they had built actually work. The building could accommodate six participants, which considering the emphasis on lab work and the construction activity was the maximum number for one instructor and an assistant to manage safely.

Upper air station at NCTI that we used for the Basic Installation Competency course. The former hydrogen shed in the background became our warehouse for materials and supplies.

My Edmonton bosses Rico and Peter were supportive of the competency program to the point of investing well over fifty thousand dollars for my course materials and supplies, plus covering my salary during all the time I spent on secondment to NCTI. The other regions also invested into the course and NCTI cleaned up the building and made it ready for our use. I visited each region to learn their unique techniques and practices that would be included in the training. After my participant manuals were approved the pilot course was held at NCTI in January 2003. The course was 14 teaching days long and the students were required to bring their own set of approved hand tools so they would gain confidence in their use.

The small class size made it easier to maintain the relaxed atmosphere that I found conducive to teaching. I played music during the lab times and invited the participants to bring their favourite CDs, as long as they weren't rap! Once the days' lecture and demonstrations were over each team was free to manage their own schedule for completing the lab work. I tried to run the course as close as possible to an actual project being installed on the road and if everything was satisfactory on Friday afternoons they could get an early start on the weekend if they wished. I maintained a conversational approach during my lectures and told a lot of 'war stories' to illustrate my teaching points. By the end of the course all six participants were helping each other and working as a single team.

Quinn's Inn in St. Andrews near Cornwall and the site of our BIC course graduation dinners.

The length of the BIC course entitled my participants to a graduation meal allowance. The participant's consensus on all my courses was to dine at Quinn's Inn in historic St. Andrews just north of Cornwall. Built in 1865 it was originally a stagecoach stop between Montreal and Kingston. In 1924 the Quinn family took it over and it now operates as a gastropub with amazing food and ambience at a reasonable cost.

BIC pilot course participants at their graduation dinner. Steve Highstead, the manager of technical training, is on the right next to me. On my other side is NCTI tech Martin Vaillancourt, my course assistant. Deanna Cadoret's husband Peter is on the left. Jessica Chaikowski and Diane Crocker, the competency program developers, also came down from Ottawa for the occasion.

The first graduation dinner was attended by Steve and the competency program developers who came down from Ottawa to get the students' feedback on my pilot course. These bun tosses were a lot of fun. On one occasion a local lady figured my students and I were having a far better time than she was, so she ditched her date and joined our group! We found out later she was related to one of our Nav Canada managers! Our grad parties usually continued well into the night back at the bar at NCTI, or if it was summer and the

weather was good, at 'Churchill' out on the NCTI lawn. A steel mock-up of the Churchill FSS cab had been built in Ottawa to verify the design met operational

The Churchill gazebo on the NCTI lawn, a favourite spot to relax.

requirements. When the frame was no longer required it was taken to NCTI and reassembled there as an outdoor gazebo. Very few besides my course participants, Steve and I knew its provenance. Steve and I would often arrange to meet for a beer at 'Churchill.'

Louise Julien and I at NCTI.

My BIC courses were huge successes! I received high praise from everyone concerned with the competency program as well as from the participants and the regional organizations. The old GMD site proved to be an excellent venue. For future courses I added a lesson dealing with fibre-optic cable handling and splicing. I had met Louise Julien at a trade show being held at NCTI during the time I was teaching the second BIC course. She was a fibre-optic specialist with Corning Glass and kindly volunteered to teach the participants on my current course about fibre-optics using Corning materials, techniques, and tools. Her demonstration during this second course was well received so I purchased a set of Corning tools and some cable. Louise kindly accepted my invitation to return to NCTI to teach her techniques to subsequent BIC courses.

Serge Roy was the technologist's manager at NCTI and my boss whenever I was working on secondment to the engineering development program. Serge enrolled some of his technologists as course participants besides providing me with as many different lab assistants as he could. NCTI's people did not get out much and operated somewhat in a bubble vis-à-vis the other Nav Canada sites. Serge wanted his staff to be able to install the training systems closer to engineering services' standards. Martin Vaillancourt, of course, was my lab assistant on more than one occasion. Former Hummer driver Deanna Cadoret was also my lab assistant, as was her husband Peter who had also participated on my pilot course. I trained six others from NCTI including Yves LeClerc. Yves drove an old van named Igor that mounted a propane BBQ, so in the interest of field-trip realism Yves backed Igor up to our building one day for a lunch of burgers and brats. Many of the NCTI technologists came over for lunch too and to see my operation. Serge showed up and tactfully ignored the beer cans that we had sleeved into empty soft drink cans.

All the technical instructors made me feel very welcome at NCTI. I visited Martin's home on a couple of occasions including a card night where I lost badly trying to play Hearts en français. The Cadorets had me to a picnic in their backyard. Fridays after school usually found a cadre of instructors enjoying fresh perch rolls riverside at the Blue Anchor, or the finest smoked brisket sandwiches at Smoked Meat Pete's in Dorion. I taught a total of eight BIC courses over four years before retirement, training something like 50 technologists in engineering installation practices. Along the way I trained Jean-Pierre Gagnon, a retired technologist from Montreal. Jean-Pierre had come out of retirement to work as a contractor developing and delivering the French version of the BIC course to students from the Quebec region.

A Serious Injury

I was in the middle of one of my courses in May 2004 when I received the phone call that all parents dread. My eldest son Scott had been injured in a motor vehicle accident and was in hospital in serious condition. I needed to get home to be with Jovanna and the boys right away, but I was the only qualified BIC instructor and no one, including myself, wanted to cancel the course that was more than halfway complete. Scott's condition was stable so I re-arranged the schedule and taught the remaining lectures by the end of the next day. My teaching assistants would take over the rest of the lab work so I could leave the morning after. Jovanna took me straight from the airport to see Scott in the hospital, where I got the details of his mishap.

He and some friends had got hold of an old K-car they intended to use in a demolition derby. They were ripping around a friend's field in it when they decided to jump a drainage ditch. All the glass had been removed from the car and Scott was wearing his helmet and dirt-bike armour, which is likely what saved his life. K-cars being what they were it simply smashed into the far bank of the ditch at 60 km/h and folded like a cheap suit. Scott actually walked out of the wreck and it was a few minutes later that he began to feel the effects. His friends took him into emergency where they discovered a concussion, broken jaw, dislocated shoulder, cracked ribs, and a crushed ear canal. Today he lives with three screws in his jaw and difficulty hearing on one side. Of course his friends were filming the whole thing and all the action is probably still out there on the web somewhere.

An Enticing Offer

I was in a very interesting position having two bosses. I was reporting to Rico in Edmonton and formally part of Peter Dawson's engineering services organization, while at the same time I was on secondment to Serge at NCTI while reporting to Steve's technical training organization in Ottawa. Both allowed me the freedom to set my own schedule so I pretty much decided who I would be working for on any given week as I fitted my assigned RCO projects in between my BIC courses to best suit my personal needs.

In 2005 NCTI ran a competition for course instructor technologists. I had completed my adult education certificate and Serge thought well of my abilities. He asked me if I was going to apply:

"You would be a real asset to our teaching staff!"

"Thanks Serge, but I still have two kids in school and there aren't the opportunities here for them like at home. They would have to leave home for post-secondary education and they would have a harder time finding work in Cornwall."

"Talk to the other instructors and techs with families; I am sure it would not be that bad, and this part of the country has a lot going for it!"

"I agree this would be a great place to work and I really enjoy teaching, but I only have three years to retirement, and I may decide to leave early. It's very likely the family would want to end up back in Alberta or even Winnipeg because that is where the roots are. Any move back west would be on my dime."

"Think it over, talk to Jovanna. The working conditions here are not as stressful as back in Edmonton from what I hear. At least think about it."

"Okay, I'll think about it and we'll talk it over at home. Thank you for the vote of confidence and the opportunity, but I really don't want to waste your time if I can't accept your offer."

We did talk about the opportunity back in Beaumont and at the end of the day we decided that although working in Cornwall would have a lot of benefits for me, it would be better for the family not to uproot and move there. The day before the competition closed Serge phoned me in

Edmonton and asked me once more to consider applying. After we talked about my reasons for not wanting to relocate he said I should go ahead and apply and if I won the job he would see what we could work out.

I got my application in two hours before the deadline the next day and in due course Serge and his team came to Edmonton to interview me. A week later I was told I had won the position! Serge was very excited and wanted me to report as soon as possible, but I brought him back down to earth by telling him once more that my family and I did not want to end up living in Cornwall after I had finished my career, also that early retirement was looking more and more likely.

I had prepared most of the BIC course materials from my home office and been given a desk at Edmonton's ATC operations centre to use whenever I needed it, so I suggested to Serge that I could continue to do course development from Edmonton while travelling to NCTI whenever necessary to prepare and teach. I pointed out I could make a lot of back-and-forth trips for the cost of a relocation across the country. Two people who were relocated from Winnipeg had negotiated a similar arrangement and never actually moved to Edmonton despite that being their reporting point. Serge thought this solution could work, but working from home was still a novel idea and HR did not want to experiment with the concept, especially over cross-country distances. Their decision was that if I was working for Serge I would have to relocate to Cornwall.

A full-time secondment to Serge would not work because engineering services, quite reasonably, did not want to carry my salary on their books if I was working elsewhere full-time. A bureaucratic solution to have NCTI swap a position or reimburse engineering services could not be worked out.

Serge then tried creating a technical training position in his organization but located at Edmonton's ATC operations centre, which meant my reporting point would be Edmonton and not Cornwall. Operational training was moving back to operations centres across the country but HR vetoed this idea too, saying words to the effect that only operational training was in Edmonton and Radio Knobs did not mix with Scope Dopes.

I then offered to relocate to Cornwall as long as I could move back to Edmonton before retirement. Nav Canada had set this precedent when the ATC controllers were moved from Moncton; they were given the option of relocating back there after a certain number of years in Edmonton. Many availed themselves of that opportunity then retired once settled in back home. I told Serge that I would guarantee him a minimum of three years at NCTI, which would take me up to my normal 2008 retirement date, if a similar arrangement could be made for me. HR said that sweetheart deal was made only for Scope Dopes and Radio Knobs need not apply.

Serge and I had tried our best but Nav Canada was showing no flexibility with any of their employees at that time. Neither was I when it came to a permanent move to Cornwall. My part-time secondment to NCTI continued as long as I was involved in the engineering competency program but I never taught any other courses at Cornwall. With the job at NCTI formally off the table Jovanna and I agreed that I would leave Nav Canada in about 18 months, at the end of 2006. I did not share this decision with anyone in the organization at the time.

During the back-and-forth with Serge and HR I was putting the final touches on the training course for General Installation Competency, or GIC. This was the second part of the engineering competency program that focussed on project management, and would teach skills such as running effective meetings, the phases of project planning and cost estimating, scheduling, and report writing. This would be a five-day course taught in a classroom environment so it would be more efficient to have me travel to the regional offices outside Quebec to deliver it. I enjoyed very much meeting up again with many of my BIC students and the other technologists and seeing how they were getting on, but honestly, although the courses were successful, my heart was no longer in it without new challenges on the horizon.

MY FAREWELL TOUR

During the final months with Nav Canada I treated many of my trips away from home as working vacations. I decided to travel with Jovanna as much as possible, at my own expense of course, to give her an appreciation of the kind of work I had been doing as well as to see some of the country I had experienced over the years. Besides our honeymoon to Europe she had not travelled much and was looking forward to some vacation time.

Our first junket was to Halifax after my delivery of the GIC course in Moncton. When the course was over I drove to Halifax to meet Jovanna's plane. Sean was able to

Swiss Air 111 memorial site near Peggy's Cove, Nova Scotia. Photo courtesy Nova Scotia Tourism.

come too so the three of us spent a week together exploring the south shore of Nova Scotia. Jovanna's father had sailed on corvettes in the Royal Canadian Navy during WWII, so we visited HMCS *Sackville*, moored just down the hill from our hotel. We went white water rafting on the Bay of Fundy tides at Shubenacadie, sailed on the *Bluenose II*, and ate fresh lobster at Peggy's Cove. We also saw the Swiss Air Flight 111 memorial near Peggy's Cove. I had previously met Vic Gerden who led the Transportation Safety Board investigation into that tragedy and I had followed it closely. The site is a very solemn and moving memorial.

After touring the East Coast I took Jovanna west to Campbell River on Vancouver Island in 2006. When my work there was done I met her plane at Comox and we drove to Victoria where we met up with our old friends Bob and Debbie Crosby. We enjoyed catching up over dinner together then we spent a day with them at Butchart Gardens.

Jovanna with Fred Lang in Victoria.

I also introduced her to Fred Lang, the former FSS supervisor from my Coral Harbour days, who is now retired with his second wife Joyce in Victoria. We walked around the inner harbour and especially enjoyed checking out the houseboat community. We fed the harbour seals herring that we bought, along with our picnic lunches, at Barb's Place then we took in Craigdarroch Castle, the stately home of the Dunsmuir family, bought nanaimo bars in the town of Nanaimo, checked out the old hippies and goats-on-the-roof at Coombs, the old-growth forest at Cathedral Grove, and finally the local market on the Campbell River wharf.

It seemed only right that Jovanna complete her coastal tour by dipping her toes in the Arctic Ocean. In 2005 Environment Canada was constructing a new upper air station at Eureka to replace the original 1947 buildings. Eureka is on Ellesmere Island not too far south of Alert, and besides the upper air program it is home to a science station that does atmospheric research under the auspices of a consortium of universities and government agencies. There is also the nearby Fort Eureka where military personnel look after the communications

and satellite links with Alert. Alert is so far north that the earth's curvature blocks it from 'seeing' communications satellites, so a radio link with Eureka is necessary in order to connect Alert with the rest of the world.

Enjoying lunch at Barb's Place, Victoria's inner harbour.

Jovanna and one of our pilots at Edmonton Flight Centre after our aborted trip to Eureka.

I was heading to Eureka to install airport radio equipment into Environment Canada's new operations building. It was cheaper to charter a flight from Edmonton instead of flying commercial to Resolute Bay and chartering from there. The winning bidder was going to fly us back and forth in a Citation business jet! We couldn't head north until the new building had been accepted from the contractors, which pushed our trip past the end of the very short summer season. The weather was good as we departed Edmonton but turned drizzly as we approached the treeline. We stopped in Yellowknife for fuel and our pilots decided we could go no further. A stubborn weather system was blanketing the high Arctic with freezing drizzle and fog and showing no sign of moving anywhere else any time soon. The Citation would undoubtedly become iced over while on the ground either in Resolute Bay or Eureka. Neither airport had a hangar or facilities for de-icing so we had to turn around. Jovanna never made it north of the treeline but Great Slave Lake substituted for the Arctic Ocean for toe-dipping. We had a good time visiting local arts and crafts shops, the Wild Cat Café, and Ragged Ass Road.

Of course the farewell tour had to include NCTI. Since becoming a conference centre several pairs of dorm rooms had been knocked together to create larger VIP rooms, each with a sitting area. As a course instructor I was able to book myself into one of these and Jovanna was able to stay with me; my favourite had an ornamental balcony with a view of the river. I brought Jovanna down from the Ottawa airport a day or two before my course ended on one of Nav Canada's regular shuttles. She toured the facility, saw my teaching setup, and got to experience the food and accommodations. Dave Kearly, a NCTI tech, had arranged the staff's annual steak and lobster dinner for that same weekend.

The 408 Squadron monument at Trenton's RCAF museum.
"And They Shall Beat Their Swords Into Ploughshares."

Jovanna and I attended Dave's food fest where she met many of my colleagues and was served far more than she could eat! We also sampled the perch rolls at the Blue Anchor and drinks at Churchill before heading off down the seaway. There was a lot to see and do so it was an entire week before we reached Niagara Falls!

We toured Upper Canada Village before stopping in Trenton to see the RCAF museum and my dad's marker at the 408 Squadron monument. We took a Thousand Islands boat tour over to Boldt Castle on the United States side of the seaway, then stopped in Kingston where we spent the night on the old Coast Guard icebreaker *Alexander Henry*. The *Henry* spent its career working out of Thunder Bay and when we visited she was being operated as a B&B by the Maritime Museum of the Great Lakes.

The next day we drove to Prince Edward County to check out their cider and cheese offerings and were not disappointed, leaving with several bottles and blocks! We skipped past Toronto and headed for Niagara-on-the-Lake where Jovanna's friend from high school, Linda Bednar, lived with her husband Jerry. The four of us had a great time

Jovanna on the bridge wing of the CCGS *Alexander Henry*.

touring the waterfront then we capped off a terrific week with an amazing dinner at a restaurant overlooking the falls before returning to Ottawa and flying home.

AND THEN IT WAS OVER

When Rico asked me to set up another installation at another remote Arctic outpost in the dead of another winter I sat down and wrote a brief memo telling him and Peter that my retirement would be effective in 30 days, on Friday, December 29, 2006. I had some vacation leave remaining that I would use up before then so my last day in the office would be December 15. I was still working out of my 'NCTI desk' at the operations centre so my exit interview was conducted there by Jim Stetson, who happened to be the relative of the Cornwall party girl! I turned in my badges and computer but was allowed to keep my cellphone as long as I assumed the billing. When asked, I told Jim my early departure was due to the labour/management issues that were still ongoing in the company, and for me the fun had gone out of the job. He said he understood, we shook hands as he walked me to the door and that was pretty much it.

The next day was Friday the 15th and I walked into my engineering services office at our north-end workshop for the last time. Thirty-three-and-a-half years of gainful employment, some would maybe say undetected crime, fit into a small box containing a file folder of commendations, whatever was in the junk drawer of my desk, plus an outdated family photo. Rico, Peter, Ken Folkers, and the three or four techs who were present in the shop that day walked me to the pub up the street for pizza and beer. That was more of a send-off than a lot of employees were getting in those days! I brought along the company clock from the wall of my cubicle and presented it to Ken "because he had a reputation as a time manager" according to Lionel L'Heureux. I gave Peter a squeeze ball from my desk drawer to help relieve his stress. I wanted to give Rico a horse whip to make him a meaner manager but he had to settle for a kiss.... Actually, I can't for the life of me remember what tchotchke I gave him from my office and when I reached out to ask him he couldn't remember either!

I had a good run and I do miss the people I worked with. Besides all my colleagues mentioned in this book there was "Grizzly," who spent many days singing loudly from the tops of antenna towers and who later went on to a career as an air traffic controller. "Ace" installed beacons and other navaids all over Winnipeg's region, and to this day he just laughs and rolls his eyes when asked how he acquired his moniker. "Lenny" and "Squiggy" spent most of their careers installing control systems. Besides our cow-tipping summer student "Big Bird," we worked with "Wee Willie," more than one "Crazy Dave," the "Great Wazoo" and a host of other colourful characters. A thousand pages could be written about them and others but their stories are not part of mine. Perhaps one day they too will enrich us with their own memoirs.

We played hard to counterbalance the stress and responsibility that came with the job, which was also coupled with some danger. I earlier related the stories of the FSS specialist who lost his fingers at Coral Harbour, and our colleague Doug who escaped a motel fire through a second floor window. A rigger fell to his death when a tower he was helping to erect collapsed at Alert. More than one technologist was electrocuted while maintaining the high-powered Northern Electric transmitters. Len Cook and his fellow passengers were lucky to escape from the aircraft they were in when it crashed while trying to take off at Arviat. Besides dealing with recalcitrant landing gear in flight, Randy Peterson and a crew of technologists worked to keep the runway lights and navaids operational at Red Lake while cut off and surrounded by a forest fire. Two riggers were shot at by some moron with a hunting rifle while they were atop a tower near Winnipeg airport. (The moron, fortunately, had poor aim. He got off with a small fine; apparently a rigger is worth only a few hundred dollars!) We drilled holes into the walls of sites lined with unpainted asbestos wallboard before we knew it was unsafe. A number of us sported electrical burns from touching things we shouldn't have, which is the reason I never wore a watch or jewellery while on the job. Many colleagues developed rare cancers that claimed them too early; radiation from high-powered equipment was a suspected cause but a link was never proven. Today all that old equipment is consigned to the dustbin of history, and while there are still hazards on the job it is much safer now than when I began my career.

EPILOGUE

A month or two after my retirement Jim Stetson invited me to lunch where he explained that Nav Canada had an urgent requirement for pre-assembled electronic equipment racks. These would be used for the digital radios that were now arriving from Park Air in quantity and needed installation as quickly as possible. Jim asked if I would take on rack assembly as a private contractor. Coffee followed lunch and we talked through a proposal wherein I would take care of the mechanical rack assembly while leaving the electronics to the techs. Before we could ink a deal Jim was told by upper management that Nav Canada was reducing the amount of contracted work due to budgetary restraints, so that ended that initiative!

I returned one final time to Nav Canada in the summer of 2008 as a contract instructor, teaching my last BIC course at NCTI. Coincidentally the course began on what would have been my normal retirement date had I remained at work! Louise, Steve, and Serge were gone and so were many of my former colleagues. My venue in the old upper air buildings was now being used to train CARS operators, so my course was pushed down into NCTI's basement, into what had been a pair of storerooms. The conditions were less than ideal.

Jovanna's cancer returned and after travelling a very rough road she passed away late in 2012. We were able to take an Alaskan cruise for our 30th anniversary and she made it to our 35th. She saw Scott married, had a final Christmas with her mom Karen and her sisters, and was able to cash the first few of her Canada Pension checks after her 60th birthday, something she had always looked forward to doing.

I began a political career as a Councillor for my town of Beaumont in 2007. Unfortunately I was retired for a second time when my bid to become Mayor came up short in 2017.

I have not flown as a pilot since our move to Beaumont but occasionally I look up to watch aircraft and ponder renewing my licence, maybe even becoming a flight instructor. Then I think about millennials in the left seat trying their best to kill me as they saw away at the controls and I laugh to myself while dragging my eyes back to the ground.

I am very fortunate to have fallen in love with Dale. She is a retired English and drama schoolteacher and now my second wife. Together we travel the world while watching our children and grandchildren grow and mature into productive members of society. We are truly blessed.

The federal bureaucracy and Transport Canada continue to bumble along, but what of Nav Canada? Without government involvement in operations the company has moved to the forefront of the latest technologies and has designed and successfully marketed air traffic management systems around the world. The government perceives Nav Canada as a success story because the company has never come back to them asking for loans or bailouts like most Crown corporations. Today Nav Canada is recognized by the international aviation community as a highly respected ANS provider, and is seen by many countries as a model of how ANS services should be delivered. Unfortunately the human cost of corporate success remains high. Layoffs and site closures continue. Employee relations had improved for a few years, but my friends who are still working report they are once again circling the drain.

The ground-based navigation aids my colleagues and I worked with are rapidly being decommissioned as satellite navigation becomes more reliable and precise, as well as more affordable for small aircraft operators. Satellite and computer technology has advanced to the point where technologists, as well as air traffic controllers and even pilots, are now considered by some to be obsolete, although the flying public is a long way from wanting humans removed from the aviation safety equation.

I agree with the flying public, and am glad my career spanned the years that it did. They were, in my opinion, the golden years for technology and technologists in aviation.

ACKNOWLEDGEMENTS

I owe a special debt to noted aviation author Garth Wallace whose funny flying books connected with me and inspired me to write. He invited me into his home, gave me valuable advice on the writing process, subconsciously kept me motivated and unconsciously became my mentor.

This book would not have been possible without the recollections of many former friends and colleagues who were happy to reconnect when I reached out. They added some of their own stories and corrected many forgotten details. My thanks and appreciation go out to Ron Brehm, Kirk Carston, Dennis Chan, Len Cook, Rob Dobson, Lorne Fehr, Chuck Frankard, Kathleen Henderson, Steve Highstead, Cliff House, Jack Ireland, Glen Kautz, Kevin Kavanagh, Dave LeBlanc, Wayne Mews, Gil Parent, Randy Peterson, Bob and Shannon Ridley, Mike Robertson, Don Ross, Ron Schmidtke, Rico Sebastianelli, Robert Stampe, and Vince Warszycki.

Bob Stampe and Pearl Gregor are both published authors who critiqued early drafts of my first chapters and I thank them both for their honest feedback and good advice. My wife Dale, as always, kept me moving in the right direction.

Shout-outs go to my copy editor Anne Champagne of Green Words, who makes me look good in print, Kim Leitch of Tandem Thinkers for keeping the lawyers at bay, and Jennifer

Chapin, Atheena, Jodi, and the rest of the team at Tellwell Publishing!

Memory fades as time passes, and despite changing details to suit my narrative some factual errors may have crept in. These are mine alone and I own them.

AUTHOR BIO

Bruce LeCren was an Air Force brat who rose to become a senior project officer overseeing the installation of electronic systems within Canada's Air Navigation System, and later in his career he taught at the Nav Canada Training Institute in Cornwall, Ontario. After retirement Bruce served two terms as a Councillor for the Town of Beaumont. Bruce holds diplomas in Electronic Technology and Adult Education. He has restored vintage aircraft for an aviation museum and contributed articles for museum and professional journals and hobby magazines. Bruce's hobbies include wine making, woodworking, and constructing scale models. Now fully retired, Bruce lives in Beaumont, Alberta with his wife Dale and their dog Sookie when they are not travelling the world.